CONCISE DICTIONARY OF LIBRARY AND INFORMATION SCIENCE

Second Edition

CONCISE DICTIONARY OF LIBRARY AND INFORMATION SCIENCE

Second Edition

Stella Keenan
Colin Johnston

BOWKER
SAUR

London • Melbourne • Munich • New Providence, NJ

Library of Congress Cataloging-in-Publication Data
A catalog record for this book is available from the Library of Congress

British Library Cataloguing in Publication Data
A catalogue record for this book is available from the British Library

Published by Bowker-Saur
East Grinstead House, Windsor Court
East Grinstead, West Sussex, RH19 1XA
Tel: +44 (0) 1342 326972 Fax: +44 (0) 1342 336198/190
E-mail: lis@bowker-saur.co.uk
Website: www.bowker-saur.co.uk

Bowker-Saur is part of REED BUSINESS INFORMATION LIMITED

ISBN 1 85739 251 5

Cover design by Juan Hayward
Typeset by Florence Production Ltd, Stoodleigh, Devon
Printed on acid-free paper
Printed and bound in Great Britain by Antony Rowe Ltd, Chippenham

Biographies

Stella Keenan has had 50 years' experience in library and information work. She spent nine years as Lecturer and Senior Lecturer at Loughborough University in the UK before becoming a self-employed information consultant in 1989. She had previously been Secretary General of the International Federation for Information and Documentation (FID) 1984–89, Executive Director of the National Federation of Abstracting and Information Services (NFAIS), Philadelphia, 1968–74, Information specialist at the American Institute of Physics, New York, 1964–68, Indexer at the H.W. Wilson Co., New York, 1958–1964 and Librarian at Zinc Development Association, London, 1955–58. She started her career in 1950 in Liverpool where she worked in the public and university library service.

She gained her MPhil at Loughborough University and is a Fellow of the Institute of Information Scientists, Associate of the Library Association and Honorary Fellow of NFAIS. She has written and edited a number of reports and proceedings and has written abstracts for Aslib's *Current Awareness Abstracts*. She edited the *Target 2000* column for *Online and CD-ROM Review* and she is currently editor of *focus*, the journal of the International Group of the Library Association.

Colin Johnston has some nineteen years' experience in academic libraries both in the UK and overseas. He was Online Librarian at the Sultan Qaboos University Main Library in the sultanate of Oman from April 1989 to April 1997. Before that he was in charge of Circulation Services at the University of Ulster at Jordanstown after serving as a subject specialist in the Ulster Polytechnic library. He has also held a number of temporary posts, including a short period with the Internet project called *Pick*, which is based in the Thomas Parry Library at the University of Wales, Aberystwyth. This project was concerned with the identification and exploitation of quality electronic sources in librarianship and information studies. He is presently in charge of lending services at Goldsmiths' College library (University of London).

He is a member of both the Library Association and the Institute of Information Scientists. He took his first degree in librarianship and classical studies at the College of Librarianship, Wales and subsequently a M.Lib in Analytical and Historical Bibliography of the seventeenth century at the same institution. He also contributes to Aslib's *Current Awareness Abstracts*. His professional interests lie in the general area of database quality, through both online and CD-ROM provision as well as a "gentle" interest in printing during the hand-press period.

Preface to the second edition

The first edition of this dictionary contained approximately 2500 terms and was published in 1996. This edition has been completely revised, with entries from the first edition being reviewed and revised where necessary and approximately 2000 new terms added. As predicted by one reviewer of the first edition, most of new terms are in the computing and telecommunications area. The growth of the Internet and the impact of the World Wide Web has added a substantial number of new terms. No terms have been deleted from the dictionary as one of the aims is to show how the language of the field has changed and also to provide definitions of terms that might be encountered in older professional literature.

With new terms being coined almost by the hour, it became very difficult to say, 'Stop and close the file'. By the time this second edition is published, a number of new terms will have emerged, but that is the nature of attempting a dictionary. Perhaps the next edition (if there is to be one) will be maintained by a Web master who will update appropriately in electronic format.

The contribution of my colleague, Colin Johnston, has been invaluable in getting this revision to the press. Without his assistance, especially in locating difficult definitions and using his knowledge in the computer and automation field, this edition would not have reached this level of completion.

When the idea of this dictionary was first suggested by editors at Bowker-Saur, my initial reaction was that I wanted to produce something that would be useful to students and educators, which would contain terms that I had come across myself during my professional career. I have tried to keep this idea in mind while compiling the dictionary so it could be said that it contains the vocabulary that I have encountered in 50 years of working in the library and information profession.

It is also important to stress that the dictionary covers library science and information science as a profession. The sixth edition of the *Concise Oxford English Dictionary* defines a profession as a vocation of calling, especially one that involves some branch of advanced learning or science. Information science developed as a profession following World War II as work in libraries and information centres attracted a broad range of individuals who came from outside the traditional library world. Many were drawn from the physical, biological and social science communities. The impact of these professionals changed the face of traditional library work.

In the UK one of the main interests in the 1950s and 1960s was the development of sophisticated and specialized classification systems, many based on the faceted classification theory of Ranganathan. In the USA the focus was on the use of computers to provide information retrieval services while the social scientists were concerned with user needs and the impact of information on society.

The increasing use of computers sparked a wide range of developments ranging from vocabulary manipulation and automatic abstracting and indexing experiments to studies of literature patterns which included both quantitative and qualitative studies and citation manipulation.

As has already been stated, the advent of the Internet and the World Wide Web in the 1990s has coloured developments in the past decade and added very considerably to terms that a person may encounter in their daily work and professional reading.

The speed with which the vocabulary has developed is an indication of how fast the Internet has been absorbed into library and information work. Undoubtedly many terms will soon be obsolete and many more terms, concepts etc. will be added or will change their meaning in the future. But this is in the nature of such a dynamic and fast-developing relationship, and it is set to continue just as the development and power of the personal computer will continue. Library and information science and the computer are inextricably mixed and the amount of jargon will continue to grow. Yet this speed may add to the confusion that surrounds new terms, and it is not inconceivable that definitions of terms may differ between editions. Perhaps a word of caution to those who coin new terms will not go amiss. Just as in the early days of online, it should be remembered that the Internet, like online, is only a means to an end and not an end in itself.

Although there have been several thesauri of information science terminology, notably by Claire K. Schultz in 1968 and more recently by Jessica Milstead in 1994, there has been no comprehensive dictionary of the field. Most of the terms contained in the *ASIS thesaurus of information science* compiled by Jessica Milstead are defined in this dictionary.

Since a profession is delineated by its language, this dictionary is an attempt to capture the terminology based on the compiler's 50 years of professional experience which has spanned traditional librarianship, information science research, professional organization management and teaching and lecturing on a number of subjects. While length of experience has been of some advantage, exposure to current usage is extremely important. As an abstractor for Aslib's *Current Awareness Abstracts*, the compiler has for the past several years been exposed to current professional terminology.

Conventional and traditional library terms have generally not been included as there are a number of excellent dictionaries and glossaries that cover this field, notably *Harrod's librarians' glossary* and the American Library Association's *Glossary of library and information science*. The definition of such terms will be found in these dictionaries, whereas this dictionary focuses on the science of librarianship and information science. In addition to these two publications, there is a wide number of dictionaries, glossaries and encyclopaedias that covers related fields which were consulted in compiling this dictionary. These are listed in the Bibliography at the end of the dictionary. It is interesting to note that even at the end of 1999 there were no substantial web pages containing useful definitions of library and information science terms available on the Internet.

The first edition of the dictionary was presented in six theme areas. This edition contains all the terms arranged in one alphabetical array, although the six themes present in the first edition are still covered. They are information sources, information handling, computers and telecommunications, management, research methodology and publishing.

Generally speaking, acronyms and system names have been excluded from the dictionary, although there are some exceptions in the telecommunications systems and publishing areas. To a certain extent, this decision is arbitrary as consideration for inclusion has been given to videotex system names and activities in the publishing area that relate to the advancement of electronic data interchange. Excluded almost entirely are names of programs or packages that are proprietary to a specific company. Search engine names are excluded with the exception of a few very early examples.

As one of the aims is to make the dictionary a 'one-stop shop' for definitions, there are no cross-references as full definitions are given under all synonymous terms. Where necessary, the field, e.g. computing or management, has been noted in the definition. The words given in bold face within a definition indicate that the word is itself defined elsewhere in the dictionary in the appropriate alphabetical place.

Stella Keenan
December 1999

Aa

AACR2
▶ **Anglo-American Cataloguing Rules, second edition** – published in 1978 (first edition USA 1966 and UK 1967) main rules for **cataloguing** material; used as the basis for **international standard bibliographic descriptions.**

Abort
▶ stopping a **function** or **computer program** before it has finished naturally. Abortion could also be caused by **software bugs, input** that the **program** cannot handle or **hardware** malfunction.

Aboutness
▶ proposition that **index terms** assigned to a **document** represent or indicate its total content which is useful to the **novice searcher** but does not cover aspects that might be of interest to a scholar or researcher.

Abridgement
▶ shortened version of a work, preparation of which does not involve rewriting or presentation in a different form.

Absolute address
▶ real and unchanging location in **computer memory.** Also called **machine address.**

Absolute cell reference
▶ in **spreadsheets,** reference to a particular **cell** or group of **cells** that do not change.

Absolute instruction
▶ **instruction** which is complete in itself and requires no further **data reference.**

Abstract
▶ concise and accurate representation of the contents of a document, usually without interpretation or bias, accompanied by a **bibliographic** citation. Specific types of abstract are **indicative, informative,** biased or **slanted.**

Abstracting
▶ process of creating an **abstract;** preparing a concise and accurate representation of document's contents.

Abstracting service
▶ organization that prepares **abstracts** and publishes them, either in **periodical** form or on a **bibliographic database.**

Academic freedom
▶ right of academic staff to think and teach in accordance with their own principles rather than institutionally prescribed philosophies.

Academic workstation
▶ **workstation** that supports all the functions required by a scholar or researcher. Also called **scholar's workstation.**

Acceleration time
▶ time required for a **computer disc** to reach normal rotating speed before it goes into action.

Accelerator board
▶ type of **expansion board** that makes a **computer** run faster. Usually contains an additional **central processing unit.**

Accent mark
▶ mark placed over or under **characters** in many languages which may affect pronunciation.

Access
▶ **1.** generally – availability to a user of items in a store; **2.** computing – method by which a **computer** refers to **records** in a **file.**

Access charge
▶ cost imposed by local telephone companies to use the local **network** to connect to international **networks.** Also called **carrier common line charge.**

Access control
▶ use of a **password** or other method to ensure that only accredited users can use a **computer** system.

Access point
▶ **1.** computing – the physical point of connecting to a **network; 2.** information handling – **index** term or **heading** in an **index, catalogue** or **database,** which is used to identify specific **records** or **entries** in a **file.** Examples are an author's name, subject term, **classification** code etc. Sometimes called **entry point.**

Access to information
▶ ability to gain **access** to a **document** or fact to make use of the information contained.

Access time
▶ **1.** – time it takes to retrieve an item that has been identified in an information store; **2.** – time taken to find **data** and transfer them to a device or a **storage** location. Usually measured in microseconds or milliseconds.

Accessibility
▶ availability of the physical form of information **storage,** such as a **catalogue.**

Accession number
▶ running number unique to each **document** which is assigned by the library in sequence as items are received; used for administrative purposes, and in some cases as the basis for **shelf order.**

Accountability
▶ liability of a person or institution to be responsible and answer for assigned tasks and duties.

Accreditation
▶ procedure used by professional bodies such as associations or institutions which leads to approval of a course of study that indicates an acceptable level of education. It is recognized by employers as a method of ensuring an adequate standard for the preparation of prospective employees.

Accrual accounting
▶ accounting method where revenues are reported when earned (accrued) and services and materials are reported as expenditures when received.

Acetate film
▶ safety film with a base of cellulose acetate or cellulose triacetate.

Acid-free paper
▶ paper which contains no free acid or has a pH value of 7 or more.

Acoustic coupler
▶ device capable of transmitting and receiving specified sound tones along telephone lines. The **digital signal** sent by the **computer** is converted to sound and transmitted to the telephone handset. At the receiving end the sound is converted back to the **digital signal**.

Acoustic hood
▶ cover that muffles sound which can be used to cover a noisy piece of equipment.

Acquisition
▶ process of obtaining books and other material for a library or **information centre**.

Acronym
▶ word formed from the initial letter or letters of the name of an organization, system or service.

Actors network theory – ANT
▶ radically different approach for executing an **information policy** using a mixture of scientific realism, discourse analysis and social constructivism.

Action learning
▶ learning by working on real problems with a focus on learning and implementing solutions.

Active database
▶ **database file** that is loaded and currently being used.

Active document
▶ **electronic document** that is loaded and currently being used.

Active file
▶ **computer file** that is open and currently being used.

Active window
▶ **window** on a **computer screen** in which a **program** is currently running and which contains a **pointer**.

ad hoc committee
▶ committee established for a limited time to deal with a specific issue or task.

ADA programming language
▶ comparatively **high-level programming language** developed and used mainly for military computing. Named after Augusta Ada Byron, Countess of Lovelace, who was a colleague and friend of Charles **Babbage**. She was involved in the development of a mechanical calculator called the **analytical engine** that he designed.

Adaptor
▶ **circuit board** which can be inserted in a **computer**, usually into an **expansion slot**, which can provide some additional facility. May also be called an **expansion board**.

ADC – Analogue-to-Digital Conversion
▶ conversion of **analogue signals** to **digital signals** for **input** into a **computer**.

Add-on
▶ connecting additional pieces of equipment to a **computer** so that it can operate more powerfully or carry out an additional task.

Add-on board/card
▶ **circuit board** which can be inserted in a **computer**, usually into an **expansion slot**, which can

provide some additional facility. May also be called an **expansion board.**

Added entry
▶ **entry** made under a **heading** of secondary importance, e.g. if **main entry** is under author's name, added entries may be made under title of document, translator's name, **series** title etc.

Addendum
▶ brief additional matter added to the end of a **document.**

Address
▶ in **telecommunications,** coded representation either of the destination of **data,** or the **terminal** from which the **data** originated; in computing, a set of **characters** that uniquely identifies a service on a **network**; place in a **computer** system where full information is stored.

Address bus
▶ electrical connections between the **microprocessor, memory** and **ports** of a **computer** which control the route for **data** items as they move from one place in the **computer** to another.

Address mask
▶ **bits** in an **Internet protocol address** which correspond to the **network address.**

Adhesive binding
▶ method of binding where glue is applied to the backs of a book's pages, which are then fixed into a cover.

Adjacency
▶ **1.** computing – in **character recognition,** refers to print where the reference lines between two consecutive **characters** are separated by less than a specified distance;

2. information handling – **proximity** of two or more words specified as a requirement in a **search statement.** In **database searching** this indicates that the words sought should be next to each other.

Admissibility
▶ performance criterion that can be expressed as the level of inconvenience (effort, time, cost etc.) experienced in fulfilling an action or providing a service.

ADONIS
▶ electronic system developed in the late 1980s by a **consortium** of major European scientific and medical publishers for the storage and supply of **full-text journals,** operated by the British Library Document Supply Centre.

Advance copy
▶ book sent out before the official publication date for **review** or promotional purposes, sometimes unbound or in a temporary binding.

Advance order
▶ order placed with publishers by booksellers in advance of a book's publication date; it may be used by the publisher as a guide to the number of copies to be printed.

Advanced power management
▶ feature designed to save power so that the **screen** is powered down. In some cases the **hard drive** is also powered down if **input** is suspended for a set time.

Aesthetic kerning
▶ adjusting the spacing between two adjacent letters to produce a better visual effect.

Affirmative action
▶ form of positive discrimination that actively favours a minority

group or an individual belonging to such a group.

Agent
▶ **computer program** that performs a small and well-defined information-gathering or processing task in the background.

Ageing of literature
▶ belief that literature on a particular subject has a finite, useful life. This depends on the subject and the idea that publications in rapidly developing fields age more quickly than those in other fields.

Aggregator
▶ **computer program** that is capable of carrying out computations on values held in particular **fields** in all **records** in a **database**.

AGLINET
▶ **Agricultural Libraries Information Network** – organization formed within the International Association of Agricultural Librarians and Documentalists for the purpose of encouraging **cooperation**.

AI – Artificial Intelligence
▶ ability of a machine to copy aspects of human intelligence such as understanding **natural language**, problem solving etc. A **computer** responds by referring to rules, which have been **programmed** into its **memory**. If it responds outside these conditions, it is said to be acting intelligently.

ALANET
▶ **electronic mail** and **information service** of the American Library Association.

Alert box
▶ **message box** in a **window** that warns the user about a **command**

and asks for confirmation that an action should be undertaken. Usually signals a potentially damaging operation.

ALGOL – ALGOrithmic Language
▶ **high-level programming language** developed in 1958 which is used for scientific, mathematical and technical problems.

Algorithm
▶ step-by-step procedure for accomplishing a specific task. Each **instruction** must be feasible and unambiguous, and the action must be completed in a finite number of steps.

Algorithmic language
▶ **computer programming language** which works using a series of defined steps rather than by trial and error; another name for a **programming language**. Examples: **COBOL**, **Fortran** and **Pascal**.

Aliasing
▶ undesirable result of a high **input** signal being poorly represented on a low-resolution device such as a **printer**, **computer monitor** or audio speaker.

Alkaline paper
▶ **acid-free paper** with a reserve or **buffer** of extra alkalinity to protect against deterioration.

All rights reserved
▶ printed notice in a **document** which indicates that use of the material is not permitted without the permission of the **copyright** owner.

Almanac
▶ publication containing useful facts and statistical information; usually published annually.

Alpha version
► early version of a **software** product.

Alphabetic subject catalogue
► **catalogue** arranged under broad **subject headings** arranged alphabetically, with each **heading** being further subdivided alphabetically. It may also contain author and **title entries** in the alphabetical sequence.

Alphabetic subject index
► **index** to a classified file of a subject **catalogue**, or to the **schedules** of a **classification scheme**.

Alphabetical order
► strict order of entries from A to Z. **Computer programs** that use **ASCII** coding cannot follow strict alphabetic order.

Alphabetico classed catalogue
► precoordinate alphabetical **subject catalogue** within which **headings** and **generic** and similar relationships are displayed.

Alphabetization
► process of putting words into **alphabetical order**.

Alphanumeric
► arrangement of **characters** which includes letters of the alphabet, numbers, **symbols** etc.

Alternate key
► **key** on the **computer keyboard**, which is used in combination with other **keys**. Often called the Alt **key**.

Alternative publication
► material that covers topics or items not normally covered by the official press, usually dealing with politically extreme right- or left-wing ideas. Sometimes called **underground press**.

Alternative title
► secondary title, usually preceded by a **colon**.

American Standard Code for Information Interchange – ASCII
► American **standard computer** code, adopted in Europe, in which eight **binary bits** can be combined to represent the **characters** on a typewriter **keyboard**. Only seven **bits** (128 possible combinations) are necessary to describe all the **characters**. The eighth **bit** is either used for **error** checking purposes or it is not used. **Data** are often transmitted between **computers** in **ASCII format**, even if the original **data** are produced in another form, such as a **word-processing format**.

ANA – Article Numbering Association
► British organization which publishes and maintains UK **EAN** coding systems and **TRADICOMS EDI standards**.

Analysis of variance – ANOVA
► statistical tool used for analyzing differences in **data sets** which allows a person to identify whether or not differences are significant.

Analytical bibliography
► study of published works which examines in detail the physical structure in terms of pages, paper, binding etc. Sometimes called **critical bibliography**.

Analytical engine
► type of mechanical calculator designed by Charles **Babbage** around 1833. His ideas were used about 100 years later to design the first **computers**.

Analytical entry
► **catalogue entry** for part of a **document**.

Analytico-synthetic classification
▶ **classification scheme** which gives the **classifier** maximum ability to construct **classification** numbers for subjects that are specifically enumerated or identified.

Analogue
▶ direct representation of a phenomenon in another form.

Analogue computer
▶ **computer** designed to perform calculations based on physical qualities rather than on coded text or numbers.

Analogue signal
▶ electrical **signal** that represents another form of energy or activity; for example, the representation of sound waves in electrical form as an audio **signal**.

Analogue-to-digital conversion – ADC
▶ conversion of **analogue signals** to **digital** for **input** into a **computer**.

Anaphora
▶ textual elements, often pronouns, that refer to previous text elements and share their meanings. They are abbreviated in subsequent references that occur in discourse to avoid repetition. They are easily understood by readers or listeners, but not recognized by **computer software** when **full-text databases** are searched.

AND
▶ **logical operator** – logical instruction in a **computer program** or statement. Often described as a **Boolean algebra** operator.

AND gate
▶ electronic device in a **digital computer** which controls the flow of signals in a logical operation.

Animation
▶ series of **images** that are slightly different which are displayed at a speed fast enough to give the illusion of smooth movement.

Annals
▶ record of events arranged in chronological order.

Annotation
▶ note included in an entry in a **catalogue**, **bibliography** etc., which provides further information about the **document**.

Annotation (computing)
▶ in **hypertext**, a new **node** which links to an existing **node**. In some cases this can be used to allow authors and readers to add additional information.

Annual
▶ **serial** issued once a year.

Annual report
▶ official publication reviewing the activities of an organization for a twelve-month period.

Annual review
▶ survey of major publications in a specific subject area over a twelve-month period.

ANOVA – ANalysis Of VAriance
▶ statistical tool used for analyzing differences in **data sets** that allows a person to identify whether or not differences are significant.

ANSI Z39.50
▶ **protocol** for use over a **network** that allows a user to frame a question that can be understood and processed by all **computers** attached to that **network**. This **protocol** can be used in searching **library catalogues**. Usually referred to as **Z39.50**.

Answerback
▶ automatic or manual response from a device which indicates that the correct device has been reached and is operational.

Ant
▶ **1.** – powerful but easy-to-use **web application** that uses a minimum of systems resources to create **web pages; 2.** – name for a **search engine**.

ANT – Apprenticeship by New Technologies
▶ French innovation that allows the general public to become familiar with different methods of accessing information ranging from **video-conferencing** and local **online information** to the **Internet**.

ANT – Actors Network Theory
▶ radically different approach for executing an **information policy** using a mixture of scientific realism, discourse analysis and social constructivism.

Antenna
▶ device which sends or transmits **telecommunication signals**. It may also pick up and receive **signals**. Earth stations and microwave transmission towers use antennae to receive and transmit **signals**.

Anthology
▶ collection of extracts from different works by a number of authors, often of poetry or essays.

Anti-aliasing
▶ method of improving **display** quality and printing of **analogue images** in **digital format** which otherwise would result in a jagged image. This is achieved by using shading to smooth lines that would otherwise be angled. With sound **signals**, a **sound card** is needed to correct the distortion.

Antiope
▶ French **videotex** system.

Antique paper
▶ paper made from esparto grass which has a dull finish and imitates handmade paper.

Antivirus program
▶ **utility** which searches both the **hard disk** and **floppy disks** for **viruses** and removes any it identifies.

Aperture card
▶ card which frames a micro **image** of the **document** indexed by **headings** on the **card**, so that **retrieval** of the **card** also retrieves the text of the **document**.

API
▶ application program interface – set of **routines, protocols** and tools for building **software applications; interface** used by an **application program** to interact directly with the **operating system**.

APL programming language
▶ interactive computer programming language which is specially useful in operations involving **arrays**.

Appendix
▶ material that supports and is attached as a separate item to a main work.

Applet
▶ computer program designed to be executed from within another **application**.

Application icon
▶ in the **Windows** environment, a **graphics image** that is represented by a miniature picture to indicate the facility that is available.

Application layer
▶ in **open systems interconnection** (**OSI**), the seventh layer which is responsible for the **applications program** for the **end user**.

Application-oriented language
▶ **computer programming language** that is suitable for writing **applications programs**.

Application program
▶ **program** or set of **programs** designed to perform a specific **application** or task.

Application program interface – API
▶ set of **routines, protocols** and tools for building **software applications**; **interface** used by an **application program** to interact directly with the **operating system**.

Applications package
▶ set of **computer programs** and related **documentation** used for a particular purpose.

Applied research
▶ collecting and analysing information that can be used to solve real-life problems.

Appraisal
▶ monetary evaluation of material for tax or other purposes according to their use and information value.

Apprenticeship by new technologies – ANT
▶ French innovation that allows the general public to become familiar with different methods of accessing information ranging from **video-conferencing** and local **online information** to the **Internet**.

Approval plan
▶ system whereby a publisher or wholesaler supplies selected material to libraries or **information centres**, who may return unwanted items.

Arbitrary symbol
▶ in **classification notation**, a symbol that has no self-evident place in the **filing order**.

Arbitration
▶ process in which an employer and employee allow an impartial third party to resolve an issue over which they are in conflict.

Archie
▶ early system which allows **indexes** in the public domain **software** to be searched on the **Internet**.

Architecture
▶ logical structure of a **computer** system; the interaction between the **hardware** and **software** that provides the facilities required.

Archival backup
▶ type of **backup** where all **files** are copied to **backup storage** device. Sometimes called **full backup**.

Archival permanence
▶ degree to which **documents** retain their original characteristics.

Archive
▶ organized body of **records** for a particular institution that contains full historical details; public **records** maintained in a **depository**.

Archive file
▶ **file** intended for long-term **storage** rather than frequent daily use. Usually stored on a removable **disk** or **tape** rather than on a fixed **disk**.

Archive storage
▶ secure **storage** of **data** that is infrequently used but may be needed some time in the future.

Arithmetic logical unit
▶ that part of the **central processing unit** that decodes **computer program** instructions, solves arithmetical problems and carries out tasks that demand the use of logic.

Arithmetic operator
▶ any operation that carries out arithmetic on numbers; symbols such as + (plus), – (minus), * (multiply), / (divide) etc.

ARPANET
▶ resource-sharing **computer network** supported by the Advanced Research Projects Agency of the US Department of Defense in the early 1970s. **Prototype** for the **Internet**.

Array
▶ **1.** computing – series of objects in computing which are of the same type and size. A one-dimensional **array** is called a **vector**, and a two-dimensional **array** is called a **matrix; 2. information handling** – set of **classes** in a **classification scheme;** all the **classes** that comprise a **facet** or **subfacet**.

Arrow key
▶ four arrow **keys** on the **computer keyboard** that can move the **cursor** up, down, to the right or to the left on the **screen**.

Arrowgraph
▶ diagrammatic representation of relationships between **concepts**, with arrows used to show **concept** relationships.

Art paper
▶ high-grade printing paper coated to provide a very smooth finish.

Artefact
▶ **object** made or modified by a human being.

Article
▶ contribution written by one or more people for publication in a **periodical** or a **newspaper**.

Article Numbering Association – ANA
▶ British organization which publishes and maintains UK **EAN** coding systems and the **TRADICOMS EDI standards**.

Articulated subject index
▶ **subject index** generated by a **computer** on the basis of a subject statement derived from a title.

Artificial classification
▶ **classification** in which accidental properties of things classified are used as the arrangement **characteristic**; sometimes called **synthetic classification**.

Artificial intelligence – AI
▶ ability of a machine to copy aspects of human intelligence, such as understanding **natural language**, problem solving etc. A **computer** responds by referring to rules which have been **programmed** into its **memory**; if it responds outside these conditions, it is acting intelligently.

Artificial language
▶ language based on a set of rules established before its use; sometimes called **synthetic language**.

Artificial neural network
▶ simulation of memory **storage**, interconnections and learning processes of the human brain.

Artwork
▶ illustrative material such as drawings, photographs, paintings etc., as opposed to text used in a publication.

Ascender
▶ part of a lower-case printed letter that projects above the main body height or **x-height**, e.g. b and h.

Ascending order/sort
▶ list arranged to start with the lowest item and goes up to the highest; could be from the smallest number to the largest or from the first letter of the alphabet to the last.

ASCII – American Standard Code for Information Interchange
▶ American **standard computer** code, adopted in Europe, in which eight **binary bits** can be combined to represent the **characters** on a typewriter **keyboard**. Only seven **bits** (128 possible combinations) are necessary to describe all the **characters**. The eighth **bit** is either used for error checking purposes, or it remains unused. **Data** are often transmitted between **computers** in **ASCII format**, even if the original **data** are produced in another form, such as a **word-processing format**.

Assembler
▶ **program** written in a **low-level language** required to translate a **program** from **assembly language** into **machine language** for direct execution by **computer**.

Assembly language
▶ **low-level programming language** which uses a symbolic **mnemonic** form of the **machine language** of a **computer**. It is used to overcome the difficulty of **programming** in machine code.

Assertive library service
▶ provision of services that anticipate information needs, rather than responding to demonstrated needs. Sometimes called **proactive library service**.

Assertiveness
▶ non-aggressive behaviour which treats people as equals; behaviour based on the conviction that one's own opinion and the opinion of others are equally important.

Asset management
▶ effective use of all the human and material resources of a library or **information service**.

Associative memory
▶ mental process of linking events so that memory of one event automatically recalls another.

Associative relationship
▶ relationship between **terms** that is not based on **hierarchy**. More usually called **related term** relationship.

Associative retrieval system
▶ **computer**-based system where a statistical value has been assigned to **terms** based on the **frequency** with which they occur together in a **document**.

Asterisk
▶ 1. computing – punctuation mark denoted by a 5- or 6-pointed snowflake shape (*) which in many **operating systems** and **applications** is used as a **wild card** symbol to represent a string of **characters**; 2. searching – it can stand for a group or combination of **characters** and is sometimes called a **wild card**; 3. arithmetic – it stands for the multiplication sign

Asynchronous transfer mode – ATM
▶ **protocol** that enables **data** (text, **video**, sound) to be transferred over a **network** by breaking the **data** into fixed-length **cells** or **packets** of 53 **bytes** and creating a fixed route for the **signal** to take, thus making it easy to track for billing purposes.

11

Asynchronous transmission
▶ in **telecommunications**, **transmission** of **data** which takes place when the data are ready rather than when an external **signal** is sent. It is designed to support **applications** that require high **bandwidth**, such as voice and **video**, together with conventional **network** traffic.

Asyndetic
▶ **catalogue** or **index** without **cross-references**.

ATM – Asynchronous Transfer Mode
▶ **protocol** that enables **data** (text, **video**, sound) to be transferred over a **network** by breaking the **data** into fixed-length **cells** or **packets** of 53 **bytes** and creating a fixed route for the **signal** to take, thus making it easy to track for billing purposes.

ATM – Automatic Teller Machine
▶ cash dispensing machine which uses credit or debit cards when authenticated by a **PIN number**. May dispense cash, balance, statement etc.

Attachment
▶ **file** that is sent together with an **E-mail** message.

Attribute
▶ **quality** or **characteristic** of an **entity**.

Attribute sampling
▶ statistical technique which estimates the rate or percentage of occurrences of a specific **characteristic** or **attribute** of a population.

Audio book
▶ book recorded on tape, designed for blind or partially sighted people. Also called a **talking book**.

Audio bridge
▶ method of connecting a small number of telephone lines to provide an audio conference.

Audio card
▶ **expansion board** which allows a **computer** to manipulate and output sounds. Also called a **sound card**.

Audio cassette
▶ **audio tape** enclosed in a plastic container.

Audio newspaper
▶ **tape cassette** containing news, magazine **articles**, sport etc., designed for blind or partially sighted people; also called a **talking newspaper**.

Audio tape
▶ generic term for sound recorded on **magnetic tape**.

Audio-visual interleave – AVI
▶ **file format** which can store moving images together with sound to ensure synchronization.

Audio-visual material
▶ items that are not completely dependent on printed words to transmit meaning as they use audio and visual **formats**. Most, but not all, audio-visual material requires some sort of **display** equipment to be used.

Audiographics
▶ **teleconferencing** system that allows simultaneous audio and **graphic** interaction that gives the impression that all participants are around the **display** unit at the same time.

Audit
▶ systematic examination of the financial records of an organization, usually conducted by an external organization.

Audit trail
▶ **1.** – tracing the steps in a financial transaction to verify accuracy; **2.** – record of **computer** operations which shows what has been done and, if possible, who did it. Used in **computer security** and accounts **programs**.

AUSINET
▶ Australian **network** offering nationwide **online access** to a range of **databases**.

Authentication
▶ in computing **verification** of the identity of a process, person or source. It may take place between a user and a **computer** or between **computers**.

Author abstract
▶ **abstract** of a **document** written by the author, often published at the beginning of the original item.

Author catalogue
▶ **catalogue** of author **entries** arranged alphabetically under authors' names.

Author language
▶ **application** which allows people without **programming** skills to write **computer programs**.

Author's proof
▶ copy of material sent to an author for checking and correction prior to publication.

Author's rights
▶ legal rights assigned to an author through **copyright** legislation.

Author-title catalogue
▶ **catalogue** which contains **entries** for both authors and titles.

Authoring
▶ used in **hypertext** systems to describe the process of generating text for a **hypertext database** and/or generating **links** between items.

Authoring system
▶ **hardware** and/or **software** needed to produce an author language. It may combine **graphics**, sound, **video** and **animation**. **Programming** skills are not needed to use an authoring system.

Authoring tool
▶ **computer program** which allows the user to write a **hypertext** or **multimedia application**. Less technical knowledge is needed and it is often used for **applications** which are a mixture of textual, graphical and audio **data**. Sometimes called **authorware**.

Authority control
▶ control of **index headings** or **access points** through the use of a list of controlled or acceptable **terms** in order to maintain **indexing** consistency.

Authority file/list
▶ established forms of **headings**, **index terms** or other items which may subsequently be used for **information retrieval**. An authority file may also contain **cross-references**.

Authorization code
▶ series of numbers or a special **password** that has to be used to start certain **computer programs** or to allow **access** to certain **files**.

Authorware
▶ **computer program** which allows the user to write a **hypertext** or **multimedia application**. Less technical knowledge is needed and it is often used for **applications** which are a mixture of textual, graphical and audio **data**. Sometimes called **authoring tool**.

Auto abstract
▶ abstract produced by computer analysis of a document; the result of automatic abstracting.

Auto dial
▶ device that responds to a specific input signal by calling a remote terminal over a network using a modem.

Auto logon
▶ device that responds to a specific input signal by calling a remote terminal over a network and identifies the user through an individual identification code.

Autoanswer
▶ feature of many fax machines and modems which answers incoming calls automatically, even when the person called is not present. Can be useful in multi-user systems.

Autochanger
▶ CD-ROM drive which stores and allows access to a number of discs on each drive, allowing automatic selection from the storage device; more usually called a jukebox.

Autocratic management
▶ management style when decisions are made by administrators or supervisors with little or no consultation with lower-level employees.

Automatic abstracting
▶ frequently occurring substantive words in a document are used to produce an auto abstract. Sentences which are found to contain the highest concentration of high-frequency words are identified and printed out in sequence.

Automatic carriage return
▶ word processing and desktop publishing feature which means that the user does not have to press the enter or return key to begin a second line of text when the first one is full.

Automatic dictionary
▶ dictionary of machine-readable words or codes used in a machine coding or translating system where the computer can substitute words or codes in one language for those in another.

Automatic extracting
▶ process where summaries of documents are processed automatically to produce indicative abstracts. One method is to select sentences based on sentence importance and measured by means of linguistic analysis of sentence structure.

Automatic indexing
▶ using the computer to assign index terms based on the frequency of word occurrence in the document.

Automatic speech processing
▶ ability of a computer system to understand and act on spoken input; more usually called speech recognition or voice recognition.

Automatic teller machine – ATM
▶ cash dispensing machine which uses credit or debit cards when authenticated by a PIN number. May dispense cash, balance, statement etc.

Automatic translation
▶ translation of material from one language to another language automatically.

Autoredial
▶ feature of many modems which automatically redials a fixed number of times until the number required is connected.

Autosave
▶ saving of **computer files** without
the user typing the save command;
saving a **file** at intervals to provide
automatic **backup**.

Auxiliary schedule/table
▶ subdivision tables that supplement
classification schedules in
classification schemes which are
used to develop **notation** for specific
subjects.

Auxiliary storage
▶ non-volatile devices, such as
computer tapes, disks etc. used to
store **data** and **program** instructions.
Also called **secondary storage** or
mass storage.

AVI – audio-visual interleave
▶ **file format** which can store
moving images together with sound
to ensure **synchronization**.

AZERTY
▶ continental European typewriter
keyboard which places the letters a,
z, e, r, t, y in this order on the top
row.

Bb

Babbage, Charles (1791–1871)
▶ inventor of a mechanical calculator called the **analytical engine** which introduced **concepts** that were later used in electronic **computers**.

Babble
▶ **noise** from other sources that can interfere with a **signal**. Also called **crosstalk**.

Back file/issue/number
▶ numbers that precede the current issue of **serial** item such as a **periodical**.

Back up
▶ copy of a **file, disk** or tape for security purposes; used to restart the **program** should something go wrong with the equipment or the **data**.

Back-end processor
▶ **processor** used for a special purpose under the control of the **central processing unit**; purpose may be for working out arithmetic or logic functions, or working with **databases**.

Back-of-the-book index
▶ **index** provided at the back of a published book, usually prepared by the author or an **indexer**.

Backbone
▶ main **communication** path in a **network**; the main **cables** or connections that carry most of the traffic.

Backbone provider
▶ American development using the **Internet protocol** developed in the **ARPANET** project which linked regional **supercomputer** centres known as backbone providers.

Background noise
▶ in computing extraneous matter such as static in an electronic **transmission** or random **dots** on a scanned **image**.

Background printing
▶ printing a **document** while doing other work on the **computer**.

Background processing
▶ **computer** operation which cannot be seen and does not involve the user. Several jobs can be done simultaneously by using background processing.

Backing store
▶ store for **data** which is not a working part of the **computer memory**. Used to hold **programs** and **data** which can be read and used by the **computer** in the course of a main **program**.

Backing up
▶ copying **data** from one **computer disk** to another in order to safeguard the **data**.

Backlist
▶ titles of books that a publisher keeps in print and available.

Backlit display
▶ liquid crystal display (LCD) unit
that uses back lighting in order to
improve the contrast.

Backplane
▶ large circuit board containing
sockets into which other circuit
boards or expansion boards can be
plugged. Also called mother board.

Backslash
▶ character sign \ used in MS.DOS
and Windows to identify the root
directory on a disk.

Backspace
▶ moving the cursor in a backward
direction; could delete the preceding
character.

Backtracking
▶ problem-solving method which
tries out various combinations until a
successful one is identified.

Backup copy
▶ copy of computer programs and
files, often in a removable medium
such as a floppy disk or tape, that
can be used to restore damaged or
lost files.

Backup storage
▶ storage medium that is capable of
preserving large amounts of
computer-generated information,
including images, sound, video etc.;
storage device that is used to hold
archived data.

Backup utility
▶ computer program designed to
carry out backup actions
automatically on selected data.

Backward compatibility
▶ ability of a higher-grade hardware
or software to function effectively
with lower-grade items; ability of
more recent programs or operating

systems to allow material produced
on earlier versions to be fully usable.

Backward recovery
▶ method of recovering original
data from a database after a system
failure.

Backward search
▶ word processing facility in which
a word or phrase is searched in
reverse with the direction of the
search being towards the start of the
document rather than towards the
end.

Baconian classification
▶ knowledge classification proposed
by Francis Bacon in 1605 based on
the use of three facilities: memory,
imagination and reason.

Bad break
▶ wrong hyphenation of a word at
the end of a text line.

Bad page break
▶ position at the start of new page
that splits text badly or splits a table.

Bad sector
▶ portion of a disk that does not
read or write data correctly.

Balance sheet
▶ written financial statement
showing the assets and liabilities of
an organization at the end of a fiscal
period.

Balanced tree
▶ in a tree structure each path from
a remote leaf or branch to the main
root is of the same length.

Ball printer
▶ impact printer that uses a small
metal ball to print characters.
Sometimes called a golfball
printer.

Band
▶ range of **frequencies** between two limits.

Bandwagon effect
▶ joining a movement or activity which is currently popular and seems to be sure of success.

Bandwidth
▶ difference between upper and lower **frequencies** that can be carried over a given **transmission** medium. Voice **signals**, for example, range from 300 to 3400 **hertz (Hz)** and use a **bandwidth** of 3100 **Hz**.

Banner
▶ **heading** such as a name or a title that stretches across the top of a **document**.

Bar chart/graph
▶ graphically displayed statistical **data** that use equally wide bars of varying height proportional to the **data** being displayed.

Bar code
▶ type of code to label retail products where the product is electronically scanned at the place and time of purchase; symbol defined as a **European article number** which contains the **ISBN** of a book.

Bar-code scanner
▶ optical device that can read **data** from **documents** bearing **characters** recorded as parallel bars to form a **bar code**. The **characters** are translated into **digital signals** for **storage** or processing.

Bare board
▶ **circuit board** which has no components in it; usually refers to a **memory expansion board** that does not yet have any **memory chips** mounted on it.

Base address
▶ starting **address** for a block of **data**.

Base font
▶ **font** in a **word processing** or **desktop publishing program** used as a **default** at the start of each **document**.

Base number
▶ value on which a numbering system is founded; the **binary** system uses base 2, **octal** system uses base 8, decimal system uses base 10 and the **hexadecimal** system uses base 16.

Baseband transmission
▶ type of **data transmission** in which a single **medium** such as wire can carry only one **channel** at a time; direct **transmission** of digital **signals**.

Baseline
▶ line on which printed **characters** are placed.

BASIC – Beginners All-purpose Symbolic Instruction Code
▶ **high-level programming language** which was developed as an easy-to-use introduction to **computer programming**.

Basic Input Output system – BIOS
▶ set of **instructions** that tells the **computer** how to function, receive **instructions** or transfer **data**; that part of the **operating system** which controls **communication** with the **monitor screen, keyboard, printer** and other **peripherals**.

Basic research
▶ original investigation directed towards the advancement of knowledge and the discovery of new facts, theories and laws.

Bastion host
▶ type of **firewall** that provides **access** security incorporating a **gateway**.

Bat file
▶ **file** name that ends in .BAT in MS-DOS and related **operating systems** and contains a list of **DOS commands**.

Batch
▶ collection of **computer** operations processed as a single unit and at the same time.

Batch processing
▶ processing of **data** by a **computer** which accumulates **transactions** and processes them as a single unit (a **batch**), rather than as they arise.

Batch command
▶ single **instruction** which causes a number of relatively simple **commands** to be carried out on a **batch file**.

Batch file
▶ **program file** that contains a sequence or collection of **commands**.

Batten system
▶ **indexing** system developed by W.E. Batten which coordinates single attributes; sometimes called **peek-a-boo system** because of the use of holes on cards which have to be compared to retrieve relevant items.

Battery pack
▶ rechargeable battery used in **portable computers**.

Baud
▶ unit measuring the speed of **transmission** of **data elements** over **telecommunications** lines. The speed in bauds is the number of discrete **signal** events per second. If each

signal event represents one **bit**, a baud is the number of **bits per second**.

Baud rate
▶ operating speed of a device or **communication channel** expressed in terms of pulses per second. Usually expressed in two figures, for example 300/1200, the first indicating sending speed and the second receiving speed.

Baudy language
▶ graphical language for conveying feelings; based on a pun on **baud**/body language. Sometimes called **smileys** or **emoticons**.

Bayesian function
▶ mathematical expression based on Bayes' theorem which states that additional information (if and when available) can sometimes help to alter or improve decision quality.

BBS – Bulletin Board System
▶ **computer** that allows users to **log on** from **remote terminals,** exchange messages and often **download programs**.

BCD – Binary Coded Decimal
▶ method of representing decimal numbers in **binary** by converting each decimal **digit** separately, each **digit** being represented by four **binary digits**. The resulting number is not the same as a number in **binary notation**.

BEDIS – Book Electronic Data Interchange Standards
▶ **Book Industry Communication (BIC) working party set up in 1987 which develops and approves **standards** that are used in **electronic data interchange** (EDI).

Beep
▶ short tone used to attract the attention of a user or operator. Also called a **prompt**.

Beginning of file – BOF
▶ **code** number used in a **computer** system to mark the start of a **data file**.

Behavioural science
▶ any science that studies the behaviour of man and the lower animals in their total environment using observation and experiment. Recognized behavioural sciences include psychology, sociology and anthropology.

Bell-shaped curve
▶ frequency distribution which is shaped like the vertical cross-section of a bell.

Bells and whistles
▶ slang expression to describe elaborate features added to a **computer program**. Usually describes features that are confusing and unnecessary.

Beltel
▶ South African **videotex** system.

Benchmark
▶ 1. computing – **program** designed to test and compare the performance of different **computers**;
2. research – reference point or criterion which can be used for measurement.

Benchmark test
▶ test run to compare pieces of equipment to measure speed and/or accuracy.

BER – Bit Error Rate
▶ measurement of the total number of **bits** received with **errors** relative to the total number received and expressed as a figure to the power of ten. Also called **error rate.**

Berne Convention
▶ **copyright** agreement signed in 1886 which provides protection for library and artistic works in those countries who have signed the agreement.

Bernoulli disk
▶ flexible, **magnetic disk** which is sealed inside a hard case. It can hold up to 150 **megabytes** of **data** and must be used with a special **Bernoulli drive**.

Bernoulli drive
▶ type of **disk drive** which can read a **Bernoulli disk**.

Bespoke software
▶ **software** that has been designed for a specific user or purpose.

Beta software
▶ **computer software** that has not yet been completely tested and may still contain problems or **bugs**.

Beta test
▶ last test carried out on a **software program** before it is released. The purpose is find out and correct any **bugs** or problems before the **software** is made available for purchase.

Beta version
▶ **software** version that is almost ready to be released.

Biannual
▶ publication issued twice a year.

Bias
▶ 1. generally – degree of departure from the average of a set of values from a reference value;
2. information handling – reflection of social attitudes or local needs in

the construction or use of **indexing** tools.

Bibliographic citation
▶ details of an item enabling it to be identified completely and unambiguously.

Bibliographic classification
▶ **classification scheme** developed by H.E. Bliss and published in 1910 which organized knowledge on the basis of **educational and scientific consensus**. Revised by Jack Mills in the 1970s.

Bibliographic control
▶ general term covering a range of bibliographic activities, including standardization of **bibliographic descriptions**, distribution of **union catalogues** etc.

Bibliographic coupling
▶ technique used to assign automatically a subject relationship between papers on the basis of **references** cited in common.

Bibliographic data element
▶ item used to provide unique information on a particular item, e.g. author, title, language etc.

Bibliographic database
▶ **database** containing information relating to documents (books, **articles**, **reports** etc.) The information normally contains details of authorship and title, together with place and date of publication. Some **databases** contain **abstracts** and each item is **indexed** to facilitate search and **access**. Sometimes called a **reference file**.

Bibliographic description
▶ set of **data elements** used to identify individual items such as author, title, language etc.

Bibliographic instruction
▶ American term for formal instruction for users and potential users of academic library and **information services**; called **user education** in the UK.

Bibliographic record
▶ **record** of an item which contains full details in a particular **format**, such as a **MARC record**.

Bibliographic service/utility
▶ organization that maintains **online bibliographic databases**.

Bibliography
▶ list of material or **documents** dealing with a particular subject area, individual etc.; study of books as physical objects; systematic study of the physical and textual **characteristics** and properties of books and other material relating to the transmission of texts and the techniques of printing and publishing.

Bibliometrics
▶ use of mathematics and statistical techniques to study **communication** patterns and publishing in the distribution of information; related to **scientometrics**. Originally called **statistical bibliography**.

Bibliotherapy
▶ therapy that uses reading material to help patients with their mental, emotional and social problems. The process has three stages: reader identification with the character in the book; catharsis; and insight.

Bi-directional
▶ device that functions in two directions such as carrying **signals** to and from a **peripheral** device.

Bi-directional printing
▶ printing in both directions used by many **dot matrix** and **inkjet printers** to achieve extra speed.

BIC – Book Industry Communication
▶ British organization established in 1991 to promote **electronic data interchange** (**EDI**) in the UK **book trade**.

Bidding
▶ process of tendering prices for specific services or equipment by potential suppliers.

Biennial
▶ publication issued every two years.

Biff
▶ to notify a person that they have incoming **E-mail** messages.

Big Endian
▶ memory addressing system in which numbers that occupy more than one **byte** in memory are stored with the uppermost 8 bits at the lowest address. Derived from 'Gulliver's Travels' by Jonathan Swift where there was a dispute about which end of the boiled egg should be broken first.

Bildschirmtext
▶ West German and Austrian **videotex** system.

Billion
▶ number equal to one million million in the UK; number equal to one thousand million in the USA.

Bimonthly
▶ publication issued every two months.

Bin
▶ **1.** – holder for paper fitted to a photocopier or **printer**; **2.** – folder for discarded **computer files**, also called **recycling bin**.

Binary
▶ number system in which there are only two **digits**, 0 and 1; the equivalent of an on/off switch where 1 means voltage is present and 0 means zero voltage.

Binary addition
▶ basic arithmetic operations performed by **computers**. It is the key to understanding how machines can do arithmetic.

Binary code
▶ code made up two numbers – 0 and 1.

Binary coded decimal – BCD
▶ method of representing decimal numbers in **binary** by converting each decimal **digit** separately, each **digit** being represented by four **binary digits**. The resulting number is not the same as a number in **binary notation**.

Binary digit – bit
▶ **digit** on the **binary** scale of **notation**, either 1 or 0. The smallest unit of information recognized by a **computer**. **Computers** usually store information as a series of **bits**.

Binary file
▶ **file** containing **bits** or **bytes** that do not necessarily represent printable text. Often used to denote any **file** that is not a **text file**.

Binary fraction
▶ fraction which uses the powers of 2 rather than the powers of 10.

Binary Large OBject – BLOB
▶ **database field** which contains unstructured **data** such as digitally encoded **images** or sounds.

Binary notation
▶ writing of numbers to the base 2, so that the position of the **digits** in a number designates powers of **2.**

Binary number
▶ number expressed in **binary notation,** a system which uses only two **digits** – 0 and 1.

Binary search
▶ **search** technique in which items are divided into two parts, where one part is rejected and the process is repeated until an item with the required property is found.

Binary transfer
▶ **file transfer protocol** which allows **binary files** to be transferred between **computers.**

Binary tree
▶ **tree structure** in which each branch consists of two **branches** only.

Binaural
▶ method of recording two audio **channels.**

Binaural sound
▶ method of recording sound so that it sounds like stereo when it is played back.

Binomial classification
▶ **classification** which consists of two, or in some cases three, terms.

Biobibliography
▶ list of an author's or a number of authors' works which includes biographical details.

Biometrics
▶ 1. generally – study of measurable biological characteristics;
2. computing – in **computer security,** the **authentication** techniques that rely on measurable physical characteristics that can be checked automatically.

Bionics – BIo electrONICS
▶ design of electronic systems using biological principles.

BIOS – Basic Input Output System
▶ set of **instructions** that tells the **computer** how to function, receive **instructions** or transfer **data;** that part of the **operating system** which controls **communication** with the **monitor screen, keyboard, printer** and other **peripherals.**

B-ISDN – Broadband Integrated Services Digital Network
▶ **standard** for transmitting voice, **video** and **data** simultaneously over fibre optic telephone lines.

BISAC
▶ **electronic data interchange** (EDI) **standards** for the USA and Australia.

Bistable
▶ **circuit** or device that has two possible states – on and off.

Bisynchronous
▶ regular exchange of **synchronization signals** between **communication** devices.

Bit – binary digit
▶ **digit** on the **binary** scale of **notation,** either 1 or 0. The smallest unit of information recognized by a **computer. Computers** usually store information as a series of **bits.**

Bit density
▶ number of **bits** contained in a **storage** area of a **magnetic tape** or **magnetic disk**.

Bit error rate – BER
▶ measurement of the total number of **bits** received with **errors** relative to the total number received and expressed as a figure to the power of ten. Also called **error rate.**

Bit pad
▶ **input** device which uses a **stylus** or **cursor** moved by hand over a flat surface. Also called a **graphics tablet**.

Bit rate
▶ speed at which **bits** are transmitted, usually expressed as **bits per second (bps)**.

Bit stream
▶ sequence of **bits** which is usually regarded as potentially endless and occurring at regular intervals.

Bite
▶ BInary digiT – either 0 or 1 when these **digits** are used in **binary notation**, smallest unit of **data** a computer system can handle.

Bit handling
▶ manipulation of individual **bits** in a **byte**.

Bitmap
▶ method of producing high-resolution **computer** pictures in which every **pixel** is described by a **binary digit**.

Bitmap display
▶ **screen** on which each displayed **pixel** corresponds to one or more **bits** in the **computer's** **video memory**.

Bitmap image
▶ **image** composed of individual **pixels** which are described by **binary digits**.

Bitmapped graphics
▶ **computer graphics** which use a full **matrix** of **pixels**, with each **pixel** having its own code; also called **raster graphics**.

BITNET – Because It's Time Network
▶ one of the early large US **networks** connected to EARN in Europe, NETWORTH in Canada and GULFNET in the Middle East.

Bits per inch – bpi
▶ density of **data** contained in a **storage** medium such as **magnetic tape**.

Bits per second – bps
▶ speed of **transmission** of **data** from one **computer** to another.

Bitwise
▶ operation that is performed in **bits** rather than decimal numbers.

Bitwise operator
▶ operator that manipulates individual **bits**.

Black box
▶ any item of equipment which carries out a specific set of **functions** but whose detailed operation is not known, or not specified. Usually used in discussions between the technician and the lay person to convey the **functions** performed and the **inputs** or **outputs** available to the person using the system.

Black box metrics
▶ **evaluation** method which looks at system performance as a whole without reference to internal details.

Blad
▶ mock-up of a book with a **book jacket**, cover and some indication of

contents prepared prior to publication for promotional and display purposes.

Blank character
▶ space which results when the space bar is pressed. Sometimes called a **space character**.

Blanket agreement
▶ agreement which covers a number of items.

Blanket order
▶ ordering system where a publisher or book supplier agrees to supply a library or **information centre** with one copy of all publications without return privileges.

Bleed
▶ printed matter where the text or illustrations run to the edge of the page.

Bleeding
▶ printing ink or colour which has run into surrounding areas.

Bleep
▶ audible **signal** which acts as a warning.

Blind copy receipt
▶ message sent to a number of **users** whose identities are not known to other recipients.

Blind dialling
▶ **modem** facility that allows for dialling a number even if the line seems to be dead; can be used on private lines.

Blind keyboard
▶ **keyboard** which does not provide a **visual display** or **hard copy** of **data** entered; the **output** is stored directly on **tape** or **disk**.

Blind reference
▶ **reference** to an **index heading** which does not exist in an **index**.

Blink
▶ on and off flashing effect which makes a **cursor, character,** word or phrase become prominent on the **screen**.

Blink speed
▶ rate of flashing effect on a **screen**.

Blip
▶ unwanted **signal** on a **display screen** or a **document** mark.

Bliss classification
▶ **bibliographic classification scheme** developed by H.E. Bliss and published in 1910 which organized knowledge on the basis of **educational and scientific consensus**. Revised by Jack Mills in the 1970s.

Bloatware
▶ slang term for **software** that has many features and requires a great deal of **disk** space and **RAM (random access memory)**.

BLOB – Binary Large OBject
▶ **database field** which contains unstructured **data** such as digitally encoded **images** or sounds.

Block
▶ information units that are handled as a single item; block size may be fixed or variable.

Block copy
▶ copying a marked section of **data** or a section of a **file** from one place to another in a **document** that has been produced by **word processing**.

Block delete
▶ removing a marked block of **data** from a **document** or **file**.

Block length
▶ number of **characters** in a block of **data**.

Block move
▶ moving a section of a **file** from one place to another within the same **file**.

Block of data
▶ set of **data** items that belong together.

Blow-up
▶ photograph, **book jacket**, illustration or page of a book that is enlarged for exhibition or promotional purposes.

Blueprint
▶ original set of **specifications** or a design in graphical form.

Blurb
▶ description of a book prior to or upon publication to promote sales, often containing quotes from **book reviews**; information about a book which appears on the **book jacket**. Sometimes called a **puff**.

Board
▶ **printed circuit board** for a **computer**. Sometimes called a **card**.

Body
▶ main text of a **document** excluding **headings**, **references**, **footnotes**, **captions** etc.

Body type
▶ type used for text rather than **headings** which is usually between 8 and 12 **point** in size.

BOF – beginning of file
▶ **code** number used in a **computer** system to mark the start of a **data** **file**.

Boilerplate
▶ text or **graphics** element that is meant to be used over and over again; final **document** that has been put together using standard sections of text held in a **word processing** system.

Boilerplating
▶ assembling a final **document** using standard text that has already been prepared.

Bold face
▶ heavy black **typeface**.

Bomb
▶ slang expression for something that has failed; concealed fault in a **computer program** which has been placed there deliberately to cause system failure.

Book club
▶ commercial organization that sells books to members, usually at a slightly lower price than the **retail price**; members usually have to agree to buy a certain number of books per year.

Book drop
▶ box or chute that allows readers to return books when the library is closed.

Book Electronic Data Interchange Standards – BEDIS
▶ **Book Industry Communication** (**BIC**) working party which develops and approves **standards** that are used in **electronic data interchange** (**EDI**).

Book fair
▶ trade exhibition for book publishers, book buyers and authors.

Book fund
▶ amount of money available for the purchase of books and other materials and services.

Book Industry Communication – BIC
▶ British organization established in 1991 to promote **electronic data interchange (EDI)** in the UK **book trade**.

Book jacket
▶ paper cover for a book, often used for promotion and containing quotes from reviews etc. Also called a **dust jacket** or **dust wrapper**.

Book number
▶ number, letter or symbol which identifies an individual work from other items; number which determines the order in which items are stored on a shelf. Sometimes called a **call number**.

Book-oriented indexing
▶ **indexing** where the conceptual level of a **document** is analyzed and the messages and **concepts** recognized. After recognizing the conceptual level, **indexers** move the terminological level and express the **concepts** in **index terms**. May also be called **entity-oriented indexing**.

Book plate
▶ label attached to the inside front cover of a book to indicate ownership.

Book review
▶ **evaluation** of a book in a **journal** or **newspaper**.

Book trade
▶ commercial arrangements for the distribution and sale of books, covering retail book stores, **booksellers**, publishers etc.

Book Trade Electronic Communications Committee – BTECC
▶ Committee established in the UK in 1988 to examine the common concerns of various sectors of the book world, encourage standardization and develop **electronic data interchange (EDI)**.

Book vendor
▶ American term for a supplier of books to libraries.

Book week
▶ local or national event which focuses on books, reading and the use of libraries, often aimed at children.

Bookbinding
▶ process which hold together the separate pages of a book.

Bookbot
▶ shopping **robot** that specializes in searching for books on the **Internet** bookstore sites, presenting the results in a consolidated and compact **format** that allows for comparison shopping.

Booketeria
▶ self-service library in rural areas of the USA which are not directly served by the public library.

Booklet
▶ small book with paper covers. Sometimes called a **brochure** or **pamphlet**.

Bookmark
▶ **1.** – mark a **document** or mark within a **document** for later **retrieval**; **2.** – remembered position in a **file** that is being edited; remembered **address** on the **World Wide Web** which can be accessed directly by the user.

Bookseller
▶ person in the business of selling books; owner of a bookshop.

Bookworm
► **1.** – moth or beetle larva that eats into the paper or covers of a book; **2.** – person who is a voracious reader.

Boolean algebra
► theory of mathematical logic developed by George Boole in the mid-nineteenth century. The algebra deals with classes, propositions etc., associated with such operators as **AND, OR, NOT**, IT, THEN and EXCEPT, and has wide applicability in **computer** analysis because it expresses logical relationships in a form that can be accommodated within the **binary** system of **digital computers**.

Boolean logic
► form of expression based on **Boolean algebra**, which specifies a logical possibility of a thing existing or not existing.

Boolean searching
► method of searching where the query is expressed in subject words using the **Boolean algebra** operators AND, OR and NOT etc.

Boot
► short for **bootstrap**.

Boot disk
► **disk** or **diskette** that can be used to start the **computer**.

Boot record
► **file** contained on the first sector of a **computer disk** which contains information about the **disk**. Damage to this **file** can render the **disk** virtually unusable.

Bootleg
► illegal copy of recorded material.

Bootleg software
► **computer program** obtained illegally; proprietary **software**

transferred illegally to a user who has not been authorized.

Bootlegging
➤ unauthorized commercial recording or dealing in live performances.

Bootstrap
► method of getting a **computer** started when switching on for the first time and there is no **program** in store to load any other **programs**. May refer to the actual instructions that load the first **program**.

BORIS
► Canadian **videotex** system.

Bot
► **computer program** that gathers information or performs some other function according to a specific schedule; short term for a **robot** which is a **computer program** that runs automatically.

Bottom margin
► blank space at the foot of a page.

Bottom-up management
► **management** style which pays a great deal of attention to the concerns of lower-level staff who thereby play a major role in policy development.

Bounce
► to return a piece of **E-mail** to its sender because there is a problem at the receiving end.

Bounce message
► message sent to a sender of **E-mail** to explain why it is not possible to deliver the message to the intended recipient.

Bound term
► term joined to another to modify the meaning of a commonly used term, e.g. high temperature.

Bounding box
▶ rectangle that determines the position, size and shape of a **graphic image** or **video** clip.

Box file
▶ rigid container that can hold flimsy material such as correspondence or newspaper **cuttings**.

Bowdlerize
▶ to edit or expurgate the text of a work to change or delete supposedly objectionable words or passages; named after Thomas Bowdler who produced an expurgated edition of Shakespeare in 1818.

bpi – bits per inch
▶ used for measuring density of **data** in a **storage** medium.

bps – bits per second
▶ speed of **transmission** of **data** from one **computer** to another.

Bracket
▶ **characters** that enclose text; could be round brackets ( ), sometimes called **parentheses,** or **square brackets** [ ].

Bracket, square
▶ generally used in quoted text to indicate text not in the original document. Used in a **cataloguing record** to indicate information that has been added by the cataloguer which does not occur on the item being catalogued.

Bradford distribution
▶ **bibliometric** distribution function that describes **journal** productivity, i.e. the number of contributions made in a given subject area.

Bradford-Zipf distribution
▶ studies which have compared **Bradford distribution** and **Zipf**

distribution to show that these are two different ways of examining the same phenomena.

Bradford's law
▶ law developed by C.S. Bradford in the 1930s which states that, in a given subject field over a given period of time, a relatively small number of **journals** will publish a relatively high proportion of material, and that a large number of **journals** will publish a relatively small proportion of material. Also referred to as Bradford's law of scatter, or Bradford's curve when displayed on a graph.

Braille
▶ system of reading and writing for blind or partially sighted people developed by Louis Braille, in which letters are formed by raised **dots** embossed on paper in groups of six – three high and two wide.

Braille keyboard
▶ **computer keyboard** designed for visually handicapped users which uses **keys** which correspond to the **code** used in the **Braille** language.

Braille tactile display
▶ **computer** read-out device for visually handicapped users which uses a set of pins that can be felt by the user with positions that correspond to the standard **Braille** language code.

Branch
▶ **1.** computing – **command** to move to another section of a **computer program; 2.** information handling – in a **tree structure**, a branch is a single line which ends in a leaf.

Branch instruction
▶ **instruction** that tells the **computer** to move to another part of the

program, for example the GO TO statement.

Branching classification
▶ **classification scheme** with two or more subclasses or main **branches**.

Breadboard
▶ special **circuit board** used to design new electronic **circuits**. Components can be plugged in and connected by hand.

Break
▶ action or **key** pressed to stop a **computer program** operation.

Break even point
▶ point at which expenditure and income are balanced evenly without profit being made.

Break key
▶ special **key** on a **keyboard** that halts the execution of a **computer program**. May need to be pressed in conjunction with the **control key**.

Breakdown
▶ work stopped because of mechanical failure.

Bridge
▶ device that connects two **networks** together; matching **communication** equipment that ensures power losses are minimized; **hardware** or **software** that allows parts of an old system to be used in a new system.

Bridgeware
▶ **software** used to make transferring from one **computer** system to another easier.

Broad classification
▶ **classification** system which provides broad general **classes** without subdivision.

Broad System of Ordering – BSO
▶ system developed to act as a **switching language** between **classification** systems and **thesauri**.

Broadband
▶ **communication channel** with a **bandwidth** greater than a voice-grade **channel**, and therefore capable of higher-speed **data transmission**.

Broadband ISDN – B-ISDN
▶ **standard** for transmitting voice, **video** and **data** simultaneously over **fibre optic** telephone lines.

Broadband transmission
▶ type of **data transmission** in which a single wire **medium** can carry several **channels** at the same time.

Broadcast communication network
▶ **communication network** where all **nodes** or stations share a common **medium**, such as radio **frequency**. All messages transmitted by any **node** are received by all stations in the **network**.

Broader term – BT
▶ in a **thesaurus**, the formal **hierarchical relationships** between a genus and its species are indicated by **narrower term** (**NT**) and **broader term** designators.

Broadsheet
▶ uncut sheet of paper; paper printed on one side only. Another name in the UK for a quality daily **newspaper**.

Broadside
▶ publicity leaflet in the USA.

Brochure
▶ small book with paper covers. Sometimes called a **booklet** or a **pamphlet**.

Broken order
► material arranged out of sequence to provide better **access** or service.

Brouter
► device for connecting **computer networks** that uses both a **bridge** and a **router**.

Brownout
► extended period of insufficient power line voltage which could damage **computer** equipment.

Browser
► **computer program** that allows users to read **hypertext files** on the **World Wide Web**; it can also provide tools for **navigation**. Sometimes called a **client program**.

Browsing
► looking through a store of **documents** at random, with no conscious **search strategy**; choosing from among a number of **documents** by examining each item.

Brussels Convention
► revision of the **Berne Copyright Convention** and signed in 1948.

BSO – Broad System of Ordering
► system developed to act as a **switching language** between **classification** systems and **thesauri**.

BT – Broader Term
► in a **thesaurus**, the formal **hierarchical relationships** between a genus and its species are indicated by **narrower term (NT)** and **broader term (BT)** designators.

BTECC – Book Trade Electronic Communications Committee
► committee established in the UK in 1988 to examine the common concerns of various sectors of the book world, encourage standardization and develop **electronic data interchange (EDI)**.

BTW
► **E-mail** abbreviation for by the way.

Bubble memory
► type of **storage** in which information is stored using magnetic spots or bubbles on a **silicon chip**. The presence or absence of a bubble in a particular location can be used to denote a **binary digit**.

Bubble sort
► **algorithm** for arranging items in order where pairs of **data** items are exchanged repeatedly until they are put in order.

BUBL – Bulletin Board for Libraries
► electronic bulletin board for **JANET user group**.

Budget
► spending plan for the money available to provide a service or activity.

Budget hearing
► formal session to review the **budget**, which allows the person responsible to make a presentation to support **budget** items.

Budgetary control
► periodic review of actual against estimated expenditure established by a **budget**.

Budgeting
► developing a plan of future expected income and expenditure for a specific time period and activity.

Buffer
► **1.** computing – temporary **storage** location that holds **data** which are being transferred from one location to another; a **circuit** used to isolate one **circuit** from another; **2.** printing

– substances or mixtures of substances used to control the acidity or alkalinity of paper.

Bug
▶ **error** in a **computer program**; the process of correcting such **errors** is called **debugging**.

Bug patch
▶ routine or **instruction** which is added to a **computer program** to circumvent a **bug**.

Building block
▶ self-contained unit that can be joined to others in a system.

Built-in
▶ describes a feature which is already included in a system.

Built-in clock
▶ clock inside a **computer** which holds the date and time in **memory**. It can put the time and date on a **file** displayed on the **screen**. It can also be used to date stamp.

Built-in font
▶ type **font** that is built into the **hardware** of the **printer**. **Dot matrix** and **laser printers** come with at least one such **font**. Also called a **resident font**.

Built-in function
▶ **function** that is built into an **application** which can be accessed by **end users**.

Bulk erase
▶ wiping all **signals** from a **disk** or a **magnetic tape**.

Bulk storage
▶ system which allows large amounts of **data** to be stored, usually with rather slow **access** times.

Bullet
▶ **character** that is often a filled circle or square which is used to mark items in a list.

Bulletin board
▶ form of **electronic mail** in which all messages are sent to a common **receiver** (i.e. the bulletin board). System users have **access** to all the messages.

Bulletin board system – BBS
▶ **computer** that allows users to **log on** from **remote terminals**, exchange messages and often **download programs**.

Bundle
▶ **1.** computing – number of **optical fibres** gathered together; **2.** management – offering of a group of items for sale cheaply, possibly with something extra added.

Bundled software
▶ **software** sold in combination with **hardware**.

Bureau
▶ office that offers special services such as **word processing** or **desktop publishing**.

Burst mode
▶ mode for rapid **data transmission** between the **central processing unit** and **peripheral** devices.

Burster
▶ machine which cuts continuous stationery into separate sheets.

Bus
▶ parallel group of wires that carries **digital data** inside a **computer**. It provides an interconnected system **path** over which information is transferred from any one of many sources to any one of many destinations.

Bus controller
▶ regulating mechanism that handles **data** flow through a **computer**.

Business application
▶ **computer program** designed for business use such as inventory control or payroll.

Business information
▶ details of commercial activities covering financial statements, products, market share etc.

Business information system
▶ **information system** that carries details of commercial activities covering financial statements, products, market share etc.

Business link
▶ **one-stop shop** for **business information**.

Business plan
▶ plan for a specific activity or service which provides details of cost, growth expectation, marketing details etc.

Busy signal
▶ **signal** sent along a **communication** line to indicate that a device cannot be used because it is already in use.

Button
▶ in **Hypertext/Windows**, an **icon** that represents the activation of some event, or activates a process.

Buzzword
▶ description of a word which is popular with a group of people.

Byline
▶ line of type at the beginning of a **newspaper** or **journal** article, giving the author's name or affiliation.

Byte
▶ group of eight **bits** that form a **character**, which may be a letter, a number or a control combination.

Cc

C
► high-level computer programming language which is very compact and uses a few short instruction words and symbols to control a large amount of computing action.

C++
► derivative of C computer programming language used to write operating systems, business software and games.

Cable
► transmission link between devices in a computer system; in the communications industry it usually refers to fibre optic cable.

Cable broadcasting
► broadcasting using a network of cables with metal conductors or optical fibres for distribution of sound and visual programmes, with the capability of sending signals to a large number of users.

Cable modem
► modem designed to operate over cable television lines.

Cable network
► cable television station that also includes the television sets which are connected to a network. Users usually have to pay for services.

Cable television
► television broadcasting system where signals are received by a central elevated antenna and transmitted to homes via cable. Sometimes called CATV (community antenna television).

Cableless LAN
► local area network which uses radio, microwave or infrared links rather than cables.

Cache
► in local area networks, the amount of random access memory (RAM) available to store data that might be used again; Internet data such as web pages and images are saved on a person's hard disk.

Cache memory
► form of buffer memory which can be accessed very rapidly.

CAD – Computer-Aided Design
► use of computer or graphics terminals in manufacturing processes, and for advertising and animation. It involves the use of modelling, analysis, simulation and optimization of design.

CAD/CAM system
► use of a computer and graphics terminal for design purposes and to control the manufacturing process.

CAE – Computer-Aided Engineering
▶ use of **computers** to analyse a design that has been generated either manually or by **computer** to stimulate action.

CAI – Computer-Assisted Instruction
▶ method of teaching that uses **computers** to ask questions and provide answers.

CAL – Computer-Aided Learning
▶ use of a **computer** to promote learning.

Calendar date
▶ date expressed as month, day and year as opposed to a **Julian date**.

Calibration
▶ **1.** generally – comparing the quantity of a known **standard** to correct the value; **2.** computing – adjusting a **monitor** or **joystick** to respond correctly to movements or **signals**; adjustment of **image** values to ensure faithful rendering of colours and grey tones when **output** to a **printer**.

Call
▶ statement that tells a **computer program** to obey a **subroutine**.

CALL – Computer-Assisted Language Learning
▶ **computer programs** which help a person to learn a foreign language. Often produced together with **videos** and **cassettes**.

Call forwarding
▶ service offered by some telephone companies where telephone calls can be forwarded automatically to a different number.

Call number
▶ number, letter or symbol that identifies an individual work from other items; number that determines the order in which items are stored on a shelf; sometimes called a **book number**.

Call scheduling
▶ **fax** and **modem** feature that allows outgoing calls to be made when telephone time is less expensive.

Call waiting
▶ facility where the telephone **beeps** to show that there is an incoming call when the telephone is in use.

Callback
▶ user **authentication** scheme where the user dials the **computer** giving **password** and **login** identification. The **computer** breaks connection and uses an **auto-dial modem** to confirm the user identity and reconnect for use.

CALS – Computer-Aided Logistics and Support
▶ development of **standard formats** for **documentation** and distribution **media** and the development of **standards** for electronic **storage** and distribution of information from one company to another.

CAM – Computer-Aided Manufacturing
▶ use of **computers** to control manufacturing processes.

Camcorder
▶ compact, portable **video** camera with built-in **video cassette** recorder and microphone.

Camera-ready copy
▶ material ready to be photographed to make a printing plate; **document** suitable for microfilming.

Campus environment
▶ large area where there are a great many users connected by several

networks. Examples are a university or a hospital.

Campus-wide information network – CWIS
▶ **interactive networked information retrieval system** which provides **access** to items of information for a particular academic institution and its members. A typical CWIS will provide an easy-to-use **interface** tailored for the non-expert and have the ability to handle a diverse range of structured and unstructured textual information.

Cancel command
▶ used when a user changes their mind so the **computer** returns to the previous **display** or **command**.

Candidate descriptor
▶ **term** suggested for inclusion in a **thesaurus**.

Canned software
▶ **computer programs** available to a wide number of users.

Cap height
▶ **font size** determined by the height of the **capital letter** measured in the **point** unit.

Capacity
▶ amount of information that a **storage** device can hold, usually measured in **bytes**, **megabytes** or **gigabytes**; ability of a **computer** or **peripheral** to manage a **task** or series of **tasks**.

Capital letter
▶ letter in **upper case** rather than **lower case**; first letter of a word in **upper case**.

Captain
▶ Japanese **videotex** system.

Caption
▶ text placed under or at the side of an illustration.

Capturing technology
▶ **input devices** that collect and convert information into **digital** form.

Card
▶ **1.** computing – removable **printed circuit board** that is plugged into a **computer** to perform a specific **function**; **2.** information handling – used in **cataloguing** to provide an **entry** for an item, usually 3×5 inches in size.

Card catalogue/index
▶ physical form of **catalogue** in which each **entry** is made on a separate **card** and the **cards** are filed in a specific order.

Career path development
▶ planned **professional development** towards a defined goal or objective.

Caret
▶ mark used in a **proof** to indicate that **character**(s) or word(s) have been omitted. The mark is usually repeated in the **margin** with the missing letter(s) or word(s) written beside it.

Carpel tunnel syndrome
▶ form of **repetitive strain injury** of the wrist which is attributed to excessive work with a **keyboard**.

Carrel
▶ traditionally, a small room near a reference library or collection which may be allocated to a user for continuous research and where working papers may be kept. More recently, a work table or area that is partially screened to provide a limited amount of privacy.

Carriage
▶ printing head of a **printer** which has to be returned to the left hand side of the page to start printing a new line of text.

Carriage return
▶ **key** or **character**, which when activated, ends a line of type and brings the **cursor** down to the start of the next line.

Carrier common line charge
▶ cost imposed by local telephone companies to use the local **network** to connect to international **networks**. Also called **access charge**.

Carrier signal/tone/wave
▶ **signal** that consists of packages of information.

Cartesian coordinate
▶ system of determining position by reference to two axes at right angles to each other.

Cartographic material
▶ material representing any part of earth or heaven.

Cartography
▶ act or study of drawing maps.

Cartridge
▶ **1.** generally – portable container for film (**video cassette**) or **magnetic tape**; **2.** computing – removable, self-contained part of a **computer** usually contained in a plastic case.

Cartridge font
▶ plug-in **cartridge** for a **laser printer** which adds one or more **fonts** to the built-in **font** set that exists on the **printer**.

Cascade window
▶ arrangement of **screen windows** where each **window** partially overlaps with a previous one such

that the **cursor** can be clicked on any **window** without needing to move a **window** out of the way. Sometimes called **staggered window**.

Cascading menu
▶ **menu** set in which successive portions overlap each other and are still visible on the **screen**.

CASE – Computer-Aided Software Engineering
▶ sophisticated **computer**-based tools that help **software** designers such as **systems analysts** and **programmers** to build **applications programs**.

Case
▶ cover for a commercially published book.

Case conversion
▶ changing of a text **attribute** such as changing from **capital letters** to **lower case**; **word processing program** feature which uses a **command** or **hot key** to change the **case** of a **character** such as changing from **upper case** to **lower case**.

Case sensitive
▶ recognition of the same letter of the alphabet when one version is in **upper case** and one in **lower case**.

Case study
▶ detailed analysis of a particular event, activity, institution etc.

Cash flow accounting
▶ accounting method where revenues are reported when received and expenditures reported when cash is disbursed.

Casing
▶ **1.** computing – solid protective box which houses a **computer** or piece of delicate equipment; **2.** publishing – hard cover on a book as opposed to a paperback. Such a

book is usually described as **hard bound**.

Cassette
▶ portable container for film (**video cassette**) or **magnetic tape**.

CAT – Computer-Aided Translation
▶ use of **computers** to assist in the translation of information from one spoken language to another. Also called **machine-aided translation**.

Cataloging in source
▶ in the USA provision of bibliographic **data** on material in the process of publication and often printed on the **verso** of the **title page**. The **data** are included in the Library of Congress and the British Library **MARC** files. Called **cataloguing in publication** (**CIP**) in the UK.

Catalogue
▶ list of materials available in a particular collection, arranged in a systematic order.

Catalogue card
▶ **card** that contains a single **catalogue entry**.

Catalogue code
▶ set of rules providing guidance in preparing **entries** for items in a **catalogue** to ensure consistency.

Catalogue entry/record
▶ information relating to an item that follows well-defined rules, such as **AACR2,** which is interfiled with other **records** to form a **catalogue**.

Cataloguing
▶ processes involved in constructing a **catalogue**: describing **documents** so as to identify and characterize them; providing **entry points** peculiar to the **document**, e.g. author **headings** or title **headings**; providing for

subject and **format** information. Sometimes used to include the process of **classification**.

Cataloguing in publication – CIP
▶ provision of bibliographic **data** on material in the process of publication and often printed on the **verso** of the **title page**. The **data** are included in the Library of Congress and British Library **MARC** files. Called **cataloging in source** in the USA.

Cataloguing rule
▶ rule which sets out how to prepare **entries** in a systematic way for **cataloguing** items in a collection.

Catchment area
▶ area from which a library or **information service** expects to draw its user community.

Category
▶ grouping of related **documents**; general **concept** that applies to a great deal of material which can be used to group other **concepts**.

Cathode ray tube – CRT
▶ electronic **display** device, similar to a television picture tube, used to display information including **graphics**. Its surface provides the **screen** in **visual display units** and word processors.

CATV – Community Antenna TeleVision
▶ television broadcasting system where **signals** are received by a central elevated **antenna** and transmitted to homes by **cable**.

CB radio – Citizens band
▶ cheap popular system of two-way radio **communications**, usually between lorry and truck drivers.

CBT – Computer-Based Training
▶ use of a **computer** system to present questions, explanatory text,

illustrations, and sounds to assist a person to learn a skill which could be manual or intellectual.

CCITT – Consultative Committee for International Telephone and Telegraph

▶ international **standards** organization of **PTT** authorities which is responsible for creating communication **protocols** to provide global **compatibility** for **voice transmission, data transmission** and **video transmission** using computing and **telecommunications** equipment.

CCL – Common Communication Language

▶ **command language** established in the early days of searching on more than one **host**. **Common command languages** were particularly valuable when **host computers** were first connected in a **network**, as the searcher could more easily switch from **host** to **host** during a **search**.

CCTV – Closed-Circuit TeleVision

▶ television system that uses a **cable** to send television **signals** to a limited number of **monitors**.

CD – Compact Disc

▶ **optical storage medium** on which an **analogue signal** is recorded in **digital** form in a **read-only memory**. It is a 4.75-inch diameter plastic **disc** coated with reflective material which is read by a laser. The audio CD plays one side only and can hold up to 75 minutes of recorded music. CDs can also be used for the storage and retrieval of a wide range of digitally encoded **data**.

CD rewriter

▶ compact disc rewritable format – blank **compact discs** which can be recorded over and over again like blank **audio tapes**.

CD-I – Compact Disc Interactive

▶ CD **format** developed by Philips and Sony which provides audio and **digital data**, still **graphics** and limited **motion video** that allows for **interactive** use.

CD-R/CD-Recordable

▶ recordable version of a **CD-ROM**, having the same **storage** capacity and is read in the same manner as normal **CDs**. They are less durable, but recordings can now be made over a number of recording sessions.

CD-Recordable drive

▶ device which allows **CD-ROMs** to be made at the **desktop**. It is useful for **prototyping** titles destined for conventional production, final production of **discs** for limited distribution or single use and **archiving**.

CD-ROM

▶ rigid disc that is similar to the music **compact disc** (**CD**) but contains information in a **read-only memory** instead of music. It can store between 550 and 680 **megabytes** of computerized **data** and can be accessed by a **personal computer** with the appropriate **drive** capability.

CD-ROM drive/player

▶ equipment (**hardware**) needed to read a **CD-ROM** disc.

CD-ROM networking

▶ provision of multiple, simultaneous and **remote access** to **CD-ROM**-based information over a **network** system.

CD-ROM/XA – CD-ROM/eXtended Architecture

▶ **specification** developed by Sony, Phillips and **Microsoft** that allows different data types such as audio, **video**, compressed **video** and graphics to be stored on a single **CD** which permits the interleaving of sound and **video** with **animation** and sound **synchronization**.

CD-RW disc – CD-ReWritable disc
▶ type of **CD disc** that allows the user to write on it in multiple sessions. It can be used like a **floppy disk** or **hard disk**.

CD-WO – Compact Disc Write Once
▶ **CD-ROM** disc and **drive** technology that allows a user to write **data** to a **disc** once only. It is useful for storing **archive** material or testing a **CD-ROM** before it is duplicated.

CD-WORM – Compact Disc Write Once Read Many
▶ **CD format** similar to **CD-ROM** which can be written once but read many times.

CDS/ISIS – Computerized Documentation System/Integrated Set of Information Systems
▶ minicomputer/microcomputer version of the generalized system developed by Unesco in the 1980s to handle non-numeric **databases** widely used in developing countries.

CDTV – Commodore Dynamic Total Vision
▶ **multimedia** system developed by Commodore.

Cedilla
▶ **accent mark** under the letter c used in certain languages to change the pronunciation or differentiate one letter from another.

CEEFAX
▶ **teletext** system operated by the British Broadcasting Corporation in the UK.

Cell
▶ location on a **spreadsheet**; box which holds information.

Cell definition
▶ content of a **spreadsheet cell**.

Cell format
▶ way in which information is arranged in a **spreadsheet cell**.

Cell protection
▶ option which prevents the content of a **cell** on a **spreadsheet** being altered.

Cell relay
▶ **wide area network** technology which allows the high-speed **transmission** of fixed-length short **data packets** or **cells**. Also called **fast packet switching**.

Cellular communication
▶ **communications system** which divides a geographic region into sections called **cells** in order to gain the best use out of a limited number of **transmission frequencies**.

Cellular radio
▶ radio **transmission** used for mobile **communications**. Geographical areas about three miles across are divided into cells with individual frequencies and a **computer** automatically changes **frequency** as users move between cells.

Cellular telephone
▶ portable telephone which uses **cellular radio** techniques to carry voice-related information.

Celluloid
▶ cellulose nitrate which was once used as a film base.

Censorship
▶ prohibition against publishing or distributing material that is

considered to be objectionable for social, political, religious or other reasons.

Central data access
▶ use of one **computer** in a **network** to control all **data processing**.

Central memory
▶ place in a **computer** where instructions and **data** are stored for fast **access**. May also be called **core storage** or **main memory**.

Central processing unit – CPU
▶ heart of the **computer**. It contains the arithmetic and logic units, the core **storage** and the control unit, which directs and coordinates the operation of the **computer** and its **peripheral** units. It thus carries out all the arithmetic, logic and control operations.

Centralized cataloguing
▶ **catalogue records** created by a centralized agency, such as a major library or **bibliographic service**.

Centre alignment
▶ centring a line of print on a page.

CEO
▶ chief executive officer of an organization.

Certificate authority
▶ trusted organization that confirms the identity of a person or an organization and issues **digital certificates**.

CGA – Colour Graphics Adapter
▶ old **graphics** system for **PCs** which has been superseded by **VGA (video graphics array)** systems.

CGM – Computer Graphics Metafile
▶ **standard format** that allows for the exchange of **graphic images**.

Chain
▶ in a **classification scheme**, divisions that are subordinate to each other.

Chain indexing
▶ **subject index** procedure where each item is entered in hierarchical order from the **broadest term** to the **narrowest term**.

Chain printer
▶ **line printer** with **characters** mounted on a continuous belt which rotates at high speed.

Chain search
▶ method of **searching** which leads from one **record** to another until the appropriate **record** is found or the end of the **chain** is reached.

Challenge handshake authentication protocol – CHAP
▶ type of **authentication** in which the agent (usually a **network server**) sends the **client program** a key which is used to encrypt the user name and **password**.

Challenge-response
▶ **authentication** technique where an individual is required (challenge) to provide some private information (response). **Smart cards** may use this system: when the user enters a **code** (challenge) the system responds and allows the user to **log on**.

Channel
▶ pathway along which **signals** are transmitted; allows information to be sent directly to an individual's **personal computer**.

Channel bonding
▶ technology that combines two telephone lines into a single **channel** which effectively doubles **data transfer** speeds.

CHAP – Challenge Handshake Authentication Protocol
▶ type of **authentication** in which the agent (usually a **network server**) sends the **client program** a **key** which is used to encrypt the user name and **password**.

Character
▶ combination of **bits** within a **computer** system representing either a printed **character** or a control combination such as **carriage return**, line-feed, end of text, end of message etc.

Character block
▶ set of **dots** that make up a character.

Character code
▶ **code** that gives each **character** a number which is stored in the **computer memory**.

Character printer
▶ **printer** which prints one **character** at a time and is limited to a **fixed-pitch font output**.

Character reader
▶ device used to scan and record **characters** or symbols that are converted into **digital data**.

Character recognition
▶ use of **pattern recognition** techniques to identify **characters** (especially **alphanumeric**). There are several techniques, e.g. **magnetic ink character recognition (MICR)** and **optical character recognition (OCR)**.

Character set
▶ collection of numbers, letters, **graphics** and **symbols** that can be generated by a particular system.

Character string
▶ series of **characters** that can be manipulated as a group.

Character-based interface
▶ traditional user **interface** where all **screen images** are made up of text **characters**.

Characteristic
▶ in **classification**, distinctive property or feature by which a **class** is defined in a **classification scheme**.

Characters per inch – cpi
▶ measurement of the number of **characters** that a **printer** can print in an inch of space.

Characters per second – cps
▶ measurement of the speed of **data transmission**.

Charge-coupled device
▶ **semiconductor** device used in **digital** cameras, **videos** and **scanners** that records **images** electronically by converting light into electrical **signals** that are then stored by the computer.

Charging system
▶ **1.** computing – procedure by which an **information service provider** can seek remuneration from a client for carrying out a particular task or providing a service;
2. management – any method of recording loans and returns of material by users in a library.

Chassis
▶ case or framework that holds a machine.

Chat
▶ **real-time communication** between two users via a **computer**.

Chat room
▶ electronic **forum** where users communicate with each other in **real time**.

Chatline
► interactive talk program operating over a network.

Check bit
► bit used for error detection; it is not used for data but is used to check that the other bits are valid.

Check box
► in Windows, list of options that can be switched on or off.

Check digit
► extra digit placed at the end of a number to check for errors in data or transmission. Usually generated using an algorithm.

Check mark
► cross or tick in a box next to a menu option to show if the option is used or not used.

Chemical notation
► words and rules to identify and classify chemical compounds.

Chemical pulp
► raw material made up of wood fibres from which harmful ingredients that can cause paper to deteriorate have been removed.

Chemical structure retrieval
► information retrieval techniques used to index and retrieve information about chemical compounds based on their chemical structure.

Chi-squared distribution
► sampling distribution derived from the sum of the squares of the deviations from the mean obtained from a large number of random samples of the same size drawn from a normally distributed population.

Chi-squared test
► significance test that compares frequencies derived from sample data with expected frequencies predicted by hypothesis.

Child directory
► sub-directory of another directory; directories on a hard drive are children of the main root directory.

Child program
► computer program which is called into action by another program.

Chip
► sliver of silicon that contains the electrical circuits for a computer. It is usually between 1 and 5 cm in length and has between six and 40 external connections. The type normally found in computer systems is called a logic chip. Commonly called a microchip.

Chip count
► number of integrated circuit chips on a board.

Chronological order
► arrangement of records according to the order in which the data was input.

CIM – Computer Input Microfilm
► microfilm used for high-speed input of information into a computer.

CIM – Computer Integrated Manufacturing
► fully automated production system where all the actions and processes, from production design and quality control to order entries, are programmed into robots and electronically-controlled machines. The process is controlled by a centralized database shared by all organizational departments.

CIO
▶ Chief Information Officer; senior executive responsible for establishing corporate **information policy**, **standards** and **management** control over all information resources.

CIP – Cataloguing In Publication
▶ provision of bibliographic **data** on material in the process of publication; often printed on the **verso** of the title page. The **data** are included in the Library of Congress and British Library **MARC** files; called **cataloging in source** in the USA.

Cipher
▶ method of altering **characters** in order to make **data** unreadable. Used in **encryption** techniques.

Ciphertext
▶ text that has been encrypted which will require a **key** or **password** to decipher.

Circuit
▶ **path** round which an electric **current** flows. In **telecommunications,** a means of two-way **communication** involving go and return **channels**.

Circuit board
▶ flat plastic or laminated plate with thin copper strips that connect different electronic components.

Circuit switch
▶ unit which initiates, maintains and ends **communications** connections.

Circuit-switched network
▶ **network** in which **transmission paths** are switched to make connections between **terminals** for the duration of a connection.

Circuit switching
▶ in **telecommunications**, individual **circuits** are interconnected through successive exchanges to provide continuous **transmission**. Also called **line switching**.

Circumflex
▶ printed **accent mark** that is similar to a small upside-down v placed above a letter in some languages to change the pronunciation or differentiate one letter from another.

CIS – Competitive Information System
▶ service that contributes to the financial and commercial success of a company by analysing market, competitor and world activities.

CISC – Complex Instruction Set Computer
▶ **computer** with a conventional set of **instructions** written in **assembly language**.

Citation
▶ **reference** to a **document** or part of a **document** from which a passage is quoted, or to a source regarded as an authority for a statement or proposition.

Citation analysis
▶ study of the links made between **documents** through **bibliographic citations**.

Citation factor
▶ number of **citations** received by a **document** or group of **documents** divided by the number of **document citations** over a specific time period.

Citation impact factor
▶ number of times **documents** are cited in relation to amount published. A way of assessing the relative importance of one research **journal** with respect to other **journals** by taking the ratio of the total number of times the **journal** is cited during a specific period

divided by the number of items published by that **journal** over the same or an earlier period.

Citation index
▶ **indexing** process which indexes **source document** and cited **documents**.

Citation order
▶ in **classification**, the order in which elements of **notation** are synthesized to express a superimposed or composite **class** when using a **faceted classification scheme**; the order in which **characteristics** of a division are applied to produce subclasses in an **enumerative classification scheme**.

Citation searching
▶ process where those **articles** mentioned as **references** are searched in a **database**. The assumption is that a subject relationship exists between citing and cited material.

Citizens band – CB radio
▶ cheap popular system of radio **communications**, usually between lorry and truck drivers.

CKO
▶ Chief Knowledge Officer; principal person in an organization who has responsibility for identifying and distributing relevant information to those who could use it within the organization.

Claim
▶ request sent by a library or **information service** asking a supplier to deliver previously ordered material which is overdue.

Class
▶ group of **concepts** or items assembled by some common **characteristic**; the major subdivisions of a **classification scheme**.

Class list
▶ list of books assigned to the same **class** in a **classification scheme**, usually arranged in **class** number order.

Classed catalogue
▶ **catalogue** with three or four separate sequences: author; title; classified **subject catalogue**; arranged by **classification** symbols or **notation** order, with an alphabetical **subject index** to the classified section. Also called a **classified catalogue**.

Classification
▶ process of determining the subject content of an item and assigning to it the appropriate classification number, **code** or **notation** from a **classification scheme**. Grouping together of like things according to some common quality or **characteristic**.

Classification scheme
▶ list of **classes** whose relationships are displayed in a **systematic order** according to their subject and, possibly, their physical form.

Classificationist
▶ person who develops a **classification scheme**.

Classified arrangement
▶ grouping together in an organized and logical manner of material that deals with a common subject and held in a collection. This refers both to the arrangement in a **classified catalogue** and the physical location of items.

Classified catalogue
▶ **catalogue** with three or four separate sequences: author; title; classified **subject catalogue** arranged by **classification** symbols **or notation** order, with an alphabetical **subject index** to the classified section. Also called a **classed catalogue**.

Classified material
▶ items of a secret or confidential nature which are subject to restricted **access**.

Classified order
▶ arrangement of books and other material or **entries** in a **catalogue** according to a particular **classification scheme**.

Classified subject catalogue
▶ **catalogue** where the access points are **classification** symbols or **notation** taken from a **classification** scheme.

Classifier
▶ person who assigns **classification** numbers to items using a specific **classification scheme**.

Clean boot
▶ starting a **computer** with only those **files** and **programs** that are absolutely necessary for the **operating system**.

Clearing house
▶ organization that collects and maintains **records** of publication, research and other activities planned or in progress in a specific subject area. Sometimes called a **depository**.

Click
▶ to press and release the **mouse button** quickly.

Click-and-drag
▶ holding down a **button** on a **mouse** or other **pointing device** to move **data** to another position and then releasing the **button**.

Client
▶ **1.** computing – **application** that runs on a **personal computer** or **work station** and relies on a **server** to perform some operations; **2.** management – person who uses an **information service**.

Client program
▶ **computer program** that allows users to read **hypertext files** on the **World Wide Web**; it can also provide tools for **navigation**. More often called a **browser**.

Client/server
▶ arrangement whereby **computers** can make use of **software** and **data** held on a central **computer;** the client is the **computer** requesting the service and the **server** is the **computer** providing it.

Client/server architecture
▶ **network architecture** in which each process or **computer** in the **network** is either a **client** or a **server**.

Client/server network
▶ **network** organization in which a central **dedicated computer**, the **server**, looks after such tasks as security, user accounts, printing, **file** sharing etc. while the **terminals** and **work stations** (**clients**) connected to the **server** run **standard applications**.

Cliometrics
▶ application of **econometrics** in economic history.

Clip art
▶ pictures that are supplied in a **computer** system that are ready for use. Often used in **desktop publishing**.

Clipboard
▶ in **Macintosh/Windows** a temporary **storage** location that is always available when a user needs to transfer information during a **Windows** session.

Clipper chip
▶ security **chip** that changes **data** into a **cipher** text for **transmission** and which has to be deciphered on receipt. It can be decrypted by the

US government which has tried to make the use of the **chip** compulsory in the USA.

Clipping
▶ item cut or clipped from a newspaper or periodical. Also called a **cutting** or **press cutting**.

Clock speed
▶ measurement of how fast a **microprocessor** runs.

Clock/calendar board
▶ **circuit board** which is usually an integral part of the **mother board** that shows the precise time and date which is used in a **computer**.

Clone
▶ copy or duplicate of something which is compatible with the original; could be a **computer, microprocessor chip, printer** or other device that performs in the same way as another device.

Clone tool
▶ device present in paint and photopaint **programs** that facilitates duplication of an area without the need to define the outline of an area or **object**.

Close
▶ stop using a **file** or **application** so that **programs** or **files** can be shut down.

Closed access
▶ material that is not directly available for public use.

Closed architecture
▶ **computer** design which does not allow other manufacturers to make and sell **add-on boards**.

Closed-Circuit Television – CCTV
▶ television system that uses a **cable** to send television **signals** to a limited number of **monitors**.

Closed entry
▶ in **cataloguing, entry** for a **serial** publication or work in several volumes which is complete or where the library has no additional items, so that no further information needs to be added to the **record**.

Closed indexing
▶ **indexing** a set of **records** using a limited number of **terms**.

Closed User Group – CUG
▶ used mainly in the context of **viewdata/videotex** and refers to a group of users who are allowed **access** to **data** or information which is not made available to other users of the system.

Clump
▶ group of associated **terms** based on their co-occurrence in texts within which there are more connections between terms than between those terms and members of other clumps.

Clumped catalogue
▶ **catalogues** from several organizations brought together and made available in a **virtual environment**. They can be searched together as though they were a **union catalogue**.

Cluster
▶ **1.** computing – a group of **terminals** and other **computer** devices connected so that they operate together; **2.** information handling – group of items such as **index terms** or **documents** normally determined by statistical analysis to be associated with each other in some way.

Cluster analysis
▶ process by which subjects are grouped by their overall similarity with specific **characteristics**.

Cluster sampling
▶ sampling method in which population elements are selected from groups or **clusters** of the population rather than from the whole population.

Clustering
▶ **documents** divided into groups of subject areas on the assumption that ideas that deal with the same subject will have similar **journal reference** patterns and will refer to each other.

CMYK (cian/magenta/yellow key)
▶ four colours (including black) used when printing in colour. Cian may be spelt cyan.

Coaxial cable
▶ **communication cable** consisting of an inner central **conductor**, usually of copper, insulated from an outer **conductor**, also usually of copper. When high **frequencies** are passed down such a **channel** there is a very low loss of energy. Several **cables** can be combined to form a single **bundle**.

COBOL – COmmon Business Oriented Language
▶ **high-level programming language** designed especially for the manipulation of business **data**. It uses **terms** which are related to ordinary English words.

Cocitation
▶ two or more authors, **documents** or **journals** that are cited at the same time by another **document**.

Cocitation analysis
▶ analysis of the **frequency** with which two or more works are cited together by later authors. As the number of authors that cite earlier works grows then those works are said to be strongly cocited.

Cocitation indexing
▶ technique developed from **citation indexing** which pairs **documents** that have been cited in common with other **documents** on the assumption that **documents** cited frequently in common with other **documents** are likely to have a subject relationship.

Code
▶ use of signs and **symbols** to represent letters or whole words.

CODEC – COmpressor/DECompressor
▶ technology for compressing or decompressing large amounts of **data** such as sound and **video files**.

Coden
▶ unique code for **serial** titles developed by the American Society for Testing and Materials which assigns a five-**character** code plus a **check digit** to each unique title.

Codex
▶ ancient book composed of separate writings fastened together to open like a modern book.

Coding
▶ translating written information such as subjects into **symbols** according to a prearranged system or code.

Coefficient
▶ number that serves as a measure of a relationship between **variables** and **parameters**.

Cognition
▶ mental process by which knowledge is acquired that includes perception, intuition and reasoning.

Cognitive model
▶ provision of examples in **cognition** that can be imitated to help a person learn new behaviour styles.

Cognitive network
▶ **network** plus a set of processes in the **network** that stores information, processes and adds to it and selects and makes inferences from it.

Cognitive science
▶ scientific discipline that studies the human mind and how it works; covers the processes involved in acquiring knowledge, learning, language, thinking, reasoning, memory etc.

Cognitive style
▶ distinctive pattern of **cognition** that characterizes individuals.

COLD – Computer Output on Laser Disc
▶ **document storage** technique in which scanned **document images** are stored on a **laser** or **optical disc**.

Cold boot/start
▶ clearing of a **computer memory** and the starting up of the **operating system** after a **computer** has been completely shut down.

Collapse
▶ compression of a **hierarchy** so that only the roots of each **branch** are visible.

Collateral reference
▶ direction between two **subject headings** at the same level.

Collating sequence
▶ **alphabetical order** of all **characters** represented on a **computer** including **digits**, **punctuation** marks and special **characters**.

Collation
▶ description of a **document** which describes the item as a physical object in terms of its size, number of pages etc.

Collection assessment
▶ systematic evaluation of the size, appropriateness and usefulness of a library collection in terms of the goals, patrons and programmes of the sponsoring organization.

Collection development
▶ planning material **acquisition** to meet users' needs in both the short- and long-term future.

Collection management
▶ application of quantitative techniques such as **cost-benefit** studies to **collection development**.

Collective bargaining
▶ negotiation between an employer and a union or other group representing workers to reach agreement on wages, working hours etc.

Collision
▶ situation when two **hosts** transmit at the same time on a **network** so that **information packets** collide and become corrupted.

Collocation
▶ arrangement of subordinate **classes** in a **classification scheme** by degrees of likeness.

Colon
▶ punctuation mark (:) used to link related **classes** in the **Colon Classification**.

Colon Classification
▶ **classification system** developed by S.R. Ranganathan in 1933 based on a minimum of enumeration coupled with freedom to synthesize **notation** elements. It is an **analytico-synthetic classification** based on careful division of each subject fields into **facets**, often defined as **PMEST** (Personality, Matter, Energy, Space and Time).

Colophon
▶ details of printer, place and date of printing found at the end of a printed book.

Colour depth
▶ measurement of the number of colours a **web** camera or **scanner** can pick up measured in **bits**. The more **bits** in the measurement the more colours a **scanner** or **web** camera can see.

Colour graphics adapter – CGA
▶ old **graphics** system for **PCs** which has been superseded by **VGA (video graphics array)** systems.

Colour monitor
▶ **monitor** that can display **images** in many colours.

Colour printer
▶ **printer** that can print in more than one colour.

Colour resolution
▶ number of **bits** per **pixel** in a coloured **image**.

Colour separation
▶ process of separating artwork into the four basic process colours cyan, magenta, yellow and black.

Colour transparency
▶ positive colour photograph on a transparent film.

Column
▶ information set out in a narrow strip down a page.

Column graph
▶ type of presentation **graphic** in which numerical values are illustrated using horizontal columns.

COM – Computer Output Microfilm/Microform/Microfiche
▶ instead of producing paper **output**, COM systems reduce the same information to **microform**, thus offering a number of advantages over paper **output** such as speed, economy, ease of distribution and **storage**.

Command
▶ **instruction** to a **computer** to carry out a step in a **program** or automated **function**.

Command button
▶ in **Windows**, a facility that initiates immediate action.

Command-driven program
▶ older type of **computer program** in which each action is started by a **command** word or phrase, followed by pressing the Enter or Return **key**.

Command interface
▶ user **interface** that requires the user to enter **commands** at the **command prompt**.

Command language
▶ **1.** computing – **high-level programming language** used for communicating with an **operating system**; **2.** online searching – the **command language** is used to facilitate a dialogue between a user and a **host computer**. It consists of a restricted range of **instructions** and **terms** used by the searcher to instruct the **computer** to perform certain operations.

Command line interpreter
▶ that part of the **operating system** that receives and obeys **commands** typed in by the user.

Command processor
▶ that part of the **operating system** that receives and executes **operating system commands**.

Comment
▶ in **programming**, a message that reminds the **programmer** or tells a new **programmer** what a set of **instructions** mean.

Commentary
▶ explanatory or critical notes relating to a specific text.

Common carrier
▶ private or public corporation responsible for the provision of **telecommunications** services to the public. It is primarily concerned with the use of authorized equipment and **protocols**. Examples are BT in the UK and AT&T in the USA.

Common carrier network
▶ government-regulated **telecommunications network** service available to the general public that exercises no control over the message content they carry. **E-mail** is an example.

Common Command Language – CCL
▶ **command language** established in the early days of **searching** on more than one **host**. **Common command languages** were particularly valuable when **host computers** were first connected in a **network,** as the searcher could switch more easily from **host** to **host** during a **search**.

Common facet
▶ **facet** for a commonly occurring aspect such as time or place which is used to subdivide **classes** in a **classification system**.

Common subdivision
▶ division that is used throughout a **classification scheme** to subdivide any subject to identify physical **format**, language, country etc.

Commonwealth Scientific and Industrial Research Organization – CSIRO Network (CSIRONET)
▶ **computer network** offering **online access** within Australia to the **databases** of CSIRO.

Communication
▶ process of transferring information from a source via a **transmission medium** to one or more receiver. The transmitting source should express the information clearly, the **medium** used should convey the information efficiently and the receiver should understand the information received.

Communication buffer
▶ device that provides temporary **storage** of **data** that is being sent or received to allow for differences in the speed and availability of various devices.

Communication channel
▶ link between two **computer terminals** to provide both an outward and a return **path**.

Communication format
▶ **format** for the exchange of information with other systems.

Communication network
▶ physically dispersed **computers** connected by **telecommunications channels**. Sometimes called a **telecommunications network**.

Communication port
▶ connection that links a **computer** to a **telecommunications** system.

Communication protocol
▶ convention which allows messages to be exchanged.

Communication server
▶ **standalone** device which directs and organizes **communication** from a **network** to a **mainframe computer** and vice versa.

Communication skill
▶ ability to communicate effectively with individuals or groups.

Communication theory
▶ mathematical theory which describes how information is transmitted from a source via an encoder through a **channel** to a decoder and then on to a **receiver**.

Communications link
▶ **path** that systems must use to transfer information; **hardware** and **software** which allows remotely-sited **computers** to exchange **data**.

Communications package
▶ set of **computer programs** which allows the use of a **modem** to communicate with other **computers**.

Communications satellite
▶ **satellite** used for channelling radio, television or **data signals** from one point on the earth to another point.

Communications software
▶ **software** that makes it possible to send and receive **data** over telephone lines using **modems**.

Communications system
▶ all the equipment which must be connected together in order to send and receive messages.

Communications technology
▶ devices, methods and **networks** that transmit information in **digital** form.

Community information
▶ information relating to a particular community, usually collected by a public library, covering leisure activities, local organizations etc.

Community information service
▶ provision of relevant information to a local community on request; for example, health and education information.

Community library
▶ public library or centre that provides reference, advice and other services to a particular community in addition to a loan collection.

Community profile
▶ **demographic** study of a community in terms of social and educational factors.

Compact disc – CD
▶ **optical storage medium** on which an **analogue signal** is recorded in **digital** form. It is a 4.75 inch plastic **disc** coated with reflective material which is read by a laser. The audio CD plays one side only and can hold up to 75 minutes of recorded music. CDs can also be used for the **storage** and **retrieval** of a wide range of digitally encoded **data**.

Compact disc interactive – CD-I
▶ set of rules or a **standard** created for **compact discs** which can be used to store information. Combination of television and computing systems that use **data** on a **compact disc**. The user can make choices on how to move through the **disc**.

Compact disc-recordable – CD-R
▶ recordable version of a **CD-ROM**. CD-R discs combine magnetic and optical technology and allow **data** to be overwritten.

Comparative librarianship
▶ study of libraries and library systems in two or more national or cultural environments to compare their **characteristics**.

Compatibility
▶ 1. computing – ability of two (**hardware/software**) devices to work in conjunction. **Computer compatibility** usually means **software** compatibility. If a **program** can be run successfully on two **computers** without alteration, then the **computers** are said to be compatible; 2. information handling – in **classification** and **indexing**, the degree of similarity between two systems.

Compendium
▶ work containing in a compact **format** the substance or general principles of a larger work; a comprehensive summary of a larger work.

Competency-based education
▶ educational process based on proven ability to perform specific tasks.

Competitive information system – CIS
▶ service that contributes to the financial and commercial success of a company by analysing market, competitor and world activities.

Competitive intelligence
▶ company information that relates to market competitors etc.

Compilation
▶ 1. computing – translation of an encoded **source program** into **machine readable** code; 2. information source – collection of material from a number of different works which are published together.

Compiler
▶ **program** which translates another **program**, usually an **application program**, from a high-level form of a language, such as **COBOL** or **BASIC**, into **machine code** for execution by a **computer**.

Component
▶ one piece of equipment or electronic device.

Component software/ componentware
▶ **software** designed to work as a component in a larger **application**.

Composite subject
▶ subject that includes more than one unit **concept** which expresses complex ideas.

Composite video
▶ **video signals** that combine **video pixel** information in **monochrome** or colour with the electronic synchronization **signals** which control the **screen** picture.

Composition
▶ setting type for reproduction; overall **page layout** of type and graphics on a page. Sometimes called **page makeup** or **page layout**.

Compound document architecture
▶ **document** interchange system developed by Digital Equipment Company in the mid-1980s which aims to facilitate the integration and interchange of different **data** types.

Compound subject
▶ subject which requires more than one word to express its meaning in a **heading**; it may be expressed as a phrase or a combination of words, with the separate words being divided by punctuation.

Compressor
▶ any electronic device that compresses the range of a **signal**.

Compressed file
▶ **file** which has been reduced to the smallest possible size. Sometimes called a **packed file**.

Compression
▶ coding **data** to save **storage** space or **transmission** time.

Compulsory arbitration
▶ process where an employer and a union are required by law to submit their differences for consideration by a third party and to accept its decisions.

Computability
▶ extent to which a problem can be solved by **computer**.

Computational error
▶ **error** caused by arithmetical rounding or problems caused by numbers that are too large or too small to be represented correctly by a **binary** fraction.

Computational linguistics
▶ use of **computers** to study human languages and how to make **computers** understand information expressed in human languages.

Computer
▶ machine which can accept **data** in a certain form and process them to give results or to control a process; it can **input** and store **data**, operate a **program** and **output** results to the user.

Computer-Aided Design – CAD
▶ use of **computer graphics** to design products for manufacture and building, and for advertising and **animation**. It involves the use of **modelling**, analysis, **simulation** and optimization of design.

Computer-Aided Engineering – CAE
▶ use of **computers** to analyze a design that has been generated either manually or by **computer** to stimulate action.

Computer-Aided Instruction – CAI
▶ method of teaching that uses **computers** to ask questions and provide answers.

Computer-Aided Manufacture – CAM
▶ use of **computers** to control the manufacturing process.

Computer-Aided Phototypesetting
▶ use of a **computer** to prepare material for printing using an optical system.

Computer-Aided Software Engineering – CASE
▶ sophisticated **computer**-based tools that help **software** designers such as **systems analysts** and **programmers** to build **applications programs**.

Computer-Aided Translation – CAT
▶ use of **computers** to assist in the **translation** of information from one spoken language to another. Also called **machine-aided translation**.

Computer-Aided Typesetting
▶ use of a **computer** at any stage of the typesetting or composition process.

Computer animation
▶ creation of moving **images**, especially of cartoons or special effects, using a **computer**.

Computer application
▶ use of a **computer** to deal with a specific problem.

Computer architecture
▶ layout of the internal **hardware** of a **computer**, including the electronic components and connections to the **central processing unit** (CPU).

Computer art
▶ art produced using a **computer**.

Computer-Assisted Language Learning – CALL
▶ computer programs which help a person to learn a foreign language. Often produced together with videos and cassettes.

Computer-Based Training – CBT
▶ use of a computer system to present questions, explanatory text, illustrations and sounds to assist the user to learn a skill which could be manual or intellectual.

Computer capacity planning
▶ ensuring in a cost-effective way that an organization will have adequate computing resources to meet future needs.

Computer chip
▶ sliver of silicon that contains the electrical circuits for a computer.

Computer code
▶ instructions given to a computer to cause it to execute a program. High-level code means a program written in a high-level language; machine code means a code directly executable by the computer.

Computer conferencing
▶ facility for holding meetings controlled by a computer that allows people in different locations to talk to each other directly. Sometimes called teleconferencing.

Computer crime
▶ theft, fraud or other crimes involving computers.

Computer ethics
▶ responsible use of computers and computer networks.

Computer fraud
▶ breaking into or misusing computer systems for illegal purpose. Sometimes called hacking.

Computer game
▶ game controlled by the computer in which the computer may oppose the human player. It typically uses fast animated graphics and synthesized sound. Also called video game.

Computer generation
▶ broad group of computer classification: first generation was made from valves and wire circuits in 1940s and 1950s; second generation from early 1960s was based on transistors and printed circuit boards; third generation from late 1960s used integrated circuits; fourth generation used microprocessors, large scale integration and sophisticated programming languages; fifth generation is based on parallel processing and very large-scale integration.

Computer graphics
▶ use of computers to generate and display pictorial images. Images may be generated using vector or raster graphics.

Computer imaging
▶ use of computers to generate and display pictorial images. Also called computer graphics.

Computer Input Microfilm – CIM
▶ microfilm used for high-speed input of information into a computer.

Computer Integrated Manufacturing – CIM
▶ fully automated production system where all the actions and processes from production design and quality control to order entries are programmed into robots and electronically controlled machines. The process is controlled by a centralized database shared by all organizational departments.

Computer language
▶ language used by a **programmer**
or user to give **instructions** to a
computer.

Computer literacy
▶ awareness of computing
capabilities and an ability to
recognize and articulate problems
that can be solved with the aid of
computing technology. It does not
imply the ability to **program**
computers.

Computer literate
▶ having a working knowledge of
the way a **computer** operates and
some knowledge of **software**
programs.

Computer Output
Microfilm/Microform/Microfiche –
COM
▶ instead of producing paper **output**,
COM systems reduce the same
information to **microform**, thus
offering a number of advantages
over paper **output**, such as speed,
economy, ease of distribution and
storage.

Computer Output on Laser Disc –
COLD
▶ **document storage** technique in
which scanned **document images** are
stored on **optical disc**.

Computer peripheral
▶ any external device that is
attached to a **computer**, such as a
printer, that operates under the
control of the **computer**.

Computer power
▶ relative speed of computing; more
powerful **computers** work at a faster
speed.

Computer programming
▶ analysis of the procedures
involved in solving **programming**

problems and writing procedures in
computer program language
statements that tell the **computer**
what to do.

Computer science
▶ study of **computers**, their
construction, operation and
application, and the use **algorithms**
to solve problems.

Computer security
▶ process of protecting a **computer**,
computer network, **computer**
programs or **data** from **access** or use
by people who have not been
authorized.

Computer service organization
▶ company that provides **computer**
assistance to customers by leasing
computer time, designing and
developing customized **software** or
hardware or maintaining a
customer's **computer network**.

Computer simulation
▶ representation of a real-life
situation in a **computer program**.

Computer Telephone Integration –
CTI
▶ use of **computers** to handle and
control telephone functions such as
making and receiving calls, **directory**
services and caller identification.

Concatenate (computing)
▶ to join together two **variables** or
files.

Concept
▶ idea, as opposed to the **terms**
which are used to represent ideas.

Concept coordination
▶ analysis and **indexing** of items in
terms of single-unit **concepts**, which
permit the **retrieval** of information
via flexible combinations of **concepts**
during the **retrieval** process. Also
called **coordinate indexing**.

Concept indexing
▶ **indexing** of ideas rather than the words used by an author to represent those ideas.

Concept mapping
▶ device for representing the conceptual structure of a **discipline** or part of a **discipline** in two dimensions to demonstrate an individual's understanding of a body of knowledge and the relationships that have meaning for that individual.

Conceptual browsing
▶ process of organizing relational patterns when not all terms are known in a **database**.

Conceptual model (computing)
▶ description of a **database** or other **program** in terms of **data** or relationships.

Concordance
▶ **index** of all significant words in an author's work, giving the text **reference**, **context** and, in some cases, a definition.

Concordance file (computing)
▶ **file** of text consisting of words that are intended to appear in an **index**.

Concurrency
▶ resources or **data** that are accessed by more than one user or **application** at the same time.

Concurrent operating system
▶ **operating system software** that allows several activities or **programs** to be processed at the same time.

Condensation
▶ summary of the contents of a **document**.

Conditional branch
▶ **computer instruction** that is exercised only if certain specific conditions are met.

Conductor
▶ material that allows heat or electricity to pass through it easily.

Conference proceeding
▶ published **records** of a meeting, usually containing **abstracts** or texts of papers presented. Also called **transactions**.

Conferencing
▶ **generic** term used to cover various systems that link people together.

Confidence level
▶ likelihood that a number will lie within a range of values.

Confidentiality
▶ keeping spoken or written information from becoming public knowledge, including information held in **computer** systems.

Configuration
▶ selection or layout of **hardware** for a particular **computer** system.

Confirmation message
▶ message that asks the user to confirm that an action is to be carried out.

Connect charge
▶ charge levied on a user based on the length of time that a **telecommunication** system is used.

Connect time
▶ length of time that a user is directly linked to an **interactive computer** system.

Connection table
▶ stage in **relational indexing** where **index terms** are recorded and their

57

relation with other **terms** given a numerical weighting.

Connectivity
▶ ability of **computer** devices to send and retrieve **data** to and from each other.

Connector
▶ **1.** computing – fitting used to connect or separate two electrical devices; **male connectors** have one or more exposed pins and **female connectors** have holes into which **male connectors** can be fitted;
2. information handling – word that connects conditions in a search query such **AND, OR** or **NOT**.

Consecutive
▶ one thing following after another in order.

Conservation
▶ use of physical and chemical processes to ensure the **preservation** of books, **manuscripts** and other **records** in their treatment or **storage**.

Consistency check
▶ check to ensure that **objects, data** and items are in their expected **formats**.

Console
▶ controlling unit of a **computer** system which allows the user to communicate with the **computer**.

Consolidation
▶ merging and synthesizing information or **data** on a given subject.

Consortium
▶ formal association of a number of organizations, usually in a specific geographical area, with agreed goals and objectives. Services covered can include **collection development, cataloguing, computer** alliances, systems support, education and training, **interlibrary loans**, library automation, purchasing etc.

Conspectus
▶ overall survey or summary of a system or service.

Constant
▶ **1.** generally – value that does not change; name or symbol that does not change; **2.** computing – quantity whose value is not changed in the course of a **program**.

Consultant
▶ specialist who gives advice on specific topics.

Consultative Committee for International Telephone and Telegraph – CCITT
▶ international **standards** organization of **PTT** authorities which is responsible for creating **communication protocols** that provide global **compatibility** for **voice transmission, data transmission** and **video transmission** using computing and **telecommunications** equipment.

Consultative management
▶ **management** approach where supervisors and managers actively solicit the views of their employees before making decisions.

Consumable
▶ item such as paper, ink, ribbons, toner etc., which is used up and has to be replaced.

Content-addressable memory
▶ **storage** device whose locations are identified by their **context**.

Content analysis
▶ analysis of the content of a **document** by assigning **subject headings, classification** etc.

Contents list
▶ list of items and details of their location in a **document**, given at the beginning of a publication. Also called **table of contents**.

Context
▶ words that are expressed in a phrase to show how they are used or what they mean.

Context-free language
▶ language that uses a context-free grammar that will produce all the **strings** of that language using only those that are present in the language.

Context-sensitive help
▶ ability of some **computer programs** to pop up **help screens** with information about a **menu** feature that is highlighted or as an adjunct to a **dialogue box**.

Continuance quality improvement – CQI
▶ process that allows managers to identify poorly served groups or users in order to make such changes that meet identified needs and continue to assess service to these groups or individuals.

Continuation
▶ publication issued in successive parts or as a supplement to a later work.

Continuation order
▶ order to supply specified items, **series** or **periodicals** on a continuous basis until specifically cancelled; also called **standing order** or **till forbid order**.

Continuing education
▶ 1. – activities that staff should pursue to develop, improve and diversify their skills during their working life; 2. – form of structured education throughout an individual's life; 3. – extension of education, full-time or part-time, for young people beyond school-leaving age and adults.

Continuous paper
▶ paper that passes continuously through a **printer**, usually guided by sprocket holes along the edge.

Contract service
▶ service provided to a library or **information centre** by another library or external organization for an agreed price.

Contracting out
▶ using an external supplier to provide a service.

Contrast control
▶ knob that is used to make information on a **visual display unit** lighter or darker with respect to the background to make the **display** easier to read.

Control bus
▶ electrical pathway used to communicate control **signals**.

Control character
▶ **character** whose occurrence in a particular **context** can change a control operation. A typical example is the **character** that can initiate a **carriage return**.

Control key
▶ **key** on **PC keyboards** labelled Ctrl. It is used in conjunction with another **character** to produce a control **key** combination.

Control panel
▶ in **Windows**, a collection of **icons** which configure the basic functions of a **personal computer**.

Control unit
▶ **central processing unit** component that decodes, synchronizes and carries out **program instructions**.

Controlled term
▶ **indexing** term that has been accepted for use in an **indexing** system which has had all other connected terms identified and linked to it by **cross references**.

Controlled vocabulary
▶ fixed list of **terms** used to **index records** for **storage** and **retrieval**, with rules for selecting words and adding new words to the list.

Controlled vocabulary indexing
▶ **indexing** where terms are selected from a fixed list, which is sometimes described as an **authority list** or a **thesaurus**.

Convergence
▶ coming together of technologies which in the past have been regarded as relatively distinct, e.g. **computers**, **telecommunications** and publishing, to provide **integrated systems**.

Conversational mode
▶ **computer** system that provides immediate response to a user's **input**.

Conversion
▶ in **cataloguing**, process by which printed **records** are changed into **machine-readable records**.

Conversion program
▶ **program** that converts or changes another **program** so that it can run on a different **computer**.

Cooccurrence analysis
▶ analysis of those **index terms** that will allow satisfactory substitution and continue to retrieve relevant **documents**.

Cookie
▶ message given to a **web browser** from a **web server**.

Cooperation
▶ joint operation or action between two or more **entities**.

Cooperative
▶ association of institutions who agree to cooperate for a specific purpose.

Cooperative cataloguing
▶ sharing the work of **cataloguing** by a group of libraries or other agencies.

Cooperative multitasking
▶ type of **multitasking** in which the process controlling the **central processing unit** must offer control to other processes.

Cooperative processing
▶ system in which two or more **computers** in a **distributed network** can both execute part of a **program** or work on a **data set**.

Coordinate indexing
▶ process of analysing the information content of an item and expressing it by two or more **index** words which are manipulated to produce informational content in varied degrees of detail and/or depth. Sometimes called **concept coordination**.

Coordinate system
▶ in computing use of symbols to locate an element or point in a two- or three-dimensional **array**.

Copperplate printing
▶ printing method which uses a copper plate on which an **image** is etched.

Coprocessor
▶ additional **processor** that helps a **computer** system run faster as it takes some of the work from the **central processing unit**.

Copy
▶ in computing making an exact copy of a **file** or part of a **file** so that it can be used somewhere else.

Copy and paste
▶ process of duplicating text or **graphics** and placing the copied material in another position in the same item.

Copy protection
▶ code in some **computer programs** to prevent people from using it without permission.

Copyboard
▶ board which has a writing area that can be scanned electronically and copies printed out.

Copyright
▶ legal protection provided to authors and/or publishers against unauthorized copying of their work.

Copyright library
▶ library where material is sent for **preservation** by publishers under the provision of a **legal deposit** law or some other form of legislation. Sometimes called a **deposit/depository library**.

Copyright notice
▶ statement of **copyright** ownership in a printed **document** or a **computer program**.

Cordless mouse
▶ **computer mouse** that is not wired directly to the **computer** but communicates with a **receiver** attached to the **computer**.

Cordless telephone
▶ telephone that is not connected to a line but uses a radio link.

Core and scatter
▶ **concept** that over a period of time there will be a small number of highly-productive **journals** (core) producing most of the articles in a given subject area, and a very much larger number of **journals** that produce only a small number (scatter). Related to **Bradford's law**.

Core collection
▶ material that represents the major information interests of the users of a library or **information centre**.

Core journal
▶ **periodical** considered to be essential for a given subject area.

Core literature
▶ material considered essential for the study of a particular subject.

Core memory
▶ internal electronic **memory** of a **digital computer**. Old term for **main memory** which was made up of doughnut-shaped magnets called cores.

Core storage
▶ internal or main memory of a **computer** which holds **data** and **data processing** instructions before processing by the **central processing unit**.

Coresident program
▶ **computer program** that shares the **memory** of a **computer** with other **programs**.

Corporate author
▶ **corporate body** such as an organization or government department which produces a **document** and provides the **author entry** in a **catalogue**.

Corporate body
▶ institution or organization that has a collective name.

Corporate brain
▶ collective memory of a company, which is the basis of its ability to compete.

Corporate culture
▶ acceptance of and commitment to the perceived objectives, values and goals of an organization throughout the organization. Sometimes called **organizational culture**.

Corporate information system
▶ **information system** which provides a service to a commercial company.

Corporate intelligence
▶ total information available within a company which relates to its products and services.

Corrupted data
▶ **data** that has **errors** in it; **hardware** or **software** problems that can cause **data** to be lost or stored incorrectly.

Corrupted file
▶ **computer file** that has been damaged so that its contents are wholly or partly unstable.

Corruption
▶ unwanted changing of **data** in the **computer memory** or during replay from **backup tape** or **disk**.

Cosourcing
▶ using the services of an external organization to perform part, but not all, of a process or service. Most of the main functions are carried out internally by the principal organization. Often used as an alternative to **outsourcing**.

Cost accounting
▶ recording and controlling all expenditure of an organization in order to control specific activities. Sometimes called **management accounting**.

Cost benefit
▶ advantage stated in financial terms relating to the provision of a specific service or activity.

Cost-benefit analysis
▶ **management** technique for analysing the cost of providing a service, programme or activity where its value is stated in financial and social terms.

Cost control
▶ keeping track of expenditure in order to effect rigid control or savings.

Cost effect
▶ financial implication of a specific activity.

Cost-effects analysis
▶ **management** technique for analysing and comparing the cost of providing a service, programme or activity to determine which method of provision makes the best use of available resources.

Cost recovery
▶ gaining back the cost of providing a service or activity by special funding, charging or other means.

Courseware
▶ **software** used for training purposes or in an educational program.

Co-word analysis
▶ analysis of text which examines words occurring near each other and their frequency of occurrence in the same domain: sentence, paragraph, paper, etc.

CP/M – Control Program/Monitor
▶ widely-used **microcomputer operating system**.

CPM – Cards Per Minute
▶ rate at which a card reader operates.

CPM – Critical Path Method
▶ **management** technique for scheduling and controlling large **projects**, particularly those involving a large number of interdependent phases. It is a mathematically ordered system of planning and scheduling in which progress is monitored, automatic progress reports are written, problems analysed and **management** strategies simulated. Sometimes called **PERT**.

CPS – Characters Per Second
▶ measurement of the speed of **data transmission**.

CPU – Central Processing Unit
▶ heart of the **computer**. It contains the arithmetic and logic units, the core **storage** and the control unit, which directs and coordinates the operation of the **computer** and its **peripheral** units. It thus carries out all the arithmetic, logic and control operations.

CQI – Continuance Quality Improvement
▶ process that allows managers to identify poorly served groups or users to make such changes that meet identified needs and continue to assess service to these groups or individuals.

Crack
▶ term used by **hackers** when they break into a **computer** system.

Cracker
▶ person who breaks into **computers** via the **Internet** and uses them without authorization.

Crash
▶ sudden, complete **computer** failure usually caused by a **fault** in the **hardware** or **software**.

Crashed
▶ when the **computer** fails and completely stops.

Crawler
▶ name for a **search engine**. Automated **indexing software** that searches the **web** for new or updated **web sites**.

Cray computer
▶ very powerful **computer** which is an example of a **supercomputer** designed for **applications** that place a premium on capacity and speed.

Crippled version/crippleware
▶ demonstration **software** that has one or more critical features disabled. Used for sales promotion to allow potential purchasers to try out a particular **application**. Also called a **demo disk**.

Critical abstract
▶ **abstract** which not only represents the content of a **document** but also includes an **evaluation**.

Critical bibliography
▶ study of published works which examines in detail the physical structure in terms of pages, paper, bindings etc. Sometimes called **analytical bibliography**.

Critical error
▶ **error** which stops a **computer program** until the cause of the **error** is corrected.

Critical incidence technique
▶ specified procedures applied to **data collection** in research studies involving human activities which meet a predefined set of criteria.

Critical mass
▶ minimum number of people or things that can sustain a specific activity or service.

Critical path analysis
▶ procedure used in the **management** of complex projects to minimize the amount of time taken. It shows what activities can be run in parallel and what has to be completed before other activities can start.

Critical path method – CPM
▶ **management** technique for scheduling and controlling large **projects**, particularly those involving a large number of interdependent phases. It is a mathematically ordered system of planning and scheduling in which progress is monitored, automatic progress reports are written, problems analysed and **management** strategies simulated. Sometimes called **PERT**.

Critical thinking
▶ method of thinking which involves self- improvement using **standard** methods to assess thinking.

Crop mark
▶ mark on a printed sheet which shows the edge of physical page.

Cropping
▶ reduction of **image** size on a **screen display** by removing part of the **image** area at the top, bottom, or sides.

Cross matching
▶ comparing results obtained by different **search strategies**.

Cross reference
▶ **instruction** which leads from one **heading** to another; may be made between titles, subjects or names. Also called a **reference**.

Cross-border data flow
▶ electronic transfer of **data** or information across national boundaries; owing to regulations it is often more restricted than **communication** within national geographical areas. Also called **transborder data flow**.

Cross-database searching
▶ 1. – formulation of a **search strategy** that can be used in a number of different **databases** either separately or automatically;
2. – transferring elements of **records** found in an initial search to another **database** as **search terms**.

Cross-file searching
▶ in **online searching**, the ability to use a **search strategy** to search more than one **file** or **database**.

Cross-platform computing
▶ development of **computer programs** that can be used on different types of **computers**.

Crosshair cursor
▶ **cursor** that consists of a large cross made up of thin lines. Used especially in **programs** to make it easier to line up **objects** that are some distance apart on the **screen**.

Crosstalk
▶ **noise** from other sources that interfere with a **signal**; **interference** on a telephone line. Also called **babble**.

CRT – Cathode Ray Tube
▶ electronic **display** device, similar to a television picture tube, used to display information including **graphics**. Its surface provides the screen in **visual display units** and **word processors**.

Cryogenic store
▶ type of **memory** developed for **supercomputers** which stores

information at very low
temperatures.

Cryptographic key
▶ code used for the encryption and
deciphering of data. For security
purposes, it can be used to code data
before transmission and decode on
receipt.

Cryptography
▶ study of encryption and
decryption; usually involves taking
plain text and applying a encryption
algorithm to produce encrypted
ciphertext.

**CSIRONET – Commonwealth
Scientific and Industrial Research
Organization Network**
▶ computer network offering online
access within Australia to the
databases of CSIRO.

**CTI – Computer Telephone
Integration**
▶ use of computers to handle and
control telephone functions such as
making and receiving calls, directory
services and caller identification.

CUG – Closed User Group
▶ used mainly in the context of
viewdata/videotex and refers to a
group of users who are allowed
access to data or information which
is not made available to other users
of the system.

Cultural heritage
▶ inherited ideas, beliefs and values
that should be preserved for a
country or region to demonstrate its
development.

Cumulation
▶ publication where previous issues
of an index or a bibliography are
collected into the current issue.
Collected works of an author.

Cumulative index
▶ index containing all the items
appearing in a separate series of
indexes.

Currency
▶ degree to which information is up-
to-date and therefore still valid.

Current
▶ rate of flow of electricity through a
circuit.

Current awareness
▶ system of notifying users about
current documents and information
that have been published recently.

Current awareness journal
▶ publication containing tables of
contents pages from periodicals,
usually in a specific subject area.

Current awareness service
▶ service that alerts the user to new
information likely to be of interest to
them.

Cursor
▶ blinking line or square that
indicates the next point of data entry
on the monitor of a terminal.
Indicator on the screen of a visual
display unit which indicates, for
example, the position at which the
next character typed from a
keyboard will appear.

Cursor control key
▶ key that can be used to cause
cursor movement. May be marked
with arrows to show the direction in
which the cursor is moved.

Customization
▶ optimizing a system so that it uses
its resources most efficiently in
performing tasks. Typically, it can
involve improving one or more
aspect of system performance at the
expense of something else.

Customized software application
▶ system which has been optimized so that it can be used most effectively in performing specific **tasks**.

Cut
▶ to remove an **object** from a **document** and place it in a **buffer**.

Cut and paste
▶ use of scissors and paste to cut up and incorporate new material into existing documents.

Cut/copy and paste
▶ process of removing text or **graphics** and placing the cut/copied material in another location or another **file**.

Cut-sheet feeder
▶ device which takes one sheet of paper at a time and feeds it into the **printer**.

Cutting
▶ item cut or clipped from a **newspaper** or **periodical**. Sometimes called a **clipping, newspaper cutting** or **press cutting**.

CWIS – Campus-Wide Information network
▶ **interactive networked information retrieval system** which provides **access** to items of information for a particular academic institution and its members. A typical CWIS will provide an easy-to-use **interface** tailored for the non-expert and have the ability to handle a diverse range of structured and unstructured textual information.

Cyber
▶ prefix used to describe new things that are being made possible by the use of **computers**.

Cyberarchive
▶ **storage** and **preservation** of selected resources of both **full text** material and **web sites** available on the **Internet**.

Cybercafe
▶ cafe which not only serves food and drink but also provides **Internet access**.

Cyberethics
▶ name given to responsible **guidelines** for appropriate use of information in **cyberspace**. Sometimes called **virtual morality**.

Cyberglove
▶ device used to interact with **virtual reality** that contains **sensors** which respond to finger movements which are transmitted into the **virtual reality** system. Some gloves can measure wrist and elbow movements. Also called a **wired glove**.

Cybernaut
▶ name being proposed for library and **information workers** who deal primarily with electronic information, usually via the **Internet**; they develop **navigation** skills so that they can assist users to use these resources effectively. Sometimes called a **cybrarian**.

Cybernetics
▶ mechanical, **communication**, electronic and control systems designed to replace human functions.

Cyberspace
▶ term coined by William Gibson to describe the world of **computer networking** and the electronic environment that is developing the concept of the **information superhighway**.

Cybersurfer

▶ user of the **Internet** who can use the tools available to explore the resources offered on the **network**.

Cybrarian

▶ name being proposed for library and **information workers** who deal primarily with electronic information, usually via the **Internet**; they develop **navigation** skills so that they can assist users to use these resources effectively. Sometimes called a **cybernaut**.

Cycle

▶ complete sequence of operations; a unit of time used by the **central processing unit** to move **data** through the **computer** system.

Dd

Dagger
▶ symbol used in printing shaped like a dagger to mark a special word.

Dash
▶ character (—) similar to but longer than a **hyphen**. An **em dash** is the width of the letter M in a print **font**; an **en dash** is the width of the letter N in a print **font**.

Daisy chain
▶ connection of devices together using **cables**.

Daisywheel printer
▶ printer where **characters** are placed on the ends of spokes attached to a central point.

Data
▶ values, numbers, **characters** or symbols that have been arranged to represent information which can be **input**, processed or stored by a **computer**.

Data analysis
▶ derivation of optimal **data** structures from an analysis of patterns of **data** use.

Data buffer
▶ portion of **memory** used by **data** which is being transferred to or from a **printer**, **disk drive** or other device.

Data bus
▶ electrical **path** or **bus** that is used to carry **data** between **computer** components.

Data capture
▶ process of converting **data** from non-electronic forms (paper, **microform**, drawings etc.) into a form that the **computer** can read, store and manipulate.

Data circuit
▶ two-way means of **transmission** which uses two **channels** to transfer **data** between **computer terminals**.

Data collection
▶ covers **data** gathering and checking and transcribing it into a form that a **computer** can understand and use; gathering **data** from remote locations.

Data communication
▶ sending and receiving **data** using a **communication medium** which could be a telephone line, satellite or network.

Data compaction
▶ refers to methods used to reduce the space and time required for **data storage** and **transmission**.

Data compression
▶ reducing the size of **data elements** by changing the way in which they are coded.

Data conversion
▶ process of converting **data** from one form to another, usually from a **human-readable** form to a

machine-readable form, or from one recording **medium** to another.

Data corruption
▶ accidental or deliberate changing of **data** during **storage** or **transmission**. This can be caused by dirt or dust between the write head and the magnetic **media**, or by **transmission interference**.

Data delimiter
▶ number **code** used to mark the end of a **data file** or **data** item.

Data dictionary
▶ **file** of descriptions of **data** items held in a **database**, quoting their **formats**, usage, meaning, relationship with other items etc. **File** that holds **data** about **data** which is used by **database software** to enable **data access**.

Data element
▶ item used to provide unique information on a particular item, e.g. title, author, language etc. Sometimes called a **bibliographic data element**.

Data encryption key – DEK
▶ **key** used for the coding or **encryption** of text and to calculate the integrity of **digital signatures**.

Data entry
▶ entering **data** or **commands** into a **computer** system.

Data hierarchy (computing)
▶ **tree structure** of **data** organization where **data files** consist of **record** sets with each **record** made up of **fields**.

Data independence
▶ **database** design feature that makes it easier to **access data** without knowing where the **data** is stored.

Data integrity
▶ extent to which **data** is immune from corruption, especially when being transferred or stored.

Data Interchange Format – DIF
▶ **standard file format** for **spreadsheet** and **database applications** in which information is structured in rows and columns.

Data link
▶ **1.** computing – connection between **computer** systems that allows information sharing; **2.** information handling – link between **documents** containing the same information which is automatically updated in all **documents** when one is changed.

Data link layer
▶ in **open systems interconnection** (**OSI**), layer 2 which represents the physical medium.

Data logging
▶ usually automatic process of capturing and recording a sequence of values for later analysis and processing by **computer**.

Data mart
▶ **database** or collection of **databases** that are designed to help managers make strategic business decisions.

Data mining
▶ form of **artificial intelligence** that uses automated processes to find information and also to discover previously unknown relationships between **data**. It is used especially in the scientific and business communities for tracking the behaviour of individuals and groups, processing medical information etc.

Data network
▶ **telecommunications network** linking **computer terminals** that transmit **data**.

Data packet
▶ **data** divided into **packets** of about a hundred **bits** for **transmission** (used in **packet switching**).

Data pollution
▶ method of securing statistical **data** from **hackers** or other unauthorized users where **data** is falsified at random but does not alter the validity of statistics derived from the **data**.

Data preparation
▶ in computing, transferring information from written to **machine-readable** form.

Data privacy
▶ restriction of **file access** to authorized users; restriction on the holding of personal information on **computer** systems.

Data processing – DP
▶ includes all clerical, arithmetical and logical operations performed on **data** where a **computer** is used; the collecting, **storage**, processing and presentation of **data** as useful information.

Data processing system
▶ **computer hardware** and **software** required to carry out **data-processing** activities.

Data production
▶ mechanical process of making a **database** available for distribution in a particular **format**.

Data protection
▶ limiting **access** to personal information held in **computer files** to safeguard the **privacy** of the individual.

Data protection legislation
▶ legislation that protects people from the incorrect usage of personal information that is, **access** by

unauthorized people and the use of personal information for unauthorized purposes.

Data recovery
▶ saving **data** which has been stored on damaged **magnetic tapes** or **disks**.

Data reduction
▶ transforming large bodies of raw **data** into useful, ordered or simplified information.

Data refinement
▶ process of converting **data** into a more useful form by using knowledge about its content, structure and meaning.

Data representation
▶ **binary bit** pattern used in a system to represent **data**.

Data security
▶ control of **access** to **data** held within a **computer** system which is usually achieved by issuing a series of confidential **passwords** to authorized personnel; procedures that protect a system and its users against intentional or accidental misuse of **data**.

Data set
▶ items contained in a **data file**.

Data structure
▶ method of arranging information in the **memory** of a **computer**.

Data transfer
▶ process of transferring information from one location to another.

Data transfer rate
▶ speed at which **data** travels between devices.

Data transmission
▶ process of transmitting information in **digital** form.

Data validation
► checking on **data** that has been entered to identify **errors**.

Data warehouse
► collection of a large amount of **data** held by an organization in the belief that it will provide coherent and relevant information when searched. Users **access** information using **data mining** techniques in order to produce reports etc.

Databank
► collection of factual or numerical **data**, as distinct from a **bibliographic database** which gives **references** to **documents**. Also called a **numeric database** and sometimes used as a synonym for **database**.

Database
► **file** or systematically organized collection of bibliographic references or unit **records** representing original items, published literature or other recorded material; **data** that is stored in some form (usually electronically) which can be retrieved and manipulated; a collection of information that can be organized in some way (possibly very simply) to facilitate **storage** and **retrieval** of individual items. Today this implies **computer** storage, but could include **card indexes**.

Database management
► operation of a **computer** system to control the recording, analysis, **indexing**, **storage** and **retrieval** of **data**.

Database management system – DBMS
► **application** package which facilitates the maintenance and **searching** of **databases**.

Database producer
► organization that produces a **database**.

Database query language
► language which allows users of a **database** to formulate requests interactively and generate answers.

Database right
► European Community directive that states that any **database** is protected for a period of fifteen years against unfair extraction or re-use of content.

Database server
► **computer** in a **network** that holds and manages a **database** while the user can only manipulate the **data** and **applications**.

Database tomography
► use of a **computer**-based **algorithm** to extract and order **data** from a large body of textual material. It is a **full text** phrase association technique that has its roots in **co-word analysis** and **computational linguistics**.

Dataline
► line in a television broadcast **signal** which carries **teletext data**.

Date format
► method of writing a date using numbers; American and British styles differ, with the form representing 7th December 1999 being 12/07/99 in the USA and 07/12/99 in the UK.

Date number
► date expressed by numbers rather than words.

Daughter board
► **circuit board** that can be plugged into an existing **mother board** or **adaptor card** to add a new function to a **computer**.

db – decibel
▶ unit that measures the power of an electrical or sound **signal**.

DBMS – DataBase Management System
▶ **application** package which facilitates the maintenance and **searching** of **databases**.

DBS – Direct Broadcasting by Satellite
▶ sending television by **satellite** from a broadcasting station which is beamed to receiving dishes on earth. **Cables** then carry the **signal** to the **antenna** of television sets.

DCC – Digital Compact Cassette
▶ **magnetic tape** in a compact **cassette** box that stores **computer data** or audio **signals** in **digital format** and records **CD**-quality sound.

DDC – Dewey Decimal Classification
▶ **classification scheme** developed by Melvil Dewey, first published in 1876 and used extensively for the **shelf arrangement** of books in public libraries. It uses **decimal notation** and there are ten main **classes**.

DDD – Direct Distance Dialling
▶ automatic exchange service which allows a telephone subscriber to make telephone calls outside a local area without going through an operator.

de facto standard
▶ method used by a **vendor** or organization which is so widely accepted and used that it is considered a **standard**.

de jure standard
▶ **standard** that is the result of formal national and international processes established by national policy and international treaties.

Deacidification
▶ process which raises the pH value of paper **documents** to a minimum of 7.0 to assist in their **preservation**.

Dead key
▶ **key** on a **keyboard** which causes an action rather than typing a **character**. **Function keys** are all dead keys.

Debug
▶ identify and correct **errors** in a **computer program** or **routine**.

Debugger
▶ **software** tool to help in tracing and removing **bugs** from **programs**, e.g. by allowing traces of the **paths** actually taken through **programs** when run and causing them to stop at predetermined break-points.

Decay
▶ rate at which a **signal** or electronic impulse fades away; time taken for an impulse to fade; gradual decrease in noise.

Decentralization
▶ redistribution of functions, processes and powers from a central authority in an organization to outlying or smaller units.

Decentralized network
▶ **network** in which some or all control **functions** and services are distributed between several locations or **nodes**.

Decibel – db
▶ unit that measures the power of an electrical or sound **signal**.

Decimal classification
▶ generally any **classification scheme** using a **notation** based on decimal numbers. Sometimes used as the name of the **Dewey Decimal Classification**.

Decimal notation
▶ fractional **notation** using a base of 10, so that there are ten notational divisions available at every step. It can be subdivided infinitely by inserting subdivisions using the next decimal place.

Decipher
▶ convert a coded message into readable text; read difficult handwriting.

Decision making
▶ deciding on actions related to the **management** of a system or service.

Decision Support System – DSS
▶ **computer** system having a range of tools designed to help in the process of **decision making**. Normally comprises a method of capturing and storing relevant **data** plus a means by which the **data** can be manipulated in order to explore alternative **models** and consequences of actions.

Decision table/tree
▶ list of possible courses of action or choices to be considered in describing or solving a problem, together with actions that need to be taken.

Decision technology system
▶ system that supports all phases of the **decision-making** process.

Deckle edge
▶ rough edge of handmade paper.

Declare
▶ in computing stating the **attributes** of a **variable**.

Declassification
▶ assigning **classified material** to a less restrictive security **classification**, usually making it accessible to a wider group of users. Also called **downgrading**.

Decoder
▶ electronic **circuit** used to select one of several possible **data** pathways.

Decryption
▶ decoding or translating information from an unreadable or secret **format** so that it can be read.

Dedicated computer
▶ **computer** used for a specific **function** or series of **functions** or **applications**.

Dedicated line
▶ **telecommunication** link (usually a telephone line) reserved for the sole use of a particular customer. Sometimes called a **leased line**.

Dedicated server
▶ depending on the **network** configuration, a single **computer** dedicated exclusively to running the **network operating system** and servicing the users on the **network**. In a **peer-to-peer** network it is configured to be a potential **file** server.

Dedicated storage
▶ **storage** which is reserved for a specific user, **application** or other defined purpose.

Deductive database
▶ **database** that hold rules in addition to storing **data**. These rules are applied when the **database** is altered. A conventional **database** holds only **data** and any rules or **algorithms** used to alter **data** are held in appropriate **programs**.

Default
▶ option assigned by the **computer** if no other **instruction** is received.

Default configuration
▶ **instructions** automatically carried out by a device or a **program** in the

absence of specific **instruction** from a user.

Default directory
▶ **data directory** which is automatically selected by a **program** to find **files** associated with its operation or containing **data** that is needed.

Default drive
▶ **disk drive** that a **computer** will automatically select when not told specifically which **drive** to use.

Default font
▶ **font** which will be automatically selected for printing or for **screen display** when no **font** is specified.

Default logic
▶ formal reasoning system in which some rules or facts take priority over others.

Default value
▶ operational condition used by a device automatically when a value is not selected. Sometimes this value cannot be selected until after the device is switched on.

Defragmentation
▶ reorganization of a **file** from scattered parts of a file on a **disk** into a set of contiguous sectors.

Degradation
▶ decline in **computer** system during its operation; loss of **signal** or picture quality.

DEK – Data Encryption Key
▶ **key** used for the coding or **encryption** of text and to calculate the integrity of **digital signatures**.

Delimiter
▶ **character** used to mark the end of a **field**, or a pair of **characters** that

mark the boundaries, for example, of a **string** of **characters.**

Delivery time
▶ time interval between the start of **transmission** at an initiating **terminal** and the completion of reception at a receiving **terminal**.

Delphi study
▶ method of predicting trends or events based on the opinions and assessments of advisors or experts who receive **feedback** and revise their opinions until a consensus is reached.

Demo disk
▶ **disk** used to demonstrate **software,** usually holding part of a **program** or only allowing the **program** to carry out certain operations. Usually used in sales promotion. Also called **crippled version** or **crippleware**.

Democratic network
▶ **network** in which each **computer** in the **network** has equal priority on **data** and resources.

Demodulation
▶ process of converting a **signal** after **modulation** to its original form.

Demodulator
▶ device that changes **data signals** such as **analogue** to **digital**.

Demographic study
▶ statistical study of a specific population.

Demographics
▶ study of population statistics.

Demonstration program
▶ experimental or innovative **program** run for a limited time to test its potential and value.

Dependent variable
▶ **variable** that is, or is thought to be, affected by an **independent variable**.

Deposit/depository library
▶ library where material is sent for **preservation** by publishers under the provision of a **legal deposit** law or some other form of legislation. Sometimes called a **copyright library**.

Deposit collection
▶ collection of material from a single publisher placed in a library or **information centre** to be made generally available.

Deposit copy
▶ free copy of a new publication sent to the **copyright** office and **legal deposit libraries**.

Depository
▶ organization that collects and maintains **records** of publication, research and other activities planned or in progress in a special subject area. Sometimes called a **clearing house**.

Depth indexing
▶ **indexing** of each specific subject identified in the text of a **document**.

Deregulation
▶ allowing state-owned companies to supply equipment and services from more than one source.

Derived indexing
▶ **indexing** method by which **index** terms are derived from words in the title or the text of a work.

Deselection
▶ discarding from stock materials that are considered to be of no further use. Also called **negative selection** or **weeding**.

Descender
▶ part of a lower case printed letter that extends below the **baseline** (**x-height**), e.g. p and g.

Descending order/sort
▶ arrangement of a list where numbers are arranged with the largest one first and continuing to the smallest; letters are arranged with the last letter of the alphabet first and the first one coming last.

Descriptive bibliography
▶ detailed physical description and study of books.

Descriptive cataloguing
▶ that part of the **indexing** process which is concerned with identifying and describing a **document** by recording information such as title, author's name, **edition**, **imprint** details, **collation**, **series** details etc.

Descriptive statistics
▶ statistical methods used to describe the collection of precise quantitative **data** that can be used to facilitate **communication** and interpretation.

Descriptor
▶ **term** first used by Calvin Mooers in the mid-1960s who proposed that there was a basic set of approximately 250–350 **terms** for a specific subject area that would form the foundation of an **indexing** system; these were known as **Mooers descriptors**. Now generally used in **indexing** to indicate a **term**, **notation** or other **symbol** that designates the subject of an item.

Desktop
▶ in **Windows applications**, refers to the **screen** background which is similar to the surface of the desk used at work or at home.

Desktop computer
▶ alternative name for a **micro-computer**.

Desktop conferencing system
▶ early **conferencing** system which has the video camera attached to the **PC** and the **video output** appears on the **PC** screen.

Desktop publishing – DTP
▶ **microcomputer** system linked to a **laser printer** which produces high-quality **documents** with text and **graphics** being composed on the **screen**.

Desktop video
▶ use of a **personal computer** to view and control moving or still **video** pictures.

Destination address
▶ place which is unique in the **network** to which a **packet** of **data** is sent.

Destructive read
▶ **computer printout** or **data transfer** that erases the source **file**.

Deviation
▶ value of a **variable** measured from a standard point, usually the **mean**.

Device dependent
▶ ability of a machine to function only with a specific device.

Device driver
▶ **software** that allows the **computer** to instruct a **peripheral** device such as a **printer**.

Device independent
▶ ability of a **program** to work with a **screen format** or **printer** without the need for configuration; ability to function with a wide variety of **hardware**.

Dewey Decimal Classification – DDC
▶ **classification scheme** developed by Melvil Dewey, first published in 1876 and used extensively for the **shelf arrangement** of books in public libraries. It uses **decimal notation** and there are ten main **classes**.

Diacritical
▶ mark added to a letter to indicate a specific phonetic value.

Diagnostic aid
▶ **software** or **hardware** device that can identify faults in a **computer** system.

Diagnostic message
▶ **error message** that describes the source of problem in a **computer**, **computer peripheral** or **computer program**.

Diagnostic program
▶ **program** used to detect equipment malfunctions.

Diagnostic test
▶ test use to check a system to see if there is a problem with equipment.

Dial-up connection
▶ connection between **computers** established by dialling a telephone number via a **modem**.

Dial-up networking
▶ **computer networking** that relies on **communications** through ordinary telephone lines using a **modem**.

Dial-up system
▶ system where **terminals** have **access** to a **computer** via a **modem** attached to a telephone **network**. **Access** is provided by dialling the telephone number for a **computer** system.

Dialog box
▶ in **Windows**, a box that requests information from and provides information to the user.

Diazo process
▶ method of copying **documents** by exposing them to sensitized paper.

Dibit
▶ **digit** made up of two **binary bits**.

Dictionary catalogue
▶ **catalogue** which has author, **title** and **subject entries** interfiled into one alphabetical sequence.

Dielectric
▶ insulating material that allows an electric field to pass but not an electric current.

DIF – Data Interchange Format
▶ **standard file format** for **spreadsheet** and **database applications** in which information is structured in rows and columns.

Diffraction
▶ spreading or bending of light, radio or sound waves caused by contact with objects.

Diffusion of innovation
▶ spreading of new and innovative technology through an industry or country with social or economic consequences.

Digest
▶ 1. computing – selection of messages that have been posted to a **newsgroup** or a **mailing list** which is formatted and sent on to another **mailing list** or **newsgroup**.
2. information handling – systematically arranged **compendium** or summary of literary, historical, legal or scientific material.

Digit
▶ any number from 0 to 9 in the decimal system.

Digital
▶ **data** represented as a set of **digits**, usually **binary**, which uses the two digits 0 and 1. In computing, the unit used is usually a **bit**.

Digital-analogue converter
▶ converts **digital signals** into **analogue signals**.

Digital audio
▶ audio tones represented by **machine-readable binary** numbers.

Digital audio disk
▶ method of recording sound by converting and storing **signals** in **digital** form on a **magnetic disk**.

Digital audio tape
▶ tape that records **data** in **digital** form.

Digital camera
▶ camera that takes pictures with a charge-coupled device and transmits them directly to a **computer** or records them on **disk** without using film.

Digital cash
▶ system that allows a person to pay for services or goods by transferring money from one computer to another.

Digital certificate
▶ attachment to an electronic **message** used for security purpose. Usually used to verify the identity of a user sending a message and to provide the receiver with the means to encode a reply.

Digital compact cassette – DCC
▶ **magnetic tape** in a compact **cassette** box that stores **computer**

data or audio **signals** in **digital format** and records **CD** quality sound.

Digital computer
▶ **computer** that works with **data** represented by **binary numbers** or **codes**.

Digital data
▶ information recorded as a sequence of numbers and **digits**.

Digital data service
▶ service offered by **telecommunications** companies for transmitting **digital data** as opposed to voice.

Digital data transmission
▶ method of sending **data** by **computer** by converting all **signals** into numeric codes which are usually **binary** before **transmission** and reconverting them on receipt.

Digital electronics
▶ technology that is the basis of **digital** techniques. Low-power miniature **integrated circuits** or **chips** are used to store, code, transmit, process and reconstruct information of all kinds.

Digital image
▶ set of **pixels** (picture elements), similar to dots on a **newspaper** photograph or grains on a photographic print, which make up a picture.

Digital imaging
▶ **storage** and use of pictures in **digital** form. The image can be moved or its size changed.

Digital information
▶ any information held in **digital format**.

Digital library
▶ library which looks and feels like a paper-based library but where items have been stored in **digital** form and stored for **access** in a **network** environment which can be used by users in remote locations.

Digital logic
▶ use of **AND, NAND, OR** and **NOR** functions as pairs of **bits** and the **NOT** function as a single **bit**.

Digital monitor
▶ **monitor** that accepts **digital** rather than **analogue signals**.

Digital Object Identifier - DOI
▶ unique identifier of any piece of intellectual content in any form together with a system for using that identifier to locate **digital** services on the **Internet**.

Digital optical recording
▶ recording of **digital** information using **optical** (i.e. **laser**) techniques.

Digital paper
▶ thin material used for storing **data**.

Digital photography
▶ production and manipulation of **digital** photographs that are represented by **bitmaps**.

Digital plotter
▶ **computer output** device which draws **graphic images** on paper under the control of **digital signals**.

Digital press
▶ printing press where the image is transferred to the printing **drum** by electronic methods.

Digital signal
▶ electrical **signal** made up of discrete pulses coded to represent information.

Digital Signal Processing – DSP
► manipulation of **analogue information** such as photographs or sound that has been converted into **digital** form.

Digital signature
► piece of **data** that identifies the originator of a **document**, created by encrypting the contents of a **document** using the originator's **cryptographic key**; **binary number** used as an identification **code** for a device such as a **CD-ROM**.

Digital Simultaneous Voice and Data – DSVD
► **digital** technology for concurrent voice and **data transmission** over an **analogue** telephone line.

Digital-to-analogue converter
► device that changes a **digital signal** to an **analogue signal**.

Digital transmission
► **transmission** of **signals** that vary in step with the **input signal** rather than continuously; usually transmitted in **bits**.

Digital Versatile (or Video) disc – DVD
► **medium** that can store huge amounts of **data** on a **disc** similar to a **CD-ROM**. It can include movies with excellent sound and picture quality.

Digital video
► **video signal** represented by **machine-readable binary** numbers to describe a finite set of colours and luminescence levels.

Digital video interactive – DVI
► **compression** system used for storing **video images** on **computer**.

Digital watermark
► method of protecting the rights of **digital information** owners. They differ from printed ones because they are usually hidden from the user and can be applied to different types of **media** including text, **images** and sound.

Digital zoom
► allows even greater magnification than the usual optical **zoom** which is the normal camera method for magnifying a scene. Each dot is blown up to provide the increased magnification with some quality loss.

Digitization
► **1.** – **conversion** of printed text into **digital** form which is sometimes done by passing it through **optical character recognition (OCR) software**. Sometimes referred to as electrocopying; **2.** – converting material into **digital** form.

Digitizer
► device that converts an **analogue video signal** into **digital** so that **video images** can be **input**, stored, displayed and manipulated by **computer**.

Digitizing pad/tablet
► device which can be used to supplement the **keyboard** and the **mouse** to provide **computer input**.

Digraph
► two letters written and pronounced as a single **character**. Also called a **diphthong** or **ligature**.

Dingbat
► small picture or **symbol** such as a star, **bullet** or arrow which is used to attract the attention of the reader.

Diode
► electronic device which permits current flow in one direction but restricts it in the opposite direction.

DIP – Document Image Processing
▶ operation where a large number of documents are digitized for easy storage, handling and rapid retrieval using a digitizer or scanner. Management operations include fast image capture and relatively simple indexing, networking and workstation organization.

Dip switch
▶ small switch which is used to change the settings on a device or machine.

Diphthong
▶ two letters written and pronounced as a single character. Also called a digraph or ligature.

Direct access
▶ ability to go directly to a desired item in a storage and retrieval system without having to search sequentially through the file.

Direct access memory
▶ type of memory that stores information or data at a specific address. Floppy disks and hard disks provide direct access memory.

Direct address
▶ number which is part of a file and can be used as a file reference number.

Direct Broadcasting by Satellite – DBS
▶ sending television by satellite from a broadcasting station which is beamed to receiving dishes on earth. Cables then carry the signal to the antenna of television sets.

Direct Distance Dialling – DDD
▶ automatic exchange service which enables a telephone subscriber to make telephone calls outside the local area.

Direct mail
▶ advertising sent directly to prospective purchasers.

Direct Memory Access – DMA
▶ method of moving data between storage devices without going through the central processing unit.

Direct Read After Write – DRAW
▶ in optical digital discs, information once written cannot be erased. The DRAW technique allows immediate identification of errors. These can then be corrected by rewriting data in a new section of the disc, and erasing the address of the incorrect section from the computer memory.

Direct voice input
▶ input of information into a device such as a computer using the human voice without an intermediate stage of keyboarding.

Directive
▶ official communication issued by a manager instructing subordinate staff to take particular actions.

Directory
▶ 1. computing – list of the files held in the backing store of a system, usually maintained by the operating system; 2. information source – printed book containing lists of names of residents or organizations in a geographical area or individuals in a particular trade, profession etc.

Disassembler
▶ program that works with low-level computer languages to change the machine language code into assembly language.

Disaster dump
▶ recording the state of a computer system to a disk when a power failure or error is detected.

Disc image
▶ exact representation of **bits** that will be distributed on a **CD-ROM** in the order that they will appear on a disc.

Disc library
▶ **CD-ROM drive** that stores and allows **access** to a number of **discs** on each **drive,** which allows automatic selection from the **storage** device; sometimes called an **autochanger** or **jukebox.**

Discipline
▶ organized field of learning dealing with basic subject areas into which all knowledge can be divided.

Discount
▶ percentage deducted from the **retail** or **list price** of a publication.

Discourse analysis
▶ processing of multi-sentence texts using **natural language** processing.

Discourse generation
▶ generation of multi-sentence texts.

Discretionary fund
▶ money that may be used at the discretion of the person in charge of an institution or department.

Discretionary hyphen
▶ **hyphen** that is used only when a word falls near the end of a line. Sometimes called a **soft hyphen.**

Dish aerial
▶ circular concave directional aerial used to pick up long-distance **transmissions.**

Dish antenna
▶ concave reflecting surface used to focus radio waves; a transmitting or receiving aerial shaped like a dish used to receive radio and television **signals** from a **communications satellite.**

Disintermediation
▶ cutting out the **middleman** from the traditional sales process. New technologies could mean that there will be no need for an **intermediary** to obtain information from a resource to pass on to an enquirer.

Disk
▶ magnetically-coated piece of material shaped like a phonograph or gramophone record which can store **programs** and **data** for a **computer.**

Disk bound
▶ **computer** performance limited by a slow **interface** or **hard drive.**

Disk cache
▶ portion of **RAM** used to speed up **access** to **data** on a **disk.**

Disk capacity
▶ extent to which a **disk** can contain **files,** usually expressed in **kilobytes** for a **floppy disk** and **megabytes** or **gigabytes** for a **hard drive.**

Disk crash
▶ failure of a **disk drive** which may result in **disk** damage.

Disk doctor
▶ **computer program** that examines what is stored on a **disk.**

Disk drive
▶ device that reads **data** from or writes **data** to a **disk.**

Disk drive controller
▶ **circuit** card that contains the **interface** between the **memory** of a **computer** and the **disk drive.**

Disk duplexing
▶ method of sending **data** to two **storage** devices at the same time. Sometimes called **disk mirroring.**

Disk formatting
▶ preparation of a blank **magnetic disk** so that **data** can be stored on it.

Disk map
▶ map used to keep track of **information** on a **disk**. It is usually a **bitmap** that tells the **operating system** which parts of the **disk** have been used.

Disk mirroring
▶ method of sending **data** to two **storage** devices at the same time. Sometimes called **disk duplexing**.

Disk Operating System – DOS
▶ **operating system** that controls all activities in a **computer** system.

Disk pack
▶ group of **hard disks** where each **disk** has a **read-write head** but the group is treated as a single unit.

Disk track
▶ concentric circle on a **disk** where **data** is stored.

Diskette
▶ small **disk**; a **floppy disk**.

Diskless workstation
▶ **computer** that contains no **disk drive** for either **hard disks** or **floppy disks** and can only operate through a **network**. It is impossible to spread a **virus** from such a machine.

Display
▶ showing **data** on a **monitor** screen.

Display font
▶ elaborate type style, which is used to gain attention or as **headings**.

Display mode
▶ setting that controls the type of information shown on a **visual display unit**.

Display panel
▶ small panel which can display information on a piece of equipment that does not have a **screen**.

Display technology
▶ creation of **output devices** for the **display** of digitized information. Devices include **computer display screens**, **digital** television sets for automatic picture adjustment, top-of-set boxes for **video**-on-demand, **printers**, **digital video discs (DVDs)**, **voice synthesizers** and **virtual reality helmets**.

Dissemination
▶ distributing or sending information to a user population.

Dissertation
▶ treatise prepared as part of an academic study leading to a higher degree. Also called a **thesis**.

Distance learning
▶ educational process where students learn from local centres or from their homes using material supplied to them in printed or electronic form and/or via television, radio etc. Sometimes called **off campus education** or **open learning**.

Distance teaching
▶ instruction where the teacher and student are not in direct contact but communicate with each other by correspondence, radio, television, **CCTV**, **computer-aided learning** etc.

Distributed architecture
▶ **local area network (LAN)** which uses a shared **communication** medium such as a **bus** or a **ring**.

Distributed database
▶ **database** made up of **computer files** which are stored in a number of separate locations in a **computer** system.

Distributed logic
▶ systems where logic, or intelligence, is distributed in the system rather than located centrally.

Distributed network
▶ network in which processing activities may take place in a number of different locations.

Distributed processing
▶ processing of data at different physical locations in a distributed system.

Distributed relative
▶ related subject that has been scattered by the subdivisions used in a classification scheme.

Distributed system
▶ any system in which control does not reside in one place but is spread throughout the network. Several interconnected computers may share the tasks assigned to the system.

Distribution rights
▶ publisher's arrangements which give exclusive rights to distribute a publication in a specific geographical area.

DLL – Dynamic Link Library
▶ bundle of codes containing computer program subroutines that perform particular functions which can be shared by the operating system or applications.

DMA – Direct Memory Access
▶ method of moving data between storage devices without going through the central processing unit.

Docking station
▶ accessory that provides laptop computers with additional capabilities when it is used in a fixed location. This could allow connection

to a CD-ROM drive or hook-up to a printer, mouse, keyboard and monitor so that the laptop computer becomes a desktop unit.

Document
▶ generic term for the information-bearing media: books, serials, sound recordings, films, illustrations etc.

Document architecture
▶ design of a document produced using desktop publishing taking into account headers and footers, use of headings and subheadings, fonts, graphics etc.

Document assembly
▶ creation of pages using desktop publishing techniques using either a word processor or a desktop publishing program.

Document base font
▶ type font that is used for most of a document; default font which is used when no specific type style is specified.

Document delivery
▶ supplying a copy of an item which is retained by the requester as opposed to the supply of a loan copy. It also includes the purchase of photocopies, usually of journal articles, from suppliers.

Document description
▶ description of a document covering all the data that are of value in a particular system, usually including the bibliographic description and subject description which are obtained by analysing, cataloguing, abstracting or indexing the document.

Document format
▶ arrangement of a document page covering margins, headers, footers, page numbers etc.

Document Image Processing – DIP

▶ operation where a large number of **documents** are **digitized** for easy **storage**, handling and rapid **retrieval** using a **digitizer** or **scanner**. **Management** operations include fast **image capture** and relatively simple indexing, **networking** and **workstation** organization.

Document imaging

▶ process by which **documents** are converted into electronic form, usually using a **scanning** device.

Document information system

▶ **computer database** that contains **bibliographic data** for **documents** or the full **document image**.

Document management system

▶ means of managing **documents** which are usually in electronic form, although it may include non-electronic **documents** which may be indexed or referenced. It includes methods of converting existing **documents** into an electronic **format**.

Document reader

▶ **input device** that reads **characters** or marks, usually on prepared **documents** and forms. Used in **optical character recognition** and **mark sensing**.

Document retrieval

▶ process of **indexing, searching** and identifying **documents** to find the required information.

Document surrogate

▶ **1.** computing – digitized form of a **document** or **object** that acts as a replacement for the original should it be unavailable through damage etc.; **2.** information handling – something which stands in the place of **document**; often used to describe an **abstract** or a **catalogue record**.

Documentalist

▶ **information worker** concerned with the collection and distribution of information.

Documentation

▶ collection, organization and recording of **documents** for the purpose of **storage, retrieval,** utilization or **transmission** of the information contained in them. It is also used for the printed material that contains user **instructions** for a system, **hardware, database** etc.

Documentation centre

▶ place where publications are received, processed and preserved.

DOI – Digital Object Identifier

▶ unique **identifier** of any piece of intellectual content in any form together with a system for using that identifier to locate **digital** services on the **Internet.**

Dolby digital

▶ **standard** for high-quality **digital** audio that is used for the sound portion of **video** stored in **digital format.**

Domain address/name

▶ **Internet address** in conveniently readable form, usually in letters rather than numbers.

Domestic market

▶ market in the country where an organization is located.

DOMSAT

▶ Australian **communication satellite** system for domestic television and **telecommunications**.

Dongle

▶ device which contains an encrypted security code which must be present before a **program** can operate; intended to prevent **software piracy**.

DOS – Disk Operating System
▶ operating system that controls all activities in a computer system.

Dot
▶ character (full stop or period) often used in file names and Internet addresses.

Dot matrix
▶ pattern or array of dots used for the presentation of characters, used in visual display units and some printers.

Dot matrix printer
▶ printer that uses a series of small dots to form a character. Also called a matrix printer.

Dot pitch
▶ spacing of red, green and blue phosphor dots on the screen of a colour monitor.

Dots per inch – dpi
▶ measurement used to define printer and scanner resolution. The more dots per inch and the smaller the dots, the better the image.

Double click
▶ to press and release the mouse button quickly twice.

Double density disk
▶ floppy disk that can store twice the amount of data as an ordinary floppy disk. Now almost obsolete.

Double quote
▶ use of inverted commas (" ") to enclose text that is taken from another source.

Double sided disk
▶ floppy disk that can hold data on both surfaces.

Double speed
▶ compact disc drive or other device that retrieves data faster than other units.

Doughnut chart
▶ form of pie chart in which different data can be displayed and differentiated by shading.

Downgrading
▶ 1. information handling – assigning classified material to a less restrictive security classification, usually making it more accessible to a wider group of users. Also called declassification; 2. management – lowering the grade of an individual or a job to a lower grade.

Downlink
▶ satellite earth station that receives signals from a satellite.

Downloadable font
▶ type font that can be transferred to the memory of a printer from a computer rather than being built into the memory of the printer or plugged in as a cartridge. Also called soft font.

Downloading
▶ transfer of information from one computer to another; the process of transferring data or other information held on a remote computer system to a personal computer file, which usually has a smaller storage capacity.

Downsizing
▶ substituting smaller and usually cheaper computers for larger ones; moving from a large and usually more expensive system to a smaller and usually less expensive one.

Downtime
▶ time when a computer or an automated system is not in operation due to repairs, maintenance or faults.

Downward compatibility
▶ ability of a new **software** version to use **files** created by an earlier version.

Downward reference
▶ direction from a more to a less comprehensive **heading** in a **catalogue** or **index**; in a **thesaurus** a direction from a **broader term** (**BT**) to a **narrower term** (**NT**).

DP – Data Processing
▶ includes all clerical, arithmetical and logical operations on **data** where a **computer** is used; the collecting, **storage**, processing and presentation of **data** as useful information.

dpi – dots per inch
▶ measurement used to define **printer** and **scanner** resolution. The more dots per inch and the smaller the dots, the better the **image**.

DPS – Data-Processing System
▶ **computer hardware** and **software** required to carry out **data-processing** activities.

Draft mode
▶ printing mode in which text is printed as quickly as possible without regard to print quality.

Draft quality
▶ setting on some **printers** that provides low-quality copy usually used for correction purposes.

Drag
▶ moving an **object** using the **mouse**.

Drag and drop
▶ opening an **application file** quickly by picking a **file icon** and dragging it into the **icon** of an **application program**; ability to move text or **graphics** by dragging it into a new position using the **mouse**.

DRAM – Dynamic Random Access Memory
▶ **computer memory** that is inexpensive as it holds **data** for only a short period and requires a refresh **signal** to be sent to it periodically.

DRAW – Direct Read After Write
▶ in **optical digital discs**, information once written cannot be erased. The DRAW technique allows immediate identification of **errors**. These can then be corrected by rewriting **data** in a new section of the **disc**, and erasing the **address** of the incorrect section from the **computer memory**.

Drawing management system
▶ electronic **index** to engineering drawings that may be stored in electronic **format** or as paper **documents**.

Drive
▶ device that operates a **disk** on a **computer**.

Drive bay
▶ blanked-off space on a **personal computer** which is designed for extra **floppy disk drives** and similar devices.

Driver
▶ **program** that manages an **input** or **output** device.

Drop cap
▶ first letter of a text paragraph that may be enlarged and/or decorated to make it larger than the remaining text.

Drop-down list box
▶ box containing **menu** items which drops down from a **menu** line when the main **menu** item is clicked.

Drop-down menu
▶ menu that appears when a particular item in a **menu** bar is selected.

Drum
▶ cylinder coated with magnetic recording material with facilities for tranferring information to or from it into a **computer.** Now superseded by **disks.**

Drum printer
▶ **line printer** which has **characters** mounted on a cylinder.

Drunk mouse problem
▶ inability to make the **screen cursor** or **pointer** move smoothly. This can be caused by dirt on the **mouse** ball.

Dry running
▶ checking by hand, usually using paper and pencil, the progress of test **data** through a **computer program** before it is actually run.

DSK – Dvorak Simplified Keyboard
▶ form of typewriter **keyboard** designed to make the most frequently used **keys** most easily available, which can lead to improvements in typing speed and accuracy.

DSP – Digital Signal Processing
▶ manipulation of **analogue information** such as photographs or sound that have been converted into **digital** form.

DSS – Decision Support System
▶ **computer** system having a range of tools designed to help in the process of **decision making**. Normally comprises a method of capturing and storing relevant **data** (**database**) plus a means by which the **data** can be manipulated in order to explore alternative **models** and consequences of actions.

DSVD – Digital Simultaneous Voice and Data
▶ **digital** technology for concurrent voice and **data transmission** over an **analogue** telephone line.

DTP – Desktop publishing
▶ **microcomputer** system linked to a **laser printer** which produces high quality **documents** with text and **graphics** being composed on the **screen**.

Dual-density disk
▶ **magnetic disk** with twice the **storage** capacity of a standard **disk** but with the same dimensions.

Dual dictionary
▶ printed **index** of two identical parts published in duplicate, which allows for the manual comparison of **document** numbers contained under each **subject heading** so that matching numbers can be identified by eye.

Dual processor
▶ **computer system** based on two **CPU**s. One is normally dedicated to **information processing** while the other deals with system operation.

Dub
▶ adding sound to film after the film has been shot; often used to add subtitles in another language.

Dublin core
▶ **metadata application** developed by OCLC at its headquarters in Dublin, Ohio. It contains 15 descriptive elements and is intended for searching for information on the **Internet**.

Dumb terminal
▶ **terminal** with no independent processing capability of its own. It can send and receive information but has no intelligent features.

Dump

▶ transfer of **data** from one **computer storage** area to another, or to a **printer** or **disk**. A **screen** dump is where **data** on a **screen** is transferred to a **printer** for printing.

Dummy

▶ copy of a potential book with a **casing** or binding and blank pages; complete job layout, showing page arrangement, illustrations etc.

Duplex

▶ method of **data transmission** where **data** can be transmitted in either direction.

Duplexing

▶ use of duplicate components so that if one fails the system can continue to operate via the other.

Durability

▶ **1.** computing – transaction has durability if it passes the ACID (atomicity, consistency, isolation and durability) test. This set of **software** tests is used for checking **hardware** and **software** stability; **2.** management – length of time an **object** or idea remains intact and usable without significant deterioration.

Duration

▶ length of time that something will last.

Dust jacket/wrapper

▶ paper cover for a book, often used for promotion and containing quotes from reviews etc. Also called **book jacket.**

Dustcover

▶ in computing cover which protects a machine from dust.

DVD – Digital Versatile (or Video) disc

▶ **medium** that can store huge amounts of **data** on a **disc** similar to a **CD-ROM**. It can include movies with excellent sound and picture quality.

DVD-RAM

▶ type of rewritable **compact disc** that provides greater **data storage** than **CD-ReWritable disc.**

DVD-ROM

▶ read-only **compact disc** that can hold a minimum of 4.7 **Gb**.

DVD+RW

▶ another **standard** for rewritable DVD discs.

DVI – Digital Video Interactive

▶ **compression** system used for storing **video images** on **computer**.

D-VI – Digital Video Interactive

▶ brand name of Intel's **digital video** and audio products.

Dvorak simplified keyboard – Dsk

▶ form of typewriter **keyboard** designed to make the most frequently used **keys** most easily available, which can lead to improvements in typing speed and accuracy.

Dynamic data exchange

▶ link between **documents** and **applications** in which shared **data** is updated whenever **data** in the **source document** is changed.

Dynamic Link Library – DLL

▶ bundle of **codes** containing **computer program subroutines** that perform particular functions that can be shared by the **operating system** or **applications**.

Dynamic object

▶ any **object** which is embedded or linked into a destination **document** and can be edited from within a source **document** usually by a **click** on the **mouse**.

Dynamic Random Access Memory – DRAM

▶ **computer memory** that is inexpensive as it holds **data** for only a short period and requires a refresh **signal** to be sent to it periodically.

Dynamic variable

▶ **variable** whose **address** is determined when a **computer program** is run.

Ee

E-cash – Electronic cash
▶ form of **electronic fund transfer** using the **Internet**.

E-commerce – Electronic commerce
▶ shopping or trading via the **Internet**.

E-information – Electronic information
▶ any information in electronic form.

E-journal – Electronic journal
▶ usually an electronic counterpart to a conventional printed **journal**. Some electronic **journals** do not have a printed equivalent.

E-mail – Electronic mail
▶ **transmission** of letters and other **documents** from one **computer** to another through a **telecommunications network**.

E-mail address
▶ name that identifies an electronic post office box on a **network** that can receive **E-mail**.

E-mail client
▶ **application** that runs on a **personal computer** or **work station** that allows the user to send and receive **E-mail** messages.

E-text
▶ textual material produced in electronic rather than printed **format**.

E-Zine
▶ electronic version of **alternative publications** which started in the 1960s. Usually they had an ephemeral lifespan with idiosyncratic and often anti-establishment content. Usually regarded as **artefacts** of popular and/or underground culture. Name for an electronic magazine.

EAN – European Article Number
▶ **symbol** defined by the European Article Numbering system, which identifies the **ISBN** of a book in the form of a **bar code**.

EANCOM
▶ subset of **EDIFACT** chosen for use by the **book trade**.

EAPROM – Electrically Alterable Programmable Read-Only Memory
▶ type of **read-only memory** which can be erased and reprogrammed as required. Often used as a synonym for **EPROM**.

EARN – European Academic and Research Network
▶ large European **communication network** that is connected with **BITNET** in the USA.

EAROM
▶ Electrically Alterable **Read-Only Memory** - **read-only memory** which can be erased by passing an electric **current** through it so that it can be

reused. Often used as synonym for
EEROM.

Earth station
▶ large dish-shaped **antenna** that
sends and receives **signals** from a
satellite.

**EBCDIC – Extended Binary Coded
Decimal-Interchange Code**
▶ international **standard
transmission code** developed by
IBM which provides 256 unique
eight-**bit character codes**. It is used
for the exchange of **data** between
items of equipment.

**ECHO – European Commission
Host Organization**
▶ referral and enquiry service and a
host for a number of European
Community **databases.**

Echo
▶ process of sending information
back to its source for comparison
with the original. It can be used to
check the quality of the received
data.

Econometrics
▶ applying statistical methods to the
study of economic problems and **data.**

Economics of information
▶ all-embracing expression that
covers all economic aspects of
creating, providing, using and
storing information in all its forms.
Information is treated like any other
commodity.

Edge-notched card
▶ **card** for **term entry system** for a
post-coordinate index, with one or
two rows of holes along each edge.
Each hole represents a **subject
heading**, which is encoded by
clipping open appropriate holes so
that when a rod is passed through
the whole pack the required **card**
falls off.

Edge card
▶ **circuit card** that has an edge
connector which is used to add
facilities to a **computer.**

Edge connector
▶ part of some **circuit boards** that
connects the board to the **mother
board.**

EDI – Electronic Data Interchange
▶ **computer**-to-**computer** exchange of
data between trading partners using
approved **standards.**

**EDIFACT – Electronic Data
Interchange For Administration,
Commerce and Transport**
▶ United Nations rules for **electronic
data interchange** (EDI).

EDILIBE
▶ European Community-funded
project to implement and test the
EDIFACT standards in a system
which can be used for the
transmission and exchange of
electronic **data.**

EDILINK
▶ **PC software** for electronic **data**
interchange **(EDI) transmission** to
and from Dawson UK.

Edit key
▶ **function key** that carries out an
editing function or starts an editor
program.

EDItEUR
▶ Pan American Book Sector **EDI**
Group established in October 1991
with participants from 10 countries.

Editing
▶ **1.** computing – process by which a
computer record or **program** is
amended or upgraded; **2.** publishing
– process by which a **document** is
prepared for publication.

Edition
▶ all copies of a particular work in one typographical **format** printed from the same type, negative or plates.

Editor
▶ in **information technology, software** that aids the editing of a **file** or a **routine** which edits in the course of a **program**.

EDM – Electronic Document Management
▶ **management** of **documents** in all **formats** including digitizing, storing, accessing and security aspects, as well as administrative and **record**-keeping functions.

EDMS – Electronic Document Management System
▶ complete system of **document management** in all its **formats** including digitizing, storing, accessing and security aspects, as well as administrative and **record**-keeping functions.

EDP – Electronic Data Processing
▶ **data processing** performed by machines.

EDS – Exchangeable Disk Storage
▶ **disk drive** which uses a removable **disk pack** rather than a fixed **disk**.

Educational and scientific consensus
▶ Henry Bliss's statement about the structure of knowledge generally held by educated people, which should guide the **classificationist** in developing a **classification scheme**.

Educational material
▶ **audiovisual material** which has been designed and produced for educational purposes.

Edutainment
▶ **software** that is a cross between games **software** and educational and entertainment products.

EEPROM
▶ electrically erasable programmable **read-only memory**.

EEROM – Electrically Erasable Read-Only Memory
▶ **read-only memory** which can be erased by passing an electric current through it so that it can be reused. Often used as a synonym for **EAROM**.

EFT – Electronic funds transfer
▶ method of transferring funds from one account to another using **computers** and **telecommunications**. At least four types of EFT are currently in common use: transfers between **computers** at different banks; transfers between banks and other organizations; public **access** to **terminals** providing banking services; and **cards** for making direct debit payments for goods and services via an electronic link.

EFTPOS – Electronic Funds Transfer at Point Of Sale
▶ system of payment for goods by **electronic fund transfer** as they are purchased.

EGA – Enhanced Graphics Adapter
▶ **expansion card** which provides **high-resolution graphics** for a standard **PC**. Has largely been replaced by **VGA** (**video graphics array**).

Eighty-track disk
▶ **disk** which is formatted to use 80 **data** tracks. Usually used for double-density 3.5 inch **disks**.

EINO – Everything In, Nothing Out
▶ equivalent of **GIGO** (garbage in, garbage out).

EIS – Executive Information System
▶ system which collects information automatically on a customized basis from internal company **databases** and relevant external **databases** to provide a support system for executives.

Electrocopying
▶ **storage, display, dissemination,** manipulation or reproduction of print-based **copyright** works in **machine-readable** form. Conversion of printed text into **digital** form which is sometimes done by passing it through **optical character recognition (OCR) software.**

Electroluminescent display – ELD
▶ technology used to produce a thin **display screen** used in some **portable computers.** Sometimes called a **flat-panel display.**

Electron
▶ elementary particle with a single negative charge.

Electronic blackboard
▶ sending hand-drawn **graphics** over a telephone line to be displayed on a **visual display unit** or television **screen.**

Electronic bulletin board
▶ messages that can be accessed over a **telecommunications network** that are similar to notices that might be mounted on notice boards in an office.

Electronic commerce – E-commerce
▶ buying and selling products **online,** usually via the **Internet.**

Electronic cottage
▶ name given to the home when a person works at home using **computers** and **telecommunications**

to provide a link to a central workplace.

Electronic data interchange – EDI
▶ **computer**-to-**computer** exchange of **data** between trading partners using approved **standards.**

Electronic data processing – EDP
▶ **data processing** performed by electronic machines, usually computers.

Electronic document
▶ **document** that is held in electronic rather than print-on-paper **format.** Material capable of being interpreted by a **computer input device.** Sometimes called **machine-readable material.**

Electronic document delivery
▶ provision of complete **documents** via an electronic ordering and delivery process.

Electronic document management – EDM
▶ management of **documents** in all **formats** including digitizing, storing, accessing and security aspects, as well as administrative and record-keeping functions.

Electronic document management system – EDMS
▶ complete system of **document management** in all its **formats** including digitizing, storing, accessing and security aspects, as well as administrative and record-keeping functions.

Electronic filing
▶ use of a **computer** system for **filing** or locating information in an electronic **file.**

Electronic funds transfer – EFT
▶ method of transferring funds from one account to another using

computers and telecommunications. At least four types of EFT are currently in common use: transfers between computers at different banks; transfers between banks and other organizations; public access to terminals providing banking services; and cards for making direct debit payments for goods and services via an electronic link.

Electronic funds transfer at point of sale – EFTPOS
▶ payment for goods by electronic funds transfer as they are purchased.

Electronic information
▶ information in electronic form. Also called e-information.

Electronic imaging
▶ operations that modify a picture or image by enhancement, contrast or colour modification, or by using a range of operations such as pattern matching, object segregation, detection and recognition. It includes image processing, document image processing (DIP), multimedia and picture management.

Electronic journal - E-journal
▶ usually an electronic counterpart to a conventional printed journal. Some electronic journals do not have a printed equivalent.

Electronic library
▶ library which provides access not only to its own collection, but also to a range of other material located outside the library.

Electronic mail - E-mail
▶ transmission of letters and other documents from one computer to another through a telecommunications network.

Electronic mail address
▶ address used to send electronic mail to a specified destination.

Electronic mailbox
▶ place where messages sent from one computer user to another are stored before being collected by the message recipient.

Electronic message system
▶ general term which was initially used to describe communication via terminals in a communications network. It now covers a number of specialized services, such as electronic mail, teleconferencing, videotex and communication between word processors.

Electronic messaging
▶ all forms of communication using computers.

Electronic money
▶ method of payment which uses cards that can be credited with cash from the buyer's bank account. The card can then be used to purchase items up to the amount of money available on the card.

Electronic Numerical Integrator And Calculator – ENIAC
▶ first electronic calculator built at the University of Pennsylvania in the mid-1940s.

Electronic office
▶ workplace where all material is in electronic format and there is no information recorded, distributed or stored on paper. Sometimes thought of as the ideal type of office where the computer, rather than the typewriter or pen and ink, is the main tool for the production of documents, and material is generated and stored in electronic rather than paper format. Also called the paperless office.

Electronic publishing
▶ publishing information in electronic format where the user

views the material on a **screen** rather than on paper.

Electronic signature
▶ **code** which identifies the sender of a coded message.

Electronic spreadsheet
▶ **computer application** that displays and manipulates **spreadsheet data.**

Electronic text centre
▶ another name for a **digital library.** Often separate from the library holding printed material.

Electronics
▶ applying the study of **electrons** and their properties to manufactured products such as **computers,** calculators etc.

Elegant programming
▶ **computer programming** that is well structured with a minimum number of **instructions** so that the **program** is easy to understand and runs efficiently.

Elhill
▶ **software** written originally for the US National Library of Medicine to give **online access** to its **databases.**

Elite
▶ print style and type face which produces twelve **characters per inch.**

Ellipsis
▶ **1.** computing – mark consisting of three **dots** (...) which on a **computer menu** indicates that there are sub-menu items; **2.** printing – mark consisting of three **dots** (...) which indicates that some text has been omitted from a quotation.

Em character
▶ measurement of **character** spacing where one **character** is the width of the **capital letter** M.

Em dash
▶ elongated **hyphen** the length of the **capital letter** M.

Embedded code
▶ **routines** or sections written in **machine code** which are inserted into a **computer program** written in a **high-level programming language.**

Embedded command
▶ coded **instruction** in a **word processing** system which allows text on the **screen** to be manipulated such as centred; **bold face**; underlined etc.

Embedded computer
▶ **computer** that is part of a machine which is designed for a specific purpose.

Embedded indexing
▶ **indexing** provided by **software modules** which are used in **electronic documents** to generate **indexes.**

Embedded object
▶ **object** created in one **application** and embedded into a **document** created by another **application.**

Embedded system
▶ **computer** system which has been built in as part of a larger system.

Emoticon
▶ graphical language for conveying feelings; based on a pun on **baud**/body language. Sometimes called **baudy language** or **smileys.**

Empirical study
▶ study based on **data** or information gained through experiment, observation or experience which can be verified.

Employee evaluation
▶ assessing the behaviour of employees for the purpose of **career**

development. Also called **perform-ance appraisal** or **performance evaluation**.

Empty digit
▶ in **classification**, a **notation digit** that separates other **digits** and has no meaning in itself.

EMS – Expanded Memory System
▶ **standard** that defines the extra **memory** that is added to the 640 **Kb** limit of conventional **memory** in a **PC**. It can only be used by specially written **programs**.

Emulator
▶ device that behaves like another device; **hardware** or **software** which makes a system appear to other **hardware** or **software** as another system.

Emulation
▶ **1.** generally - imitation of a proposed activity to test its effectiveness; **2.** computing – ability of a **computer program** or device to imitate another **program** or device.

Emulation software
▶ **program** that directs a **peripheral** to imitate another, usually to improve performance.

En character
▶ measurement of **character** spacing which is half the length of the **capital letter** M.

En dash
▶ elongated **hyphen** the width of the capital letter N.

Encapsulation
▶ where something is contained within something else.

Encode
▶ using a **code** to represent **characters** or groups of **characters** in order to compress a **file**.

Encoder
▶ **program** or system that converts **computer data** into a **code** system that is different from the normal one used; any device that converts **data** into **machine-readable** form.

Encrypted database
▶ **database** that has been coded so that it can only be read by the **program** that created the **data**.

Encryption
▶ coding of **data** for security pur-poses, particularly when transmitting over **telecommunication** systems.

Encyclopaedia
▶ work containing information on all subjects, or limited to a special subject field, arranged in systematic order, usually alphabetical.

End key
▶ **key** which directs the **cursor** to end of a line of text. Used in conjunction with other **keys**, it can direct the **cursor** to the bottom of a page, end of **file** etc.

End marker
▶ special **character** or sequence of **characters** that marks the end of a **signal** or section of **data**.

End matter
▶ items at the end of a printed book, such as **appendices**, **bibliography**, **notes**, supplements, **indexes** etc.

End note
▶ note that explains or expands on the text of a **document**, usually placed at the end.

End of file – EOF
▶ **symbol** used to mark the end of a **file**.

End of line – EOL
▶ control **character** that marks the end of a line of text.

End of page – EOP
► **command** embedded in a **document** to indicate the end of a printed page and the start of a new one.

End-user
► person with an information need who is the final user or consumer of information.

End-user computing
► **computer** processing that is carried out when the **end user** chooses.

End-user searching
► **searching** conducted directly by the individual with the information need.

End-user surrogate
► person who undertakes a search and **retrieval** activity on behalf of another individual who has the information need. This person is usually a **retrieval** expert but may not be a subject expert.

Endless loop tape
► tape that has had its ends spliced together to make it work in a continuous loop.

Endowment fund
► money donated or bequeathed that is invested and the earnings used for a specific purpose, which is sometimes specified by the donor.

Enhanced graphics adapter – EGA
► expansion **card** which provides **high-resolution graphics** for a standard **PC**. Has largely been replaced by **VGA** (**video graphics array**).

Enhanced keyboard
► **keyboard** which uses 101 or 102 **keys** incuding **function keys** across the top, **numeric keypad** to the right

and **cursor** movement **keys** placed between the main **keyboard** and the **numeric keypad**.

ENIAC – Electronic Numerical Integrator And Calculator
► first electronic calculator built at the University of Pennsylvania in the mid-1940s.

Enriched keyword index
► automatic **index** produced by a **computer** which is checked and enhanced by a human **indexer**.

Escalation clause
► clause in a contract which entitles an author to receive increased or additional payments if the publication achieves a certain level of success.

Enterprise resources planning – ERP
► business **management** system that integrates all aspects of the business, including planning, manufacturing, sales and marketing.

Entity
► any concrete or abstract thing that exists, might exist or has existed. Examples are a person, thing, event, **object**, idea, process etc.

Entity-oriented indexing
► **indexing** where the conceptual level of a **document** is analysed and the messages and **concepts** recognized. After recognizing the conceptual level, **indexers** move the terminological level and express the **concepts** in **index terms**. Usually called **book-oriented indexing**.

Entrepreneur
► individual who develops a business using initiative and is willing to take risks.

Entrepreneurship
▶ ability to undertake a commercial enterprise in the hope that it will lead to financial gain.

Entropy
▶ degree or measurement of randomness or chaos present in a system; ability of a system to undergo spontaneous change; information that is not available in a **document** collection.

Entry
▶ in **cataloguing**, the **record** generated by a **document** in a **catalogue** or **index**.

Entry point
▶ **index** term or **heading** in an **index**, **catalogue** or **database** which is used to identify specific **records** or **entries** in a **file**. Examples are an author's name, **subject heading**, **classification code** etc. Sometimes called **access point**.

Entry vocabulary
▶ **terms** used in a **thesaurus** or **index** as **entries** including word stems and **preferred** and **non-preferred terms** that refer to the **preferred term**. Used in both **controlled** and **natural language vocabularies**.

Entry word
▶ **heading** word in a **subject heading** list which determines the place of an **entry** in an alphabetically arranged **catalogue** or **index**.

Enumerative classification scheme
▶ **classification scheme** where **notations** are not expected to be combined, and where all possible subjects are identified and put in the appropriate place in the scheme.

Environmental scanning
▶ methodology for coping with external social, economic and technological issues that may be difficult to observe or predict and which are likely to have a positive or negative impact on an organization in the future. Also called **issues scanning** or **issues management**.

EOF – End of File
▶ abbreviation indicating the end of a **computer file**.

EOJ
▶ abbreviation indicating the end of a **computer** job.

EOL – End of Line
▶ abbreviation indicating the end of a line of **computer** text.

EOP – End of Page
▶ **command** embedded in a **document** to indicate the end of a printed page and the start of a new one.

EOR
▶ abbreviation indicating end of **computer record** or **run**.

EOT
▶ **computer** statement indicating end of **transmission**.

Ephemera
▶ material that is of transitory value or interest, often stored only for a limited time; such material may acquire literary or historical significance.

EPOS
▶ electronic point of sale device.

EPROM – Erasable Programmable Read-Only Memory
▶ type of **read-only memory (ROM)** which can be erased and re**programmed** as required.

Equivalence relationship
▶ horizontal relationship between descriptors or subject headings that have the same meaning.

Erasable optical disc
▶ type of optical disc that can be erased and loaded with new data with a usual capacity of up to 25 Mb. Sometimes called a floptical disc.

Erasable storage
▶ any storage medium which can be reused, normally by recording over previous entries, e.g. an audio cassette.

Ergonomics
▶ study of relationships between an individual and the environment.

Erotic material
▶ material in any form that is considered indecent or obscene; material capable of causing sexual arousal or desire.

ERP – Enterprise Resource Planning
▶ business management system that integrates all facets of the business, including planning, manufacturing, sales and marketing.

Error
▶ message indicating that the computer has detected an error and awaits a correction.

Error control
▶ system capable of detecting errors and, in some cases, able to correct them.

Error correction
▶ correction of errors in stored or transmitted data.

Error detection
▶ techniques that can be use to detect garbled messages in communication systems.

Error message
▶ message that reports the occurrence of an error in a computer system.

Error rate
▶ measurement of the total number of bits received with errors relative to the total number received and expressed as a figure to the power of ten. Sometimes called bit error rate.

Error report
▶ list of errors detected in input data.

Error trapping
▶ program routine which will detect an error before it can cause problems.

Escape character
▶ code used to indicate that the next character will represent a function code.

Escape key
▶ keyboard key which allows the user to get out of a particular computer action.

ESPRIT – European Strategic Programme for Information Technology
▶ European Commission research funding programme for information technology projects in libraries and information centres.

Estimate
▶ anticipated cost of a specific activity or service.

ETB
▶ end of transmission of a block of data.

Etch
▶ use of acid to remove selected layers of metal from a metal printing plate or a printed circuit board.

Ethernet
▶ **local area network** developed by Rank Xerox to facilitate **communication** between **electronic office** equipment (**computers, word processors, workstations** etc.), locally or internationally.

Ethics
▶ code of conduct that should guide or govern the activity of a particular professional group.

ETX
▶ abbreviation for end of transmission of text.

Etymology
▶ study of the origin of words and their meanings.

Euronet
▶ European **packet switching network** for the transmission of **digital** information established by the European Commission, with **entry points** in each of the member states.

European Article Number – EAN
▶ **symbol** defined by the European Article Numbering system, which gives the **ISBN** of a book in the form of a **bar code**.

European Commission Host Organization - ECHO
▶ enquiry and **referral service** and a **host** for a number of European Community **databases**.

European Strategic Programme for Information Technology – ESPRIT
▶ European Commission research funding programme for **information technology projects** in libraries and **information centres**.

Evaluation
▶ measuring the performance of a system or service and assessing its effectiveness in meeting established objectives. Testing the reliability or gauging the quality of information and **data**.

Evaluation metrics
▶ systems assessment which uses both qualitative and quantitative measures; there are two forms – **glass box metrics** and **black box metrics**.

Evaluative abstract
▶ **abstract** that includes details of the value and usefulness of the item.

Even parity
▶ **parity** checking mode in which each set of transmitted **bits** must have an even number of set **bits**.

Event-driven programming
▶ **programming** in which the **computer** responds to events rather than going through a prearranged series of actions.

EVGA – Enhanced Video Graphics Array
▶ **graphics display** board providing improved **video graphics array** (**VGA**). Sometimes called **SVGA** (**super VGA**).

Evolutionary order
▶ **classification** method where subjects are organized in the order of their history or development.

Examination copy
▶ free or on-approval copy of a book provided to a potential purchaser who may place an order for a number of copies. Sometimes called an **inspection copy**.

Exchange format
▶ **data format** which allows **electronic documents** to be interchanged. Also called **interchange format**.

Exchangeable disk storage – EDS

▶ **disk drive** which uses a removable **disk pack** rather than a fixed **disk**.

Exclamation mark

▶ sign (!) which expresses surprise.

Exclusive agreement

▶ agreement where one person or company is made the sole agent for a product or system.

EXE file

▶ three letter extension to a **file name** which indicates that the **file** contains **binary program data**.

Executive information system – EIS

▶ system which collects information automatically on a customized basis from internal company **databases** and relevant external **databases** to provide a support system for executives.

Executive size

▶ paper size sometimes used in the United States that measures 7.25 × 10.50 inches.

Executive summary

▶ concise statement of the content of a **document** which covers all the important points and is usually printed as the first section, so that a reader with limited time can grasp the salient facts.

Exhaustivity

▶ measure used in **indexing** to determine how completely the **concepts** contained in a **document** have been **indexed**.

Expanded memory system – EMS

▶ **standard** that defines the extra **memory** that is added to the 640 **Kb** limit of conventional **memory** in a **PC**. It can only be used by specially written **programs**.

Expansion board/card

▶ **circuit board** which can be inserted in a **computer**, usually into an **expansion slot**, which can provide some additional facility. May also be called an **adaptor**, or add-on board/card.

Expansion slot

▶ **connector** that can be used to add additional **circuit boards** to a **computer** to provide extra facilities.

Expansive classification

▶ **classification scheme** devised by C.A. Cutter in 1891 which is now out of date.

Expert system

▶ **computer program** which relies on knowledge and reasoning to perform a difficult task usually undertaken by a human expert. An expert system usually has a limited number of experts that contribute to its development and it can be codified by rules.

Expert user

▶ user who has considerable experience with a particular system or **database**. Some **databases** and systems have a special expert user mode, different from that used by novices or beginners.

Exploded pie

▶ **pie chart** where some segments have been drawn out from the body of the pie to highlight information.

Export file

▶ **file** that is stored in a **computer** in a **standard format** so that it can be accessed by other **programs** which may be run on different **computers**.

Exporting

▶ transferring a **program** or **file** that has been created on one **computer** to another.

Expression
▶ any legal combination of **symbols** that represent a value in **computer programming**.

Expurgated edition
▶ text of a work which has had objectionable material or words deleted from it.

Extended character set
▶ set of **characters** using 8 **bits** per **character** which are represented by the numbers 128 to 255 above the normal **ASCII** set which uses 7 **bits** per **character**.

Extensible mark-up language – XML
▶ sophisticated method of presenting **World Wide Web** material.

Extension
▶ set of up to three **characters** that can be added to a **DOS file name** separated by a **dot**.

Extension campus
▶ location established by a college or university for the provision of organized programmes of study, often designed for those who for various reasons are not able to join the institution's formal student body at its main location.

Extension service
▶ provision of materials and services to individuals or groups outside a regular service area, often where no other library service is available.

External bus
▶ **bus** that connects a **computer** to **peripheral** devices.

External cache
▶ **memory cache** which is not part of the **central processing unit**.

External hard drive
▶ **hard drive** which is connected to the **computer** outside the **casing** and used by plugging it into the **parallel port** socket.

External modem
▶ **modem** which is outside the **computer casing** and is connected to the **computer** by a **serial port**.

External peripheral
▶ **peripheral** device which is installed outside the **computer casing**.

Extra-density disk
▶ **floppy disk** which has been formulated to hold up to four **megabytes**.

Extraction indexing
▶ automatic extraction of words from texts held in a **database** for **input** into **information retrieval systems** and used to search and identify **documents**. Most common form of **automatic indexing**.

Extranet
▶ name given to an **intranet** that has parts that are accessible to authorized outsiders.

Extrapolation
▶ in statistics, the process of estimating the value of a **variable** beyond its known or observed range.

Extremely low frequency
▶ **frequency** range of 100 **Hz** or lower.

Eye-strain
▶ pain in the eyes which could be caused by looking at a **monitor screen** for too long.

Ff

F distribution
▶ **sampling** distribution derived from the ratios of the variances of samples drawn from two normally distributed populations of the same variance.

Facet
▶ **classification** category or **class** or words organized by a fundamental **characteristic** of the words themselves and not by the **discipline** associated with the words.

Facet analysis
▶ analysis of words and their meanings into fundamental constituent elements.

Facet indicator
▶ **symbol** which separates parts of the **notation** of a **classification scheme**, so that it is possible to identify the **facets** from which the **notation** has been drawn.

Faceted classification scheme
▶ **classification scheme** in which simple **classes** only are enumerated, arranged in **facets** based on fundamental elements. **Composite subjects** are specified by selecting appropriate **notation** from different **facets** and combining these.

Facsimile
▶ exact copy of an original publication.

Facsimile edition
▶ exact copy of an original publication produced photographically.

Facsimile transmission – FAX
▶ method of transmitting and receiving text and **graphic** images over a **telecommunications** link, with the recipient receiving a complete copy of the original **document**.

Fact database/file
▶ **computer**-based **file** that contains actual **data** (statistics, **full text** or numerical information), as opposed to **bibliographic** or **reference databases** that contain **document** identification details rather than actual information.

Fact retrieval system
▶ **information retrieval system** which retrieves facts rather than **references**.

Factor analysis
▶ statistical technique for studying or analysing the interconnection between varying conditions or **variables**.

Fail-safe system
▶ system that can resist human **error**; **computer** warning to a user of imminent failure allowing the user to close the system down. Often called a **graceful degradation system**.

Failure analysis
▶ studying why systems and organizations fail, usually to provide guidance for future developments.

Fair employment
▶ personnel policies such as employment, promotion, compensation etc., based on a person's merit rather than factors of race, religion etc.

Fair use
▶ provision in **copyright** law that allows one copy of otherwise protected works to be made for the purpose of criticism, review or private study. Reasonable use, usually by photocopying, of material that is covered by **copyright** that does not require payment or permission. Essentially, fair use should not undermine the financial value of the original.

Fallout
▶ **performance measurement** that expresses the ratio of non-relevant **documents** to relevant ones found in a **database** when an **information retrieval system** is being tested.

Fallout ratio
▶ ratio of non-relevant **documents** retrieved in a **search** to the total number of non-relevant items in the **database**.

False drop
▶ **retrieval** of an unwanted item from a **file** or **database** as a result of an **error** in the **specification** of a request or **search statement**.

Family name
▶ name of the family to which a person belongs. Also called **proper name**.

Fanfold stationery
▶ another name for **continuous paper**.

FAQ
▶ short for 'frequently asked questions'.

Fascicule
▶ work published in parts or small **instalments**, with each part being complete in itself.

Fast Ethernet
▶ **network protocol** which provides a **bandwidth** of 100 **Mbps** as opposed to **Ethernet** which operates at 10 **Mbps**.

Fast key
▶ **key** which can be pressed to bypass **GUI** actions so that tedious **menu**, **icon** or **mouse** use can be avoided. Sometimes called **keyboard shortcut** or **quick-key**.

Fast packet switching
▶ **wide area network** technology which allows the high-speed **transmission** of fixed-length short **data packets** or **cells**. Also called **cell relay**.

Fast save
▶ **computer program** option which saves only the latest **document** changes.

Fatal error
▶ malfunction in a **computer system** that causes equipment or **programs** to cease functioning.

Fault
▶ any condition that causes **computer** equipment or **programs** to cease functioning.

Fault tolerance
▶ ability of a system to respond to unexpected **software** or **hardware** failure.

Faulty sector
▶ **disk error message** which is caused by a defective part of a magnetic surface.

Favourite
▶ frequently visited **web page address** which has been recorded by the user to allow **direct access** without having to type in the full **web address**. Sometimes called a **bookmark**.

FAX – facsimile transmission
▶ method of transmitting and receiving text and **graphic** images over a **telecommunications** link, with the recipient receiving a complete copy of the original **document**.

Fax card
▶ controller **board** on a **computer** that allows the **transmission** and receipt of **fax images** over telephone lines.

Fax modem
▶ **modem** that allows **faxes** to be sent and received by **computer**.

FD – Full Duplex
▶ **transmission** mode in which **signals** are sent along the **communications medium** in both directions at the same time.

FDDI – Fibre Distributed Data Interface
▶ 100 **Mbps access** method for sharing **fibre optic cable** on a **local area network (LAN)**.

Feasibility study
▶ objective and systematic examination of a possible set of actions which examines practicality, cost and consequences.

Feature extraction
▶ technique by which previously recorded significant features of a **signal** are identified giving it a unique identity. The features of the unknown **signal** are then compared with those previously recorded until a match is found. It is important in **optical character recognition** and **speech recognition** systems.

Feed holes
▶ small holes at the side of continuous feed **computer** paper.

Feedback
▶ response from the user which provides information on how well a search or other service is succeeding in meeting needs.

Feedback loop
▶ feature built into an **information service** which gives information back to the **service provider** on the usefulness of the material or information provided.

Female connector
▶ socket that has holes in it which can be attached to a **male connector**.

Festschrift
▶ memorial or complimentary publication consisting of contributions from distinguished professionals issued in honour of an individual.

Fibre optic cable
▶ **transmission** medium which is replacing **coaxial cables** in many areas; the **cables** are one or two orders of magnitude smaller in diameter than **coaxial cables,** with more information-carrying capacity. They are light and crush resistant, and free of electromagnetic faults.

Fibre optics
▶ use of fine strands of glass to carry lightwave **signals**. **Data transmission** is quicker, less prone to **interference** and can provide a greater number of services than metal **cable**.

Fidonet
▶ network system for **bulletin board** operators which allows **data** to be exchanged over telephone lines.

Field
▶ **1.** computing – part of a **computer record** which contains a single item of **data**. Part of a **machine-readable record** that contains information. Fields may be of **fixed** or **variable** length; **2.** information handling – portion of a **reference** or unit **record** representing a specific item of information, such as the author, title, **abstract** etc.

Field definition
▶ items that determine the use and appearance of a **database field**.

Field delimiter
▶ special **character** that shows where a **computer data field** ends.

Field format
▶ configuration of a **computer database field** in terms of the **data** to be included and size of the **field**.

Field label
▶ **character** or group of **characters** used to identify the information contained in a single **field**.

Field length
▶ number of **characters** in a computer database field.

Field mark
▶ **computer program code** that signals the beginning or end of a database field.

Field name
▶ name that uniquely identifies a field in a **database**.

Field width
▶ the maximum number of **characters** allowed in a **field**.

Fifth generation computer
▶ **computer** based on **parallel processing** and **very large scale integration**; intended for work with **artificial intelligence** and **expert systems**.

File
▶ in general any organized and structured collection of information. The **data** in such a collection are organized into items and are structured so as to facilitate **access**.

File attribute
▶ **specification** of the type of **file** for identification or protection purposes: could be read-only, **archive** etc.

File compression
▶ reduction in the number of **bits** used to represent information to reduce the **storage** area required. Sometimes called **data compression**.

File conversion
▶ process of converting from one logical structure to another; the transfer of all or part of **records** in a **file** from one **medium** to another, usually from a **non-machine readable** to a **machine-readable** form.

File extension
▶ **characters** that follow the full stop in a **file** name.

File format
▶ method of arranging information in a **file**.

File integrity
▶ extent to which any information held in a **file** (usually **computer**) is reliable and uncorrupted.

File management
▶ organization of **files** on a **storage** device. **Applications programs** may be started from **file managers**.

File manager
▶ tool which helps to organize computer files and directories, allowing a user to arrange and structure them in a helpful order.

File name
▶ name given to a file so that it can be identified and found again.

File organization
▶ basis for the arrangement of entries in a catalogue, index or computer store.

File protection
▶ method of stopping a file being deleted accidentally from a storage device.

File security
▶ protection of data against accidental loss and/or unauthorized access. Implementation usually involves the use of passwords.

File server
▶ software which collects and consolidates data from several terminals interacting with a central computer.

File shredding
▶ destruction of a database file that has been recorded by writing bytes into the disk space occupied by the file.

File structure
▶ arrangement and layout of data in a file which describes the field types, length and order.

File transfer
▶ process of transferring files from one computer system to another.

File transfer protocol - FTP
▶ standard protocol which is used to transfer files from one system to another.

Filing
▶ process of arranging documents, papers, cards, records or other items into a specified order.

Filing element
▶ word or character that is used in filing.

Filing order
▶ order in which documents or records of documents are filed according to a specific classification scheme.

Filing rule
▶ rule that determines the filing order for entries in a catalogue.

Filmstrip
▶ strip of 16 mm or 35 mm film, holding up to 50 images carrying pictures, text or captions.

Filter
▶ optical or electronic device which removes unwanted frequencies from a signal.

Filtered information service
▶ service which electronically filters or screens a large amount of information, leaving behind selected information which is delivered electronically to the client.

Finding list
▶ catalogue with very brief entries; usually only provides the location of material in a library.

Finger
▶ computer program that can be used via the Internet to obtain information about a user or users logged on to a system.

Firewall
▶ security barrier in a network that will relay only data packets that are identified, so that data can be protected from unauthorized use.

Firewall code
▶ code in a computer system that ensures that users cannot cause system or interface damage.

Firmware
▶ software which is programmed on to a PROM (programmable read-only memory) by a user.

First sale doctrine
▶ copyright law provision which allows the owner of an authorized copy of a protected work to dispose of that copy without interfering with the copyright holder's distribution rights.

First-generation computer
▶ earliest computers developed in the 1940s and 1950s made from valves and wire circuits.

First-generation image
▶ master copy of an original image, text or document.

Fixed field
▶ part of a computer record that has a specified number of characters which must always be present.

Fixed location
▶ locating documents by their fixed positions on a shelf.

Fixed-pitch font
▶ single-spaced font which allocates the same amount of space to each character. Also called monospaced font.

Flag
▶ additional information added to items of data which characterizes their type or field. Sometimes called a tag.

Flame
▶ angry or ill-considered E-mail message or newsgroup posting.

Flame bait
▶ E-mail or other Internet message intended to provoke a flame or a flame war.

Flame war
▶ angry uninformative quarrel in a newsgroup.

Flashing
▶ characters blinking on and off on a visual display unit screen.

Flash chip
▶ special type of EEPROM (electrically erasable programmable read-only memory) that can be erased by an electrical pulse rather than by ultraviolet light.

Flat content intranet
▶ intranet model where files are requested from a storage location or a server, received by a desk-top computer and viewed through the web browser.

Flat file
▶ database that has all its records contained in a single file.

Flatbed plotter
▶ computer-controlled drawing machine which consists of a flat plate on which a paper sheet is laid.

Flatbed scanner
▶ optical scanner that consists of a flat surface on which documents to be scanned are placed.

Flat-panel display
▶ technology used to produce a thin display screen used in some portable computers. Also called electroluminescent display.

Flexible bandwidth service - FBS
▶ service alternative to leased lines and multiplexors which allows the bandwidth to change to meet site requirements.

Flexible disk
▶ another name for a **floppy disk**.

Flexible notation
▶ **notation** that allows, by the addition of **symbols**, the insertion of new subjects without destroying the sequence of the **classification schedule**.

Flexiplacing/flexiworking
▶ versatile attitude to place and hours of work which allows employees a degree of freedom.

Flicker
▶ noticeable alteration of light and dark on a **screen**.

Flippy
▶ usually a double-sided **floppy disk**.

Floating graphic
▶ picture that is part of a **document** and can be moved around the page.

Floating library
▶ mobile library on a boat, which takes books to islands or other places only accessible by water.

Floating toolbar
▶ toolbar that is not in a fixed position, but can be moved to different places on the **screen** so that it does not obscure the **image** or **document** being edited.

Floating-point value
▶ number in which the decimal point can be in any position.

Floppy disk
▶ small **magnetic disk** which may be 8.00, 5.25, 3.5, or 3.0 inches in diameter. Made of a flexible material, e.g. plastic, coated with a magnetic surface. Such **disks** are relatively cheap to make and easy to handle, but have less storage space than a **hard disk**.

Floppy tape
▶ **microcomputer** memory in the form of a **cartridge** of continuous-loop **magnetic tape**.

Floptical disc
▶ type of **optical disc** that can be erased and loaded with new **data**; capacity is usually up to 25 **Mbytes**. Also called **erasable optical disc**.

Flow chart
▶ diagram using standardized symbols to show the steps in workflow for a system or procedure.

Flow charting
▶ technique for representing a succession of events by means of lines (indicating connections) linking systems (indicating processes or events). Used to plan systems and **programs**.

Flush left
▶ arrangement of text where each line starts in the same position on the left hand of the line to make a neat edge.

Flush right
▶ arrangement of text where each line finishes in the same position on the right hand of the line to make a neat edge.

Fly leaf
▶ blank page at the beginning or end of a book.

FMV – Full Motion Video
▶ system which delivers moving **video images** and sound to a **computer**.

Focus group
▶ selected individuals brought together to examine a particular topic or issue.

Folder
▶ collection of **files** in a **computer** system. Some systems call this a **subdirectory**.

Foldout
▶ page which folds out from a book or **journal**. Sometimes called a **gatefold** or **throwout**.

Follow-on posting
▶ contribution to an **Internet newsgroup** that responds to a previous posting.

Font
▶ design style applied to all numerals, **symbols** and **characters** of the alphabet.

Font card/cartridge
▶ plug-in device for a **printer** which contains additional printing **fonts**.

Font family
▶ set of print **fonts** which all have the same **typeface** but are of different size, style and weight.

Font metrics
▶ design of a **font** that specifies **character** width, height, **capital letters** etc.

Font size
▶ measure of type size stated in **points** where 1 **point** = 1/72 of an inch and describes the height of a **character**.

Foolscap
▶ British paper size measuring 8 × 13 inches, superseded by ISO A4.

Footer
▶ information that is printed at the bottom of every page of a **document**. Sometimes called a **running foot**.

Footnote
▶ statement explaining or amplifying text which is usually placed at the end of a chapter or at the bottom of a page.

Footprint
▶ area on earth which can be reached by a **satellite transmission**; area which a **printer** or other **hardware** takes up on the **desk top**.

Forbidden character
▶ **character** which is not allowed in the **data** so its appearance indicates corruption.

Forbidden operation
▶ action that is to be avoided by the **operating system** because it will result in **data corruption** or require the system to be rebooted.

Forced page break
▶ **page break** that is inserted by the user which cannot be overriden. Often called a **hard carriage return** or **hard page break**.

Forecasting
▶ predicting or calculating future events.

Foreign rights
▶ subsidiary rights which allow a publication to be translated and published in another language.

Forename
▶ **given name** that precedes a family name or surname. Sometimes called a Christian name or **given name**.

Foreword
▶ introductory text which comes before the text of a book, usually written by someone other than the author.

Form letter
▶ **standard** letter which can be sent out to a number of people.

Format
▶ appearance or make-up of a publication; **layout** or presentation of

items in **machine-readable** form; physical form of material.

Formatted output
▶ **output** which uses specified **formats** dealing with such things as **margins**, type style etc.

Formatting
▶ preparing a **floppy disk** so that the **computer operating system** can use it, by electronically laying down track location and control information on it.

FORTRAN – FORmula TRANslation
▶ first **high-level computer language**, developed in 1957 by **IBM** and used mainly for scientific, engineering and mathematical **applications**.

Forum
▶ **Internet** discussion group using a **bulletin board system**, **mailing list** or **newsgroup**.

Forward chaining
▶ method of using rules in **artificial intelligence** work where **data** is used to establish rules which lead to new facts.

Forward compatability
▶ ability of a **computer program** or **operating system** to be used by **computers** not yet in production.

Fourier analysis
▶ system by which a complex wave form is broken down into a set of pure waves (harmonics) of different **frequencies** and amplitudes.

Fourth-generation computer
▶ **computer** using **microprocessors**, **large scale integration** and sophisticated **programming languages**.

Fourth-generation language
▶ **computer program language** which needs fewer **instructions** than earlier languages to carry out the same functions. Generally more **user friendly**.

Foxed
▶ prints or pages of old books which are discoloured due to damp.

FPROM – Fusible link Programmable Read-Only Memory/Field Programmable Read-Only Memory
▶ **chip** that can be programmed by a user.

FPS – Frames Per Second
▶ number of **images** that can be captured in a second. Television-quality **video** is around 30 **frames** per second.

Fractal graphics
▶ method of defining **graphics** in a **computer** which translates the natural curves of an **object** into mathematical formulae.

Fragmentation (computing)
▶ **data** from a **file** being separated and stored in different places on a **storage disk**.

Frame
▶ single complete picture in a **video** or film recording; in a **videotex** system, a full **screen** of information (24 rows of 40 **characters** each); an area of **magnetic tape** that stores one **character**.

Frame rate
▶ speed at which **video images** are displayed.

Frame relay
▶ **packet switching protocol** for connecting devices in a **wide area network**.

Frames per second - FPS
▶ number of **images** that can be captured in a second. Television-quality **video** is around 30 **frames** per second.

Framework
▶ basic structure of a **database**, **computer program** or process.

Free indexing
▶ **indexing** method where **index terms** are selected from the words that occur in the title, **abstract** or text of the **document**.

Free language indexing
▶ use of **index terms** that are not controlled but assigned as each **document** is entered into the **file**, usually by selecting words that occur in the title, **abstract** or text of the document.

Free-text searching
▶ **searching** (usually **online** or **CD-ROM**) in which most of the **record** is used in the search process.

Freedom
▶ being free to do something without restriction.

Freedom of the press
▶ being free to write or publish anything that is legal in **newspapers** without fear of prosecution.

Freedom of information
▶ unrestricted **access** to information.

Freedom of speech
▶ being free to say anything that is legal without fear of prosecution.

Freedom to read
▶ being free to read anything that is legal without fear of prosecution.

Freenet
▶ freely available **software** in the USA, used to set up free **community information systems**.

Freeware
▶ **software** which can be **downloaded** from the **Internet** free of charge which can be kept and used by the user. The author usually retains the **copyright**.

Freeze frame video
▶ **video** that records one picture every few minutes or seconds.

Frequency
▶ used in radio **communication** to describe the number of times a regular waveform is repeated in a second.

Friendly front-end
▶ **display** or **interface** that is designed to be easy to understand and use.

Friends of the library
▶ individuals or organizations who support a library activity through direct financial and personal contributions.

Fringe journal
▶ **periodical** which has only a small number of **articles** on a particular subject area or is a relatively unimportant **journal** for a particular subject area. Sometimes called a **peripheral journal**.

Front end
▶ **terminal** or **input device** used to create or load **data** and/or **instructions**.

Front matter
▶ pages of a book that precede the first page of numbered text. Also called **preliminaries**.

Front-end system
▶ small **computer** connected to a large (**mainframe**) **computer**. Used to handle slow **peripherals** for which the power of the **mainframe** is not required.

Frontispiece
▶ pictorial material at the front of a book, usually facing the **title page**.

FSFMV – Full-Screen, Full-Motion Video
▶ **CD-ROM** system that can **display** a moving picture which is the full size of the **display** device used.

FTE – Full-Time Equivalent
▶ adding the number of part-time staff together to reach the number of full-time staff they represent.

FTP – File Transfer Protocol
▶ standard **protocol** used to transfer **files** from one system to another via the **Internet**.

FTP site
▶ **computer** that makes **computer files** available for **downloading** using **file transfer protocol (ftp)**.

Fugitive literature/material
▶ any material that, for whatever reason (form, content etc.), cannot be easily located or integrated into a library collection. Such material is often transitory making it difficult to organize for re-use.

Full backup
▶ type of **backup** where all **files** are copied to a **backup storage** device. Sometimes called **archival backup**.

Full Duplex – FD
▶ **transmission** mode in which **signals** are sent along the **communications medium** in both directions at the same time.

Full justification
▶ use of variable spacing between text words so that all lines are the same length.

Full motion video - FMV
▶ system which delivers moving **video images** and sound to a **computer**.

Full screen access
▶ **program** feature that allows the **editing** of **data** in any place on the **computer screen**.

Full stop
▶ dot character (.) placed at the end of a sentence in text; separator used in a **file** name; part of an **Internet address**. Also called **dot** or **period**.

Full text
▶ complete **document** that contains the information required. Many **information services** will supply a reference to the item required, and it may be necessary to obtain the complete item to satisfy the **information need**.

Full-text database
▶ **database** which has the complete or **full text** of **source documents** held in **machine-readable** form.

Full-text retrieval
▶ searching method where the user types in the words that could be found in the text of **documents** in a **computer database**.

Full-text searching
▶ searching a database which has the complete or full text of source documents held in machine-readable form.

Full-Time Equivalent – FTE
▶ adding the number of part-time staff together to reach the number of full-time staff they represent.

Function
▶ **1.** computing – step in an automated **task; 2.** information handling – various operations such as **cataloguing, indexing** etc.

Function code
▶ any set of **symbols** that generates an **instruction** to a **computer**.

Function key
▶ specific **key** on a **terminal keyboard,** labelled F1 to F10 or F12, which allows the user to issue a series of **commands** with a single keystroke. These **keys** can either be designated by the user or be programmed in purpose-built **terminals**.

Functional relationship
▶ in statistics, the relationship between several **variables** whereby altering one will result in corresponding alterations in others.

Futurology
▶ studying and predicting the future of specific systems or of mankind in general.

Fuzzy logic
▶ in **computing** and mathematics, a knowledge form where notions cannot be defined precisely, but depend upon **context**.

Fuzzy logic searching
▶ method of searching by **computer** which looks for **keywords** and then uses **free-text searching**.

Fuzzy set
▶ use of multivalued logic that deals with imprecision and uncertainty in

knowledge representation by using soft boundaries between logic values.

FWIW
▶ **E-mail** abbreviation for 'for what it's worth'.

FYI
▶ abbreviation for 'for your information'.

Gg

G – Giga
▶ one thousand million in engineering; in computing it refers to the closest equivalent in **binary** code: 1 073 741 824.

Gain access
▶ permitted to enter a **data file**, usually by using an accepted **password**.

Game theory
▶ branch of mathematics using statistics and **probability theory** that deals with the best choice of action when faced with a conflict of interests. It is more concerned with strategy than tactics.

Games console
▶ **computer** that can only be used to play games which are inserted into the **console** as **cartridges**.

Gamma testing
▶ third stage of **software** testing that follows **beta testing** and takes place before the **software** is released commercially.

Gantt chart
▶ diagram that shows the schedule for a series of tasks.

Gap
▶ space left between blocks of **data** on **magnetic tape**.

Gap notation
▶ in **classification** refers to arithmetical **notation** where some numbers are not used to allow new topics to be inserted in a logical sequence.

Garbage
▶ meaningless or unwanted **data**, **characters**, numbers or **symbols** that have no relation to the **data** being entered or displayed. This may be caused by **interference** in the **communication signals**.

Gas plasma display
▶ type of **screen display** that sends an electric **current** through a special gas to form **characters** on the **screen**.

Gate
▶ switch that either allows an electronic pulse to pass through or blocks it.

Gatefold
▶ page which folds out from a book or journal. Sometimes called a **foldout** or **throwout**.

Gatekeeper
▶ person who is usually part of a **user group** who collects and screens information which is then made available to other members of the group.

Gateway
▶ device that connects **networks** to provide a **path** for the transfer of **data** between different ones. Can also refer to dedicated **communication software** that allows users **access** to off-site **databases**.

Gateway library
▶ library where paper and **digital** material is stored together. Usually called a **hybrid library**.

Gaussian distribution
▶ **frequency** distribution in which the quantities are so distributed that its graphical representation is a continuous, symmetrical **bell-shaped curve**. Also called **normal distribution**.

Gazette
▶ record of public events published periodically.

Gazetteer
▶ geographical dictionary listing information about places.

Gb – Gigabyte
▶ one thousand million **bytes**.

Geek
▶ individual with a passion for **computers**, usually to the exclusion of other interests.

Gender changer
▶ type of **adaptor** used with a plug or a socket to change between a **male connector** and a **female connector**.

General classification scheme
▶ scheme which covers, or attempts to cover, all areas of human knowledge.

General-purpose computer
▶ **digital computer** which can be used for many different **applications**.

General-purpose language
▶ **programming language** whose use is not restricted to a single type or range of **computers**.

Generation
▶ for computers and computer languages, denotes the level of development reached. Earliest **computers** are referred to as **first-generation computers** with the latest being the **fifth-generation computers**.

Generic
▶ pertaining to a **class** of related things.

Generic posting
▶ posting of items under both general and more specific **headings**.

Generic relationship
▶ relationship between superordinate, subordinate, coordinate and collateral **classes**; between a thing and its kind, and between the kinds of things.

Generic search
▶ search for all the **documents** on a subject, including all subject subdivisions.

Genetic programming
▶ type of **programming** that uses the same properties of natural selection which are found in biological evolution. Randomly combined **functions** are run and, on the basis of results, are abandoned or changed until an acceptable result emerges.

Geneva Convention
▶ universal **copyright** convention convened by Unesco in 1952, which came into effect in 1955.

Genus
▶ in **classification**, a **class** or group of things which is capable of being divided into two or more groups called **species**.

Genus-species relationship
▶ relationship between a thing and its kinds.

Geographic information system – GIS
▶ **computer software** which is used to visualize and manipulate spatial **data** and provide links to other **data**.

Germanium
▶ metal that has been used to make **semiconductor** devices, now almost completely replaced by silicon.

GET
▶ **computer program instruction** to fetch **data** or a **file** from outside the **program** in use.

GHz – GigaHertz
▶ **frequency** of one thousand million **hertz** (**cycles** per second).

Ghost writer
▶ person who writes or prepares material for publication on behalf of another person; for example, the autobiography of a well-known person who will be identified as the author.

Giga – G
▶ one thousand million in engineering; in computing it refers to the closest equivalent in **binary** code: 1 073 741 824.

Gigabit Ethernet
▶ new version of **Ethernet** which allows **data transfer** of 1 **gigabit** (1000 **megabits**) per second.

Gigabyte – Gb
▶ one thousand million **bytes**.

Gigahertz – GHz
▶ **frequency** of one thousand million **hertz** (**cycles**/sec).

GIGO
▶ **garbage** in, **garbage** out. When useless or meaningless information is **input** into a **computer**, then useless or meaningless information will be **output**.

GII – Global Information Infrastructure
▶ US Vice President Gore's manifesto which calls for technical collaboration between industrialized and developing countries and **telecommunications network** investment.

GIS – Geographical Information System
▶ **computer software** which is used to visualize and manipulate spatial **data** and provide **links** to other **data**.

Given name
▶ given name that precedes a family name or surname. Sometimes called a Christian name or **forename**.

Glare
▶ light reflected from a **visual display unit**.

Glass box metrics
▶ **evaluation** method which looks inside a system and monitors the performance of the component technologies.

Glitch
▶ any disturbances such as a **power surge** that lead to a **computer** failing or making a **computer reboot**; **software error**.

Global Information Infrastructure – GII
▶ US Vice President Gore's manifesto which calls for technical collaboration between industrialized and developing countries and **telecommunications network** investment.

Global network service
▶ public automatic switched **data** service providing **access** between British **terminals** and **computer** systems in other countries. The service features **packet** assembly and **transmission** of **data**, and provides

compatibility between incompatible equipment.

Global search
▶ searching for a word or phrase throughout a complete **document, directory, subdirectory** or **file**.

Global village
▶ term coined by Marshall McLuhan to describe how the world would be affected by the **communications** revolution, leading to large amounts of information that is readily available and where people can have easy contact with each other.

Globalnet
▶ planned extension which would make **intranets** accessible in a secure and **user-friendly** manner on the **Internet**. Would join **intranets** and **extranets** into a truly global **network**.

Glossary
▶ list of **terms** in a specific subject field.

Go list
▶ terms that have been used as **index terms**.

Golfball printer
▶ **impact printer** that uses a small metal ball to print **characters**. Sometimes called a **ball printer**.

Gopher
▶ **client/server** mechanism on the **Internet** which can be used to search for information on a **network** of **databases**.

GOTO
▶ **computer program instruction** to **branch** off to a new set of **instructions** or **commands**.

Government publication
▶ official publication issued by a government publishing facility.

GPPM – Graphic Pages Per Minute
▶ speed at which **laser printers** can print non-text pages.

Grabber
▶ usually hand-shaped **icon** of a **graphics** or **desktop program** that can be used to get hold of a marked piece of text or an **image** and move it to another place.

Graceful degradation system
▶ system that can resist human **error**; **computer** warning to a user of imminent failure allowing for the user to close the system down. Often called a **fail-safe system**.

Grandfather-father-son system
▶ method of providing **data security** by storing the three most recent versions of a **master file**.

Graph
▶ method of displaying number relationships in a visual manner such as a **bar chart, columns** or a **pie chart**.

Graphic
▶ two-dimensional representation of an **image**, which could be opaque: art originals, photographs etc. Items that need to be viewed using an optical device, such as slides, **filmstrips** etc.

Graphic file format
▶ **format** in which **computer graphics** are stored and transmitted.

Graphic pages per minute – GPPM
▶ speed at which **laser printers** can print non-text pages.

Graphical user interface – GUI
▶ user connection to a **computer** system which uses graphical **symbols** rather than text.

Graphics card
▶ part of a **personal computer** that controls the **screen image**, usually provided as a three-dimensional **image**.

Graphics character
▶ shape such as a line, corner or pattern that can be typed on the **screen**.

Graphics tablet
▶ **input device** which uses a **stylus** or **cursor** moved by hand over a flat surface. Also called a **bit pad**.

Greater than operator
▶ sign (>) which means that the quantity on the left hand side is greater than that on the right.

Greeked
▶ meaningless line patterns which show the spacing and arrangement of text on a **screen** but cannot be read.

Green computer/Green PC
▶ movement towards the incorporation of energy-saving measures into the design of **hardware** and systems. **Personal computer** specially designed to minimize consumption of power by powering down unnecessary components when they are inactive.

Grey literature
▶ term often used for semi-published literature, i.e. literature which is not formally listed or priced but is nevertheless in circulation, such as institutional **reports**. Such literature is often difficult to trace.

Grey scale
▶ number of discernable shades of grey between black and white on a **visual display unit screen**.

Grey scale image
▶ **image** where colours are represented by shades of grey.

Grey scale monitor
▶ **monitor** which displays shades of grey rather then colours.

Grievance committee
▶ group of employees appointed to review and assist in the resolution of grievances between employers and staff.

Grievance procedure
▶ established process which allows an employee or group of employees to air a grievance and seek a solution.

Groos droop
▶ named after Ole V. Groos who noticed when studying **Bradford's distribution** that a curve may drop below the linear predictions of **Bradford's law**.

Group decision support system
▶ **computer**-based system, usually implemented on a **local area network** (**LAN**), which supports collaborative group work.

Group icon
▶ **icon** used to denote a group of **programs**.

Group work area
▶ section of **memory** which users of a **network** can share.

Groupware
▶ **software** designed to help small groups of users to work together more effectively.

GUI – graphical user interface
▶ user connection to a **computer** system which uses graphical **symbols** rather than text.

Guideline
▶ **1.** computing – in **desktop publishing**, **word processing** and

drawing **programs** a non-printing line that acts as a guide to **margins**, **gutters**, **page breaks** etc. and helps to determine the position of an element on a page or **screen; 2.** management – advice on a process or activity.

Guiding
▶ signs, signposts, written guidebooks or leaflets, maps, plans etc. that show a user how a particular library or **information service** is physically arranged.

Guilt screen
▶ **screen** that is displayed when **software** is used without permission, giving the name of the **copyright** owner in an effort to make people using a pirated copy feel guilty.

Guiltware
▶ type of **shareware software** that aims to make the user register and pay for **software** used by exploiting an individual's sense of guilt.

Gutenberg
▶ inventor of printing with moveable type in the 1450s.

Gutter
▶ **1.** computing – in **desktop publishing** the space between text **columns** in **documents** with more than one **column**. **2.** Publishing – blank middle space between text in an open book where the pages are bound together.

GW-BASIC – Gee Whiz Beginners' All-purpose Symbolic Instruction Code
▶ **Microsoft**'s version of the **BASIC** programming language.

Hh

Hacker
▶ person who illegally breaks into a supposedly secure **computer** system from a **remote terminal**.

Hacking
▶ illegally breaking into a supposedly secure **computer** system from a **remote terminal**. This may be done with criminal intent, as a response to the challenge of breaking into the security of the system or as a legitimate effort to uncover security weaknesses in a system.

Half duplex – HDX
▶ in **telecommunications**, transmission of **signals** along a **communications channel** in both directions, but not at the same time.

Half-life
▶ calculation of the value of a particular **document** by subtracting its publication year from the **median** publication years of the **documents** that cite it.

Halftone
▶ early printed or **monitor screen image** that is formed by varying shades of grey. Process by which photographs, drawings etc. are reproduced in toning shades of grey as opposed to black and white.

Hand-held computer
▶ **computer** that is small enough to be held in the hand.

Handbook
▶ comprehensive publication on a specific subject with concise information. Also called a **manual**.

Handout
▶ printed material distributed to give additional information to support a lecture, product **promotion** etc.

Hands on
▶ experience of actually using a machine-based system.

Handshake
▶ **signal** exchanged between two **computers** to ensure **compatibility** before **data transmission** takes place.

Handshaking
▶ exchange of **signals** between two devices which indicates that both are ready to receive and transmit **data**.

Handwriting recognition
▶ technique by which a **computer** system can recognize **characters** and other **symbols** written by hand.

Hanging indent
▶ text **format** in which all lines except the first one in a paragraph are indented. Sometimes call an **out dent**.

Hard bound/cover
▶ book with a hard cover as opposed to a paperback. Sometimes called a **casing**.

Hard card
▶ used to add more **memory** to a **computer** by being inserted into an **expansion slot**.

Hard carriage return
▶ **page break** that is inserted by the user which cannot be overriden. Sometimes called a **hard page break** or **forced page break**.

Hard copy
▶ printed **output** from a **computer** that is in permanent form. Soft copy is an **image** that is viewed on a **screen monitor**.

Hard disk
▶ **magnetic disk**, permanently installed in a **computer**, which can hold a large amount of **data**. It provides much more **storage** capacity than a **floppy disk**.

Hard error
▶ equipment **error** or malfunction in **computer processing** that is caused by **hardware**.

Hard page break
▶ **page break** that is inserted by the user which cannot be overriden. Sometimes called a **hard carriage return** or **forced page break**.

Hard return
▶ in **word processing**, creation of a line break by pressing the return or enter **key** that has the effect of starting a new line irrespective of **margin** settings. Differs from **soft return**.

Hard-sectored disk
▶ **floppy disk** that is sold ready formatted.

Hard space
▶ space typed by the user by pressing the space bar on the **computer keyboard**.

Hard vocabulary
▶ precise terminology which cannot be misunderstood, such as chemical formulae, mathematical statements etc.

Hardware
▶ the mechanical, magnetic and electronic **components** of a **computer**.

Hardwired
▶ **computer** or **peripheral** equipment connected by a **cable** to other electronic equipment.

Harmonization
▶ process of making systems, services or organizations as compatible as possible.

Harvard system
▶ method of citing **references** to written work originated by Harvard University.

Harvesting
▶ use of **robot** technology to carry out a number of automatic processes such as identifying, gathering, distributing and storing **URLs** from the **World Wide Web**.

Hash
▶ special character, #, which is a symbol used to represent a number in the USA.

Hash algorithm/code/coding
▶ numeric code that identifies an **index entry** and is the product of a **hash function**. Sometimes called **hash value**.

Hash function
▶ **algorithm** used to calculate a value or **hash code** in a **database** that uniquely identifies a **record** and retains its physical location by means of a pointer.

Hash table
▶ table composed of **hash codes** or **hash values** that provides rapid **access** to **data** by means of a **pointer**.

Hash value
▶ numeric **code** that identifies an **index entry** and is the product of a **hash function**. Sometimes called **hash code** or **hash algorithm**.

Hashing
▶ process (called **hash function**) whereby a **database record** is converted into a number that is a mathematical function (**hash code**) of the **data** that can then be used to retrieve the **record** or to check its validity. The advantage of hashing is that it makes for faster **storage** and **retrieval** of **data** than searching a simple alphabetic arrangement of **data**.

HD – High Density
▶ provision of a relatively high **storage capacity** per unit of **storage** space.

HDTV – High-Definition TeleVision
▶ television that has twice the **resolution** of normal television giving a very clear picture at about 1200 lines per **screen**.

HDX – Half DupleX
▶ in **telecommunications**, **transmission** of **signals** along a **communications channel** in both directions, but not at the same time.

Head
▶ device which reads, records or erases information on a **storage medium**.

Head crash
▶ failure of the **magnetic disk** reader caused by the **read/write head** touching the surface of the **disk** instead of floating above it.

Header
▶ **1.** computing – information on a **data packet** that precedes actual **data** and contains details of source, destination **address, error** checking etc.; **2.** information handling – **characters** at the beginning of an **index** or **catalogue entry** which indicate the **filing** position of **entries** in a **catalogue**; these may be names of authors, titles, editors etc., and **subject headings**.

Header/heading
▶ in publishing – information that is printed at the top of every page of a **document**; usually carries title and author name. Sometimes called a **running head**.

Header label
▶ precedes **data records** in a machine-based **file** and contains descriptive information about the **file**.

Help desk
▶ place (sometimes a telephone contact) where knowledgeable people can be contacted who can provide advice or assistance on a given system, service or **database**.

Help function
▶ advice contained in the **software** of a **computer** system to provide details of the different options available.

Help screen
▶ information that can be displayed on the **monitor** of a **computer**-based system to provide information about the different options available.

Helpful order
▶ order of items which guides users to related items and helps them to extend, broaden or narrow their **search**.

Hertz – Hz
▶ unit of **frequency** equal to one **cycle** per second; a **megahertz (MHz)** is a million **cycles** per second.

Heuristic programming
▶ branch of **artificial intelligence** that uses **heuristics** (common sense rules drawn from experience) to solve problems.

Heuristic searching
▶ searches where the **search strategy** may be continually modified as the results of the search start to appear.

Heuristics
▶ method of problem solving in which increases in efficiency may be traded off against finding a good solution, if not the best possible one.

Hexadecimal code
▶ **data code** which uses base 16 (as opposed to base 2 for **binary code** and base 10 for decimal **code**).

Hidden agenda
▶ undisclosed but actual aim of a particular activity or meeting.

Hidden cost
▶ administrative expense that cannot easily be identified with a specific budget line item.

Hierarchical classification
▶ method of **classification** in which a series of **classes** is divided into successive subordination.

Hierarchical database
▶ **database** that is arranged like a tree where the path starts with a broad subject and leads to more specific items.

Hierarchical file structure
▶ arrangement of **directories** in a **computer** system which is organized into **files** divided into **subdirectories**.

Hierarchical menu
▶ **menu** which has other **menus** under it.

Hierarchical notation
▶ **notation** which displays the relationship of subordination by its length, one **digit** being added for each step of division.

Hierarchical relationship
▶ relationship between **concepts** or **classes**, where one is subordinate to another as in **broader term** or **narrower term**.

Hierarchy
▶ set of **classes** organized to display their **generic relationships** of superordination, subordination and horizontal relationships between collateral and coordinate **classes**.

High density
▶ provision of a relatively high **storage capacity** per unit of **storage** space.

High end product
▶ most expensive and most promoted product in a manufacturing company's range.

High performance computing
▶ branch of **computer science** which concentrates on developing **supercomputers** and the **software** to support them.

High resolution
▶ improvement of **image** quality by increasing the number of **pixels** per square inch.

High Sierra standard
▶ **CD-ROM standard** developed in the USA by some institutions and a group of manufacturers and **software** companies which has been approved as **ISO standard** ISO 9660.

High technology
▶ very advanced technology, usually at the cutting edge of development.

High-definition television – HDTV
▶ television that has twice the **resolution** of normal television which gives a very clear picture at about 1200 lines per **screen**.

High-density disk
▶ **disk** which can be **formatted** to twice the normal capacity of 720 **K** of a 3.5 inch **disk**.

High-density storage
▶ **computer storage** capability where a very large number of **bits** can be stored.

High-level programming language
▶ **computer language** which is easy to learn and which allows users to employ terms with which they are already familiar.

High-resolution graphics
▶ **graphic displays** composed of a large number of individual dots or **pixels**. The smaller the dots, the greater the density. A **high-resolution display** should have at least 192 dots vertically and 280 dots horizontally on a standard **screen**.

High-speed printer
▶ **computer printer** which can operate sufficiently rapidly to be compatible with **online** printing.

Higher education
▶ commonly accepted as formal academic education obtained after secondary level education, usually through a university or other college of higher education. Sometimes called **tertiary education**.

Highlight
▶ make an item stand out, for example in a **search** result or on a

menu, by making it lighter or darker.

Highway
▶ **transmission** path along which **digital signals** may pass. A synonym for a **bus** or a **trunk**.

Histogram
▶ **bar graph** in which the bars represent how many times something occurs.

Historical bibliography
▶ study of history and methods of book production covering printing, binding, paper making, illustration and publishing.

Historical record
▶ any **record** (written, visual etc.) of an event that is kept possibly, but not necessarily, for a particular purpose.

Hit
▶ successful match between a **search** request and the **retrieval** of an item relevant to that request.

Hit rate
▶ percentage of successful matches to the number of **search** attempts.

Holding
▶ item in the stock of a library or **information centre**.

Holism
▶ opinion that maintains that the whole cannot be completely understood in terms of its parts.

Holistics
▶ about or involving the whole and its environment.

Hollerith card
▶ **card** used to record information which has 80 **columns** and 12 rows. **Data** is recorded by punching holes in positions on the **card** which represent **data**.

Hollerith code
▶ **standard code** for punching 80-column **punched cards**.

Hologram
▶ **image** which appears to be three-dimensional owing to light being reflected from different **image** layers.

Holograph
▶ **document** in the author's handwriting; recording on photosensitive film using two or more **laser** beams of different colours to form a single beam.

Holography
▶ creation of three-dimensional **images** using light produced by **lasers**.

Home
▶ starting position for the **cursor** on the **monitor screen** of the **computer**.

Home computer
▶ **microcomputer** intended for use in the home which can be used for a wide range of **applications,** ranging from **video** and educational games to business **programs**.

Home key
▶ **cursor** movement **key** that sends the **cursor** to the beginning of a line of text or other positions that have been set by the **computer program**.

Home page
▶ pages of information made available via the **Internet**; the main **web page** for a person or an organization. Sometimes called a **welcome page**.

Home security system
▶ **hardware** and **software** that can control and take care of such things as lights, smoke detectors, doors and windows etc. in a home.

Homograph
▶ two or more words that have the same spelling but different meanings.

Homography
▶ study of words that have the same spelling but a different meaning.

Homonym
▶ word that sounds the same and may be spelt the same but has a different meaning.

Hospitality
▶ ability to give a unique **notational symbol** to any new **class** to be added to an existing **classification scheme**, which will correctly locate that **class** in relation to other **classes**.

Host
▶ organization which makes a number of **databases** available for use. Sometimes called a **spinner**, **vendor** or **online supplier**.

Host computer
▶ main **computer** of a local or remote **network**.

Host name
▶ unique name of a **computer** on a **computer network**. Also called a **site name**.

House style
▶ **typesetting**, spelling or other conventions adopted by an individual publisher.

Hot desk
▶ office organization where desks are shared and no one individual has their own desk but uses whatever is available.

Hot key
▶ **key** combination that can execute a **computer command** using one **key** stroke instead of several that might otherwise be required.

Hot line
▶ telephone number that is provided by a manufacturer or dealer which can be used to obtain technical assistance or advice.

Hot link
▶ in **object linking and embedding (OLE)**, mechanism for sharing **data** between two **application programs** where a change to the **data** in one **application** appears automatically in the other.

Hot spot
▶ exact spot that a **mouse** or other **cursor** needs to touch to select an **object** on a **screen**; place in a **hypertext document** that must be clicked on to bring up further information.

Hot word
▶ word in a piece of text that causes something to happen when the **cursor** is activated.

Hotlist
▶ list of **documents** that a user wants to **access** frequently which can be stored on a **World Wide Web** viewer.

Hourglass icon
▶ **icon** shaped like an hourglass that shows a **computer** activity is being undertaken and the user has to wait for its completion.

House journal/organ
▶ **periodical** produced by a commercial or industrial organization for internal distribution to staff and/or external customers.

Housekeeping
▶ **1.** computing – routine **maintenance** of **programs** and other contents of a **computer**; **2.** management – routine and continuing library or **information service**

operations, such as **acquisition**, **circulation** etc.

Housekeeping system
▶ system that looks after the routine and continuing library service operations such as **acquisition**, **circulation** etc.

HRM – Human Resource Management
▶ **management** of staff including selection, **appraisal**, reward and development.

HTML – HyperText Markup Language
▶ application of a series of special **codes** that define the style and presentation of a **document**, allowing **hypertext links** to other parts of a **document** or to other **documents**. It is the underlying text language of the **web**.

HTTP – HyperText Transfer Protocol
▶ **standard** method of publishing information as **hypertext** in **HTML format** on the **Internet**.

Hub
▶ **computer** or device to which other devices are connected.

Human-computer interaction
▶ exchange of information between a person and a **computer** through the medium of a **computer interface**.

Human-computer interface
▶ connection between the user and the **computer** system **hardware**.

Human factor
▶ term used in the USA for **ergonomics**.

Human resource
▶ people who staff an organization.

Human resource management – HRM
▶ **management** of staff including selection, **appraisal**, reward and development.

Human readable
▶ information that can be read by a human being rather than in coded form which can only be understood by a machine.

Hybrid computer
▶ **computer** system which has **digital** and **analogue** devices that work together.

Hybrid computer system
▶ **computer** system that has both **analogue** and **digital computers** linked together, often for the purpose of testing or monitoring electrical instruments.

Hybrid interface
▶ connection between a **digital** and an **analogue** device.

Hybrid library
▶ library where paper and **digital** material is stored together; library which integrates print and electronic resources. Sometimes called a **gateway library**.

HyperCard
▶ very **high-level programming language** (developed by Apple) used to produce **applications** such as **computer-aided design (CAD)** packages. One of the few **computer programs** that does not require the **programmer** to have any previous experience.

Hyperdocument
▶ another name for **hypertext**.

Hyperlink/hypertext link
▶ **link** that allows the user to move between words, **objects** and **documents** very quickly.

Hypermedia
▶ application used mainly for **computer-aided instruction** (**CAI**), having the capability to link discrete blocks of information (text, sound, **graphics** or **video**) together, following different paths and attaching **links** to blocks of related information.

Hypermedia link
▶ connection made between **concepts** and terms in a **hypermedia** or **hypertext** system.

Hypermedia-based learning
▶ use of **hypermedia** for learning which allows large amounts of information to be delivered in **non-linear formats** so that users can make choices during the learning process. By **browsing** and **searching**, users can explore and interact with **knowledge**.

Hypertext
▶ non-sequential reading and writing which allows information to be connected using associative **links**; method of connecting items of information in a non-linear manner, with a **computer** automating the process of moving from one piece of information to another.

Hypertext markup language – HTML
▶ application of a series of special **codes** that define the style and presentation of a **document**, allowing **hypertext links** to other parts of a **document** or to other **documents**. It is the underlying text language of the **web**.

Hypertext system
▶ system which allows users to link information together and create trails through associated materials.

HyperText transfer protocol – HTTP
▶ **standard** method of publishing information as **hypertext** in **HTML format** on the **Internet**.

Hyphen
▶ sign (-) used to show a word that cannot be accommodated at the end of a text line has been split; used to make compound words whose meaning differs from that of the individual words.

Hyphen ladder/stack
▶ visually unpleasant appearance of **hyphens** occurring under each other on a printed page.

Hyphenation
▶ use of a **hyphen** to connect two words or numbers; use of **hyphen** when a word is broken between syllables at the end of a line to keep the right hand **margin** of text even; use of a **hyphen** to make compound words whose meaning differs from that of the individual words.

Hypo
▶ fixing solution used in photography.

Hypothesis
▶ statement about the existence of the relationship between two or more **variables** or events that are being examined or studied; tentative theory that needs to be tested in order to be substantiated.

Hz – Hertz
▶ unit of frequency equal to one **cycle** per second; **megahertz (MHz)** is a million **cycles** per second.

Ii

IAC – Information Analysis Centre
▶ formally structured organization which selects, acquires, stores, analyses, evaluates and disseminates information, usually in a specific subject area, with the main **objectives** being **evaluation** and analysis.

ibid
▶ abbreviation for the Latin *ibidem*, meaning 'in the same place'.

IBM – International Business Machines
▶ company founded by Herman Hollerith in the 1890s; today it is the world's largest **computer** manufacturing company.

IBM compatible
▶ **computer** which works in a similar manner to **IBM computers** and can use the same **programs, operating system** etc.

Icon
▶ one of a set of easily recognizable patterns or pictures on a **screen** which can be selected by a **cursor** to indicate a user's choice.

Iconography
▶ **1.** computing – symbolic represen- tation of an **object**, or operation on a group of **files**; **2.** publishing – art of illustration or representation using figures, diagrams, **images** etc.

ICR – Intelligent Character Recognition
▶ **optical character recognition** system which is capable of recognizing a wide variety of **fonts**; may be linked to a **spell checker** to reduce word **errors**.

ICT – Information and Communications Technology
▶ name for all the technologies that enable the handling of information and facilitate different forms of **communication** among human beings and electronic systems and between electronic systems.

IDC – Information Dissemination Centre
▶ formally structured organization which selects, acquires, stores and distributes information, usually in a specific subject area, with the main objective being **dissemination**.

Identifier
▶ word or phrase that describes the subject matter of an item. It is often used for **terms** that are not provided by a **controlled vocabulary** list or in a **keyword** list.

Ideograph
▶ **symbol** or picture used in written languages such as Chinese, where objects or ideas are represented without expressing the sound in its name.

Idle time
▶ time during which a machine is switched on but not actually being used.

IKBS – Intelligent Knowledge-Based System
▶ computer program which relies on knowledge and reasoning to perform a difficult task usually undertaken by a human expert. It usually has a limited number of experts that contribute to its development. Sometimes called an expert system.

ILL – InterLibrary Loan
▶ item lent by one library to another.

Illegal character
▶ character that is not a valid character.

Illegal operation
▶ action that a computer operating system will not allow to be performed.

Image
▶ computerized representation of a picture or graphic.

Image capture
▶ process of scanning an image at a certain resolution and formatting and tagging the resulting file so that it can be retrieved.

Image compression
▶ process of making images smaller by abbreviating repeated information or eliminating difficult-to-see information.

Image database
▶ database which consists of digital images and relevant text data. Images are accessed using simple protocols and can produce digital files, prints or slides. Such databases are used to store medical records, fine art collections etc.

Image grabber
▶ device used to get an image or frame from a camera or video tape and put it into a computer.

Image processing
▶ processing images using computer techniques. This can cover a variety of processes including enhancement, extraction of particular features and digital storage for transmission or later retrieval.

Image resolution
▶ fineness or coarseness of a digitized image, governed by the number of pixels (picture elements) used.

Image retrieval
▶ method of accessing images from a digital database. Various methods include use of controlled vocabulary keywords, free text searching, hypermedia annotation, icon objects etc.

Imaging
▶ process of capturing, storing and retrieving information irrespective of the original format. Methods that can be used are scanning, micrographics, use of optical disc technologies etc.

Impact factor
▶ number of times documents are cited in relation to the number of documents published. A way of assessing the relative importance of one research journal with respect to other journals by taking the ratio of the total number of items the journal has cited during a specific period divided by the number of items published by that journal over the same or an earlier period. Also called citation impact factor.

Impact printer
▶ printer that uses something to press or strike against a ribbon to print a character on a page.

Importing
▶ bringing into a **program** a **file** that has not been created by that **program.**

Imprint
▶ statement giving details about the publisher and printer of a book, usually on the reverse of the **title page**.

Incompatibility
▶ inability of devices and **programs** to operate together.

Incunabula
▶ books printed before 1500, a period often described as the cradle of printing.

Indentation
▶ placing a portion of text or the first line of a paragraph so that the left hand **margin** differs from the left of the text to make the line shorter; blank spaces left at the start of a new line or paragraph.

Independent service provider – ISP
▶ information **provider** who pays for **network** connection in order to make information available to other users.

Independent variable
▶ in statistics, **variable** that influences or is hypothesized to influence another **variable** during an investigation.

Index
▶ set of **identifiers,** each of which characterizes a **document, abstract** or other piece of information. These **identifiers** can be arranged in a variety of ways to suit user needs: alphabetically, systematically etc.

Index entry
▶ **entry** item that is included in an **index**.

Index language construction
▶ process of building **classification schemes, thesaurus** or **taxonomy** construction.

Index term
▶ word used in an **index** to identify the subject content of an item.

Indexer consistency
▶ level of agreement between indexers regarding choice of **index terms** and the number of **index terms** to be used that are necessary to reflect **document** content accurately.

Indexing
▶ process of compiling an **index**; process of analysing the information content of an item and expressing this in the language of a particular indexing system.

Indexing depth
▶ level of **specificity** in assigning **index** terms to the subject content of an item.

Indexing exhaustivity
▶ number of **index terms** assigned to a **document** that is thought to be of importance in **retrieval** and that there is an optimal level for each particular **document** collection.

Indexing language
▶ vocabulary that is used for **indexing,** together with rules for its use.

Indexing service
▶ organization that generates an **index,** usually for a particular subject area, which may be provided in printed and/or **machine-readable** form.

Indicative abstract
▶ **abstract** which indicates **document** content but provides little detailed information.

Indicator
▶ **data element** associated with a **field,** giving information about **field** content.

Indicator light
▶ small power light which indicates that the power on a piece of equipment is switched on.

Indirect cost
▶ expenditure not directly charged to a particular activity or service. Also called **overhead cost.**

Inference
▶ **problem-solving** approach that controls the reasoning process in a **knowledge-based system.**

Inference engine
▶ **processor** which draws reasoned conclusions from a **knowledge base.**

Inferential statistics
▶ statistical methods used for drawing **inferences** about a large population or group on the basis of descriptive statistics derived from small groups or samples.

Infobahn
▶ German term for the **information superhighway.**

Infomaster
▶ person or department responsible for providing information in an institution. Often the name for the person or department responsible for putting information on **World Wide Web pages.** Also called **Web master.**

Informal communication
▶ direct person-to-person **transmission** of information which takes place outside formal mechanisms such as publications etc.

Informal network
▶ personal, social and political interactions between individuals that are not formally established.

Informatics
▶ fairly common European **term** for **information technology;** national and systematic application of **information technology** to economic, social and political development; study of the structure and properties of information and the application of technology to its organization, storage, retrieval and dissemination.

Information
▶ something learned, facts that are gathered or a measure of the content of a **message.** It can be argued whether it is a product, commodity, resource or process. It can be a sensible statement, opinion, fact, **concept** or idea, or an association of statements, opinions or ideas. It is closely associated with **knowledge** in that once information has been assimilated, correlated and understood it becomes **knowledge.**

Information age
▶ since the convergence of **computers** and **telecommunications,** together with a concern for information, the 1980s onwards have been characterized as the information age.

Information analysis
▶ identification of the subject content of items by **indexing** and **classification.**

Information analysis centre – IAC
▶ formally structured organization which selects, acquires, stores, analyses, evaluates and disseminates information, usually in a specific subject area, with the main objectives being **evaluation** and analysis.

Information and communications technology – ICT
► name for all the technologies that enable the handling of information and facilitate different forms of **communication** among human beings and electronic systems and between electronic systems.

Information audit
► **management** technique that systematically collects information about a particular activity or service area in terms of the needs of the customers.

Information broker
► person who conducts a **search** for information on behalf of another person. It often describes self-employed **information consultants** who offer search and **evaluation** services to clients for payment of a fee.

Information centre
► place where **information resources** may be accessed that is staffed by information personnel.

Information chain
► links in the process of passing a request from an enquirer through an **information system** to generate information sent to the enquirer.

Information channel
► **hardware** linking two **terminals** in a **data transmission link**.

Information consultant
► person who offers **search** and **evaluation** services and advice on systems for a fee.

Information database
► any structured **file** of published literature, **data** etc. which is stored and can be accessed electronically.

Information design
► organization of the presentation of electronic information that differs radically from the traditional print approach and includes the use of **HTML, indexing, FAQs** (frequently asked questions) etc.

Information dissemination
► distribution or sending of information to a group of users or potential users.

Information dissemination centre – IDC
► formally structured organization which selects, acquires, stores and distributes information, usually in a specific subject area, with the main objective being **dissemination**.

Information engineering
► application of engineering disciplines to information systems such as **software** engineering, systems engineering, electronic engineering etc.

Information exchange
► sending information from one **terminal** to another over a **network**. Also called **information transfer**.

Information explosion
► unprecedented growth of information and **knowledge**. It is argued that the doubling of printed information every five years threatens the human ability to cope with the volume. However, it offers greater **access** to **knowledge** through technological advances in **computer** and **communications** systems. Sometimes called **publication explosion**.

Information flow
► movement of information, from its generation to its reception by an individual.

Information gathering
► process of collecting and reviewing information by any available means, including individual memory, deduction, reading published material, **communication** with other people, detection, experimentation or observation.

Information handling
► storing, processing and **retrieval** of information; all processes from selection to distribution of information to a user.

Information industry
► broad categorization of all the activities involved in information activities: education, publishing, **media**, **hardware** and **software** producers, **information providers**, libraries and **information centres** etc.

Information infrastructure
► aspects of society that provide **information transfer** facilities such as publishing, education, **information services** etc.

Information intermediary
► person who conducts a **search** for information on behalf of another person, who is often called the **end user**.

Information literacy
► ability to recognize when information is needed and to locate, evaluate and use the required information effectively. Awareness of use and potential of information and **information sources**.

Information literate
► person who is acquainted with both modern sources and **searching** skills associated with **information retrieval** and is knowledgeable in critical analysis of information.

Information management system
► system designed to organize, store, retrieve and disseminate information.

Information need
► general expression that covers any situation where information is being sought.

Information overload
► provision of too much information and **data** which overwhelms an enquirer so that it cannot be used effectively.

Information planning
► planning for the implementation and development of **information services** within an institution.

Information policy
► governmental national plan for provision of and access to information in a particular country or region.

Information presentation
► **format** in which information is found, which could be written, audio, **computer database** etc.

Information processing
► using **computers** to store, process and retrieve **data**.

Information product
► discrete package of information developed prior to specific need with the expectation of providing it to a large number of users without modification.

Information professional
► person formally engaged in the organizing, storing, managing, assessing and/or distributing of information in all forms. Includes librarians, archivists, museum curators and people dealing with **records management**.

Information provider – IP
▶ originally used mainly in the context of **viewdata (interactive videotex)** systems to describe an individual or organization providing material for the **database(s)** involved. Organization that owns information available via the **Internet** or for use in a **videotex** system. Responsible for keeping information up-to-date and accurate. Not to be confused with a **service provider**.

Information reporting system
▶ system that provides **management** with information on the day-to-day operation of an organization.

Information resource
▶ informal or formal human, printed or electronic resource that holds information that can be accessed to answer a need.

Information resource management
▶ integrated organizational strategy for both managing information and enabling resources, such as physical tools, materials, financial investments and people.

Information retrieval
▶ process of **searching** a collection of items in order to identify those **documents** that deal with a particular subject.

Information retrieval system
▶ system which allows for the collection, processing, storing and retrieving of information.

Information science
▶ field of **knowledge**, theory and technology dealing with the collection of facts and figures, and the processes and methods involved in their manipulation, **storage**, **dissemination**, publication and **retrieval**. It includes the subject areas of **communication**, publishing,

library science and **informatics**.

Information scientist
▶ professionally qualified member of an **information service** who is experienced in the exploitation of specialist subject resources (excluding recreation and formal education). Differs from a librarian in that the information scientist is more often involved in evaluating the information retrieved for the **end user**.

Information security
▶ systems and procedures designed to protect an organization's information assets from accidents or disclosure to an unauthorized person or entity. Protection of information held on **computer** from deliberate or accidental threat.

Information service
▶ storing, accessing, processing or delivering information to meet the needs of specific users. It can include traditional library and information services, comprising books, **journals**, **archives**, **standards**, **patents**, research **reports** etc., and electronic material and services, comprising **CD-ROMs**, **databases**, **software**, **electronic documents**, **multimedia**, **video** etc.

Information Service Provider – ISP
▶ **1.** computing – company that provides **Internet** connections and accounts including **E-mail** facilities to both individuals and businesses. Also called **Internet access provider**; **2.** management – traditional print and electronic scholarly publisher, trade publisher, **information aggregator, vendor** or electronic-only disseminator.

Information skill
▶ ability to communicate effectively in order to identify information needs and use available services and resources to provide a useful service.

Information society
▶ society in which the main product is information, leading to a recognition that an organization's success and growth depends upon its ability to exploit information; society in which most workers depend on the flow of information in order to perform their jobs.

Information source
▶ guide to the literature and reference sources in a specific subject area.

Information strategy
▶ policy of an organization regarding its information aims and objectives and how these are to be accomplished, e.g. by training staff, investing in **online** resources etc.

Information superhighway
▶ collection of electronic **networks** which provides **access** to many **databases**, brought about by the convergence of **hardware, software** and **networking** technologies.

Information system
▶ system which allows the collecting, processing, storing and retrieving of information to meet users' needs.

Information systems strategy planning
▶ method of determining what **information systems** should be in place within an organization over the medium to long term, to achieve business objectives.

Information technology – IT
▶ **acquisition**, processing, **storage** and **dissemination** of vocal, pictorial, textual and numerical information by means of **computers** and **telecom-munications**.

Information theory
▶ theory concerning the measurement of quantities of information and the accuracy of **information transmission** and **retrieval**; learning concerned with information **transmission** and measurement.

Information transfer
▶ sending information from one **terminal** to another over a **network**.

Information use
▶ broad expression to denote how information is used.

Information utility
▶ in the USA, a commercial organization providing **information services**.

Information village
▶ name for a central **clearing house** which provides information in electronic **format**.

Information worker
▶ general term for an individual working in the information field; person who is involved in the **collation**, organization, **evaluation**, distribution or **storage** of information in any form.

Informative abstract
▶ **abstract** which gives detailed information about the item covered and may provide sufficient detail so that the original **document** does not need to be consulted.

Informatrics/informetrics
▶ study of the quantitative aspects of information in any form and in any social grouping (scientists, librarians etc.) and includes many previous studies on the measurement of information that lie outside the scope of **bibliometrics** and **scientometrics**.

Infrastructure
▶ basic structure and **components** of a country, system or service.

Inhouse database
▶ **file** developed internally within an organization which may be restricted to that organization's personnel. Sometimes called an **internal database**.

Inhouse system
▶ **information system** that is established within an organization to meet the needs of its own staff.

Initialization
▶ preparation or formatting a **magnetic disk** to accept **data**.

Inkjet printer
▶ non-impact **printer** that forms a high-speed **image** by deflecting ink into droplets electromagnetically.

Input
▶ entering **data** into a **computer**.

Input device
▶ equipment which permits **data** and **instructions** to be entered into a **computer**.

Insertion
▶ placing **characters** or words between existing items.

Inservice training
▶ scheme of practical work, lectures etc. for trainees and junior staff.

INSET – INSErvice Training
▶ usually a day or days set aside for training when normal service activities may be suspended.

Inspection copy
▶ free or on-approval copy of a book provided to a potential purchaser who may place an order for a number of copies. Sometimes called an **examination copy**.

Installation
▶ setting up a new **computer** system or **software** package for use.

Installation program
▶ **computer program** which is used to set up a new piece of **software** or equipment.

Instalment
▶ part of a work published in **serial** form.

Instant book
▶ publication inspired by a notable event or timely issue, usually produced very quickly in paperback **format**.

Instant messaging
▶ **communication** service which allows a private **chat room** to be created between **two people**.

Instruction
▶ **command** (usually in the form of a **character string**) to a **computer** to carry out some operation.

Instructional design
▶ elements of teacher/librarian courses developed in Australia which appreciate design considerations rather than teaching basic operational and production skills.

Integrated circuit
▶ complete **circuit** where the **transistors**, resistors or capacitors etc. are formed out of single piece of silicon which may carry anything from a few dozen to several million **components**.

Integrated data processing
▶ **computer** processing that combines the operation of different system elements to increase productivity.

Integrated device
▶ device that is incorporated into another device.

Integrated information centre
▶ organizational entity which provides information and technical support to the faculty and staff of an academic unit.

Integrated library system
▶ automated package of library services that contains several functions such as **cataloguing**, **circulation** etc.

Integrated Service Digital Network – ISDN
▶ **telecommunications network** that is capable of handling **digital** traffic, either voice or **data**.

Integrated software
▶ combination of different **applications programs** into one package; set of **computer programs** which are designed to run using shared resources.

Integrated system
▶ system in which **hardware**, equipment and other system **components** are linked together.

Integration of information services
▶ process of reorganizing and reallocating tasks between services and systems with a view to reducing duplication, optimizing cost-effectiveness etc.

Integrity
▶ reliability of **data**.

Intellectual freedom
▶ general climate in a society where there are no constraints placed on the way people express themselves other than good taste and observing the unwritten general rules of society.

Intellectual level
▶ age and intelligence of a potential reader of a particular book.

Intellectual property
▶ piece of work that is the result of intellectual effort by an individual; author's right to claim ownership of a created work.

Intellectual responsibility
▶ in **cataloguing**, determining the person or **corporate body** primarily responsible for the content of the work so that a **main entry heading** can be made.

Intelligence
▶ **data-processing** capability of a **computer;** ability to learn and improve a system in **artificial intelligence**.

Intelligent agent
▶ **software object** empowered to represent someone and carry out some action. It may send a message, filter and deliver information, make a purchase or interact with another **agent**. Generally it has a purpose, destination, conditions on which to act and a set of actions it is capable of executing.

Intelligent character recognition – ICR
▶ **optical character recognition** system capable of recognizing a wide variety of **fonts**; may be linked to a **spell checker** to reduce word **errors**.

Intelligent front end
▶ system that acts as an **intermediary** between the **end user** and a **computer** system.

Intelligent interface
▶ **interface** that involves the use of a **knowledge base** (**database** which facilitates **access**) as well as the use of the **database** from which **documents** are to be retrieved.

Intelligent knowledge-based system – IKBS

▶ **computer program** which relies on knowledge and reasoning to perform a difficult task usually undertaken by a human expert. It usually has a limited number of experts that contribute to its development. Sometimes called an **expert system**.

Intelligent terminal

▶ **terminal** containing a **central processing unit (CPU)** and **memory** which can send and receive information and has the facility to store and process it independently of a main **CPU**.

Intelligent till

▶ till in a shop which is a **computer terminal** that can read and record **bar code** pricings and alter stock records as items are sold.

Interactive

▶ use of a **computer** or other device in **real time** where the user is actively involved in directing the flow of work.

Interactive routine

▶ **programming routine** in which a series of operations is performed repeatedly until a previously specified end-condition is reached.

Interactive searching

▶ method of **searching** where the searcher can adjust the **search** request as the **search** proceeds, based on responses received from the system.

Interactive system

▶ system which provides continuous **feedback** to the user while in use.

Interactive video

▶ **video** program which responds to the **instructions** of a user.

Interchange format

▶ **data format** which allows **electronic documents** to be interchanged. Also called **exchange format**.

Interest profile

▶ list of **terms** and other **search** requirements (authors' names, language etc.) that define a user's requirements.

Interdisciplinarity

▶ quality of information and **data** that is involved in more than one main subject or **discipline**.

Interface

▶ electronic connection between two **computers**, between a **computer** or a **peripheral** device or between a **computer** and a user.

Interference

▶ confusion or loss of clarity caused by unwanted **signals**, or **noise**, in a **communication system**.

Interlibrary cooperation

▶ collaborative agreements between libraries for mutual benefit. Such agreements often enable member libraries to share resources such as **network access**, **cataloguing records**, **storage** etc.

Interlibrary loan – ILL

▶ item lent by one library to another.

Intermediary

▶ person who conducts a **search** for information on behalf of an individual with an **information need**.

Intermediate index language

▶ language into which a statement or **source program** is translated before it is further translated or interpreted.

Intermediate lexicon
▶ list of terms representing concepts that appear in index vocabularies, which enables a translation from one vocabulary to another. This is accomplished by matching the terms from the vocabularies which are to be reconciled with the terms in the intermediate lexicon. Sometimes called metalanguage.

Internal database
▶ file developed internally within an organization which may be restricted to that organization's personnel. Sometimes called an inhouse database.

Internal memory
▶ internal electronic memory of a digital computer. Sometimes called a core memory.

Internal modem
▶ modem which fits into a slot inside the computer case which is directly connected to the computer board.

International Business Machines – IBM
▶ company founded by Herman Hollerith in the 1890s; today it is the world's largest computer manufacturing company.

International data flow
▶ transfer of data across national boundaries via a telecommunications system.

International Packet Switching Service – IPSS
▶ public automatic switched data service between British data terminals and computer systems abroad (and vice versa). The service features packet assembly and transmission of data, and leads to compatibility between otherwise incompatible equipment.

International Patent Classification – IPC
▶ industry-oriented classification for patents, inventors' certificates and utility models and their certificates. It was devised to facilitate world-wide research into patent rights, simplify patent processing and to meet the requirements and be a practical administrative aid to countries adhering to the IPC.

International Standard Bibliographic Description – ISBD
▶ convention used internationally for the description of documents.

International Standard Book Number – ISBN
▶ ten-digit number assigned to an edition of a work, consisting of a unique number that identifies the group (linguistic, geographical, national etc.), the publisher and a check digit to identify errors in transcription.

International Standard Music Number – ISMN
▶ unique number assigned to pieces of music.

International Standard Serial Number – ISSN
▶ eight-digit number assigned to a specific serial title consisting of seven which form the unique number for the item and an eighth which is a check digit to identify errors in transcription.

International Standards Organization – ISO
▶ body which attempts to establish international standards and to help coordinate national standards.

International Telecommunications Union – ITU
▶ telecommunications agency of the United Nations. It has three main

components: CCIR, **CCITT** and the International Frequency Registration Board.

Internerd
▶ **Internet** enthusiast who spends all free time talking, reading about or searching the **Internet** to what seems like an extreme extent to other people.

Internet
▶ collection of interlinked **networks** which developed initially from a service to the academic and research community. Users of one **network** are able to gain **access** to information and **programs** stored on **computers** linked to any other **network**.

Internet access provider
▶ company that provides **Internet** connections and accounts including **E-mail** facilities to both individuals and businesses. Also called **Information service provider**.

Internet relay chat
▶ **Internet** facility that allows several users to send and receive messages in **real time**.

Internet Service Provider – ISP
▶ company that provides **access** to the **Internet** to users.

Internet2 – I2
▶ expected sequel to the **Internet** that takes it to the next level. **I2** members will have a new powerful method of **communication** which will allow them to communicate and share information. It is being developed by about 100 universities and will offer higher **bandwidths**, live **video applications** and is expected to run 100 to 1000 times faster than at present.

Internetworking
▶ complicated process of interconnecting separate **computer** networks (**LANs**, **WANs** etc.) to form larger configurations.

Internship
▶ specific period of planned and supervised professional training in a library or **information service**.

Interoperability
▶ ability of one machine to interact usefully with others on a casual ad hoc basis without prior planning and negotiation.

Interpersonal skill
▶ effective **communication** between individuals or between an individual and other members of a group.

Interpolation
▶ estimated value between two known values.

Interpreter
▶ **program** which allows **commands**, for example, to be obeyed by a **computer** individually as they are given. An interpreter may also translate the **instructions** in a **high-level programming language** as they are encountered, and thus allow a **high-level programming language program** to be run.

Intranet
▶ **network** that is confined to a single organization, but uses **Internet**-related technologies.

Intranet document management system – IDMS
▶ system which provides organizations with **intranets** with a simple means of handling **documents** internally and ensuring that users have **access** to the latest up-to-date material.

Intrinsic value
▶ in **archives**, the appraised value and worth of a **document**.

Inventory
▶ listing of a library's stock; library stock-check undertaken periodically to give a more accurate indication of items in the collection to identify lost material etc.

Inverse/reverse video
▶ **display** that uses black text on a white background when normal **display** text consists of white text on a black background.

Inverted commas
▶ **1.** computing – symbol (") used in some **computer database programs** or in a **query language** to mark a **string; 2.** printing – symbol (") used at the beginning and end of words quoted from another source. Sometimes called **double-quotes**.

Inverted file
▶ arrangement of **records** in which all similar material common is grouped together, such as authors' names, titles, **subject headings** etc.

Inverted heading
▶ **index** or **catalogue heading** in which the word order is reversed from its **natural language** order.

Invisible college
▶ individuals engaged in a particular area of interest or research who maintain contact with each other on a professional level; more generally, all the people with whom an individual interacts on an intellectual and/or professional level.

I/O – input/output
▶ gathering information from, for example, the **keyboard** and outputting the results on a device such as a **monitor**.

IP – Information provider
▶ originally used mainly in the context of **viewdata (interactive**

videotex) systems to describe an individual or organization providing material for the **database(s)** involved. Organization that owns information available via the **Internet** or for use in a **videotex** system. Responsible for keeping information up-to-date and accurate. Not to be confused with a **service provider**.

IP – Internet Protocol
▶ **network layer protocol** for the **Internet**.

IPC – International Patent Classification
▶ industry-oriented **classification** for **patents**, inventors' certificates and utility models and their certificates. It was devised to facilitate world-wide research into **patent** rights, simplify **patent** processing and to meet the requirements and be a practical administrative aid to countries adhering to the **IPC**.

IPSS – International Packet Switching Service
▶ public automatic switched **data** service between British **data terminals** and **computer** systems abroad (and vice versa). The service features **packet** assembly and **transmission** of **data**, and leads to **compatibility** between otherwise incompatible equipment.

ISBD – International Standard Bibliographic Description
▶ internationally used convention for the description of **documents**.

ISBN – International Standard Book Number
▶ ten-**digit** number assigned to an **edition** of a work, consisting of a unique number that identifies the group (linguistic, geographical, national etc.), the publisher and a **check digit** to identify **errors** in transcription.

ISDN – Integrated Service Digital Network
► **telecommunications network** that is capable of handling **digital** traffic, either voice or **data**.

ISLN – Integrated Services Local Network
► local **computer network** technology that can handle voice and non-voice services over the same **network**.

ISMN – International Standard Music Number
► unique number assigned to specific pieces of music.

Isochronous
► processes which are time-related and must be delivered within certain time constraints.

Isolate
► single **concept, term** used in a **faceted classification scheme**.

ISP – Independent Service Provider
► **information provider** who pays for **network** connection in order to make information available to other users.

ISP – Information Service Provider
► **1.** computing – company that provides **Internet** connections and accounts including **E-mail** facilities to both individuals and businesses. Also called **Internet access provider**; **2.** management – traditional print and electronic scholarly publisher, trade publisher, **information aggregator, vendor** or electronic-only disseminator.

ISSN – International Standard Serial Number
► eight-**digit** number assigned to a specific **serial** title, consisting of seven which form the unique number for the item and an eighth

which is a **check digit** to identify errors in transcription.

Issues management scanning
► methodology for coping with external social, economic and technological issues that may be difficult to observe or predict and which are likely to have a positive or negative impact on an organization in the future. Also called **environmental scanning**.

Italic type
► slanting type style that is used for emphasis.

Item on term system
► **indexing** system in which each card represents a **concept** and **document** numbers are listed on the card; it is a **postcoordinate index.** Also called **term entry system**.

Iteration
► repeated use of a **computer program** to solve a problem.

Iterative query
► **search statement** that contains a number of intermediate **searches** performed as a single **search** operation. A subsequent refinement of the **search statement** containing some of these intermediate **searches** will be executed again, repeating the duplicated section. The process can lead to a refinement of the **search strategy** until an acceptable one is developed.

Iterative query process
► repeated modification of a **search statement** as results are retrieved to obtain optimum results.

Iterative searching
► repeated **searching** in which later **searches** are modified in the light of the results of earlier **searching**.

**ITU – International
Telecommunications Union**
▶ **telecommunications** agency of the
United Nations. It has three main
components: CCIR, **CCITT** and the
International Frequency Registration
Board.

Jj

Jabber
▶ noise on a network caused by the random transmission of data due to a malfunction.

Jacket
▶ plastic or cardboard cover of a gramophone record, floppy disk or CD-ROM.

JANET – Joint Academic Network
▶ established in 1984 to link users, primarily in academic institutions, into a computer network. Now superceded by SUPERJANET.

Jargon
▶ words or expressions (usually but not always technical) that relate to a particular discipline or profession. Sometimes seen as unnecessary or unhelpful.

Java
▶ general-purpose high-level programming language which is web-oriented and similiar to C++. It enables small applications to be downloaded to the user's computer and run by the web browser.

Job
▶ a single program or task processed by a computer.

Job assessment/audit
▶ technique of monitoring the performance of individual members of staff, with agreed objectives and criteria.

Job description
▶ formal written statement which may describe the duties, tasks and responsibilities of a specific post. Also called job specification or position description.

Job lot
▶ group of material offered at a lower than normal price to a dealer to close down or reduce the stock of a particular published title.

Job-oriented language
▶ computer language designed for the needs of a specific job.

Job-oriented terminal
▶ computer terminal dedicated to a specific job or task.

Job sharing
▶ splitting a full-time position between two people who divide the full-time hours between them.

Job specification
▶ formal written statement which may describe the duties, tasks and responsibilities of a specific post. Also called job description or position description.

Jobber
▶ in the USA, a wholesale bookseller who stocks material from a number of publishers and supplies these to retailers and libraries.

Joint Academic Network – JANET
▶ established in 1984 to link users, primarily in academic institutions, into a **computer network.** Now superceded by **SUPERJANET.**

Joint-use library
▶ public facilities such as schools, community centres etc. that double as public libraries.

Joule
▶ unit for measuring energy.

Journal
▶ **newspaper** or **periodical**; daily record of a person's work.

Joystick
▶ lever whose motions control the movement of a **cursor** or a **screen image**. It can also be used to write on a **visual display unit** (**VDU**). The name derives from an analogous lever used to control the movements of an aeroplane.

Jukebox
▶ **CD-ROM drive** which stores and allows **access** to a number of **discs** on each **drive,** allowing automatic selection from the **storage** device. Sometimes called an **autochanger** or **disc library.**

Julian date
▶ calendar expressed as a five-**digit** number where the first two **digits** represent the year followed by three **digits** representing the number of the day in the year.

Jumper
▶ small metal pin on **cards, CD-ROM drives** and **mother boards** that allows the user to change a setting by hand.

Junction box
▶ box containing a **terminal** strip which joins several **connectors**.

Junk mail
▶ useless, out-of-date information or advertising material that is mass-distributed.

Just-in-case
▶ traditional managerial approach to an **acquisitions** policy that does not take into account the changing **access** to materials or users' needs. Exemplified by the changing approach especially to **serials management** where a large complete collection of **back numbers** of a **journal** is retained just-in-case its contents will be of use.

Just-in-time
▶ new approach to **acquisitions** policy in that materials, services etc. are provided when required by library users, thereby avoiding unnecessary expense in finance, time and **storage** by keeping material that may not be needed.

Justification
▶ **1.** management – demonstrating to a funding body the need for an expenditure or an increase in expenditure for a particular activity or service; **2.** printing – spacing of words at the beginning and end of a line of type to give straight left and/or right **margins.**

Kk

k – kilo
▶ denotes a thousand (ten to the power of 3). One **kb** is 1024 **bytes**. When referring to **storage capacity** k is generally used to mean about a thousand.

Kana
▶ Japanese phonetic writing system used when printing the Japanese language on **computers**.

Kb – Kilobyte
▶ unit of measurement; in **programming** it stands for 1024, the **binary** number nearest to 1000; used to measure the memory capacity of a **computer** where 1 **Kb** = 1024 **bytes**.

Kbps – Kilobits per second
▶ measure of **data transfer** speed.

Kermit
▶ versatile **file transfer protocol** (ftp) that can be used over public telephone **networks**.

Kerning
▶ adjusting the spacing between two adjacent letters to create a better visual effect. Also called **aesthetic kerning** or **proportional spacing**.

Key
▶ marked **button** or lever which is depressed or touched to register a **character**; a group of **characters** used in the identification of an **item**, and to facilitate **access** to it.

Key combination
▶ use of more than one **key** on the **keyboard** to produce an action.

Key macro
▶ set of **instructions** which are carried out when a **key** or **key** combination is used.

Key overlay/strip
▶ paper or plastic printed strip that is placed over the **keyboard** to give details of how a **program** configures the **keys** for use in that **program**. Usually called **keyboard template**.

Keyboard
▶ **computer input** device similar to a typewriter **keyboard** used to enter **data** manually.

Keyboard buffer
▶ that part of the **computer memory** used to hold the codes that are generated when **keys** are pressed.

Keyboard layout
▶ **standard** position of **keys** on a **keyboard,** e.g. AZERY, QWERTY.

Keyboard lockout
▶ **computer program** feature that prevents use of the **keyboard** while **data** is being processed; **software** or **hardware** security system that stops the **keyboard** being used by an unauthorized user.

Keyboard shortcut
▶ **key** which can be pressed to bypass **GUI** actions so that tedious

menu, **icon** or **mouse** use can be avoided. Sometimes called **fast key** or **quickkey**.

Keyboard template
▶ paper or plastic printed strip that is placed over the **keyboard** to give details of how a **program** configures the **keys** for use in that **program**. Sometimes called **key strip** or **key overlay**.

Keyboarding
▶ action of entering **data** using a **keyboard**.

Keypad
▶ hand-held **keyboard** with fewer **keys** than a normal **terminal keyboard** which is used to **input data**.

Keyword
▶ significant **term** found in a **document**, in its title or in an **abstract**, which identifies subject content.

KeyWord And Context index – KWAC
▶ title **index** alphabetized by each **significant word** in the title, followed by the remainder of the title and then by those words that precede the significant word.

KeyWord In Context index – KWIC
▶ rotated listing, usually of **document** titles, with each **significant word** arranged in **alphabetical order** in a column with the word ordering the arrangement left in its place in the title.

KeyWord Out of Context index – KWOC
▶ rotated listing, usually of **document** titles, with each **significant word** arranged in **alphabetical order** with the word ordering the alphabetical display printed on a separate line and out of

its place in the title, usually with an asterisk (*) in place of the word.

Keyword searching
▶ searching a **file** or **database** for the occurrence of specific words to find relevant information.

kHz – kiloHertz
▶ measurement unit of **frequency** which is equal to one thousand **hertz**.

Killfile
▶ list of names and subjects which a user does not want to appear in messages sent via the **Internet**.

kilo – k
▶ denotes a thousand (ten to the power of 3). One **kb** is 1024 **bytes**. When referring to **storage capacity** k is generally used to mean about a thousand.

Kilo segment
▶ unit used to measure the amount of information transmitted. One **kilo** segment = 64 000 **characters**.

Kilobits per second – Kbps
▶ measure of **data transfer** speed.

Kilobyte – Kb
▶ unit of measurement; in **programming** it stands for 1024, the **binary** number nearest to 1000; used to measure the memory capacity of a **computer** where 1 **Kb** = 1024 **bytes**.

Kilohertz – kHz
▶ measurement unit of **frequency** which is equal to one thousand **hertz**.

Kilowatt – kW
▶ one thousand watts; measurement of electrical power.

KISS index – Keep It Simple, Sir
▶ usually refers to a **computer index** which should not be made overly

complicated. ('Sir' is sometimes replaced with 'stupid'.)

Knowbot
▶ type of **search** program that can be used over a **network**; machine that performs the functions of regular **robots** and is capable of working with a **knowledge-based system**. Sometimes called a **spider**.

Knowledge acquisition
▶ process by which an individual receives information and mentally processes it internally so that it becomes part of their **knowledge**.

Knowledge base
▶ information **file** associated with an organized collection of rules, allowing reasoned conclusions to be drawn for a particular cases; part of an **expert system** containing facts, assumptions and a set of rules describing the relationship between statements.

Knowledge-based system
▶ **computer** system which uses a **knowledge base** constructed by an expert in a particular field. The **computer** is programmed with a set of rules, advice and **case studies**. Also called **expert system** or **intelligent knowledge-based system (IKBS)**.

Knowledge engineering
▶ design, development and production of **expert systems**.

Knowledge management
▶ development and facilitation of collaborative working which recognizes the interconnected nature of people, processes and information in organizations.

Knowledge representation
▶ any process that is used to convey details of material, facts, items etc.,

e.g. **classification, cataloguing, data** coding etc.

Knowledge worker
▶ another name for an **information worker**.

Known item searching
▶ **searching** for an item that the user knows exists prior to the start of the **search**.

Kurzweil reading machine
▶ machine for blind people which converts printed matter into **computer data** using an **optical character recognition (OCR)** device. **Data** are then transformed into spoken form via **speech synthesis**.

kW – kilowatt
▶ one thousand watts; measurement of electrical power.

KWAC – KeyWord And Context index
▶ title **index** alphabetized by each **significant word** in the title, followed by the remainder of the title and then by those words that precede the **significant word**.

KWIC – KeyWord In Context index
▶ rotated listing, usually of document titles, with each significant word arranged in alphabetical order in a column with the word ordering the arrangement left in its place in the title.

KWOC – KeyWord Out of Context index
▶ rotated listing, usually of document titles, with the significant words arranged in **alphabetical order** with the word ordering the alphabetical display printed on a separate line and out of its place in the title, usually with an **asterisk** (*) in place of the word.

Ll

Label
▶ **character** or group of **characters** used to identify a specific item.

Label printer
▶ specialized **printer** that is used to print labels.

Lamination
▶ method of preserving frail or deteriorating paper using heat-sensitive thermoplastic material.

LAN – Local Area Network
▶ **computers, electronic mail, word processors** and other electronic equipment linked by **cable** and located within a limited geographical area.

Landscape
▶ **document** printed horizontally on the page, i.e. it is wider than it is high.

Language barrier
▶ situation where the required information is not available in a language that the user can understand.

Laptop computer
▶ small portable **microcomputer** powered by batteries that can be carried around and used anywhere.

Large-Scale Integration – LSI
▶ integration of many **circuits** on to one **silicon chip** which may contain between 100 and 1000 logical elements.

Laser – Light Amplification by Stimulated Emission of Radiation
▶ first developed in the 1960s, it produces a narrow high-energy light beam which is used in **optical scanning devices, optical fibre communication** systems, **printers** etc.

Laser disc
▶ **video disc** the size of a long-playing gramophone record which carries **data** on both sides; it is scanned like a **CD** and delivers a **high-resolution** picture with **digital** sound.

Laser printer
▶ high-speed, **high-resolution** non-impact **printer** which uses **laser output** technology and **xerographic** techniques.

Laser scanner
▶ device which uses **laser** technology to copy and convert material into **digital images**.

Last in first out – LIFO
▶ **queue** system which processes the last item stored first.

LAWN – Local Area Wireless Network
▶ **local area network** which uses high-**frequency** radio waves rather than wires to communicate between **nodes**.

Layer
▶ **communications architecture** which is organized using relatively independent **protocols**, each one in a different layer.

Layout
▶ arrangement of text and **graphics** to form a page or an **image**.

LCD – Liquid Crystal Display
▶ clear liquid which turns black when a voltage is passed through it. It provides a **data display** when liquid crystals are placed between a light source and the observer. Usually used in **notebook computers** and slimline **desktop monitors**.

LCSH – Library of Congress Subject Headings
▶ list of **subject headings**, initially designed for use in conjunction with the American Library of Congress **catalogue**, that employs a **controlled vocabulary** with **references** to **broader** and **narrower terms** with a subject **hierarchy**. It may or may not be used in conjunction with the **Library of Congress classification scheme**.

Leading
▶ amount of space between lines of printed text.

Leaf
▶ commonly two pages (recto: right hand page/**verso**: left hand page) is referred to as a leaf. When a printed sheet of paper is folded once, it produces two leaves; when folded twice it produces four leaves etc.

Leaflet
▶ sheet of paper folded to make two or four pages.

Learning centre
▶ facility equipped with programmed or self-directed instructional material for individual or group instruction and study.

Learning curve
▶ speed with which an individual learns a new system or process.

Learning laboratory
▶ facility equipped with programmed or self-directed instructional material for individual or group instruction and study.

Learning resource centre
▶ location that holds a comprehensive collection of all kinds of learning material together with the equipment necessary for their use by teaching staff and students. It does not necessarily include books, but in practice it often does. Sometimes called a **library resource centre**.

Leased line
▶ **telecommunications** link, usually a telephone line, reserved for the sole use of a particular customer. Sometimes called a **dedicated line**.

Leasing
▶ method of acquiring equipment by paying a rental fee for a specific period of time rather than making an outright purchase.

LED – Light Emitting Diode
▶ semiconducting **diode** that gives off light when a **current** is applied.

Left-hand truncation
▶ reducing a word to its root or stem by cutting off letters at the beginning, to allow for a search to be made for words containing the stem or root.

Left click
▶ **click** on the left hand **button** on a **mouse**.

Left justification
▶ aligning text on the left side and giving a ragged right-hand edge.

Legal deposit
▶ procedure by which publishers are legally bound to deposit one copy of every book published with specifically designated libraries.

Legal deposit library
▶ library which is legally entitled to receive one copy of all books published in a country.

Legal size
▶ paper size used in the USA for legal **documents** measuring 8.5 × 14 inches.

Legend
▶ text which explains the use of patterns or colours in a **display**.

Legibility
▶ written material that is accurate and easy to read.

LEO satellite – Low Earth Orbiting satellite
▶ **satellite** which orbits over the polar regions in a low orbit that can communicate with portable hand-held **terminals**.

Less than operator
▶ sign (<) used to indicate that the quantity on the left of the symbol is less than that on the right.

Letterbomb
▶ E-mail message containing a **code** that can act like a **virus** which affects the operation of the receiving **computer**.

Letter-by-letter arrangement
▶ arranging words in alphabetical order letter by letter, with the space between words being ignored, so that words file together. Sometimes called **something before nothing**.

Lexical analyser
▶ **program** designed to break **input instruction** into recognizable units as part of the assembly and compilation process (i.e. converting **program code** to **machine code**). It can also carry out such tasks as changing **lower case** letters to **upper case** and removing unnecessary spaces.

Lexical analysis
▶ process undertaken by a **lexical analyser**.

Lexicology
▶ branch of **knowledge** concerned with words, their history, form and meaning.

Lexicon
▶ dictionary of words arranged in **alphabetical order** in a particular language.

Liability
▶ result of an unfulfilled obligation or carrying out a prohibited act that could lead to legal action.

Liaison agent
▶ third party or go-between that enhances and encourages **communication** and **cooperation** between different organizations or individuals.

Library automation
▶ use of any automatic or semi-automatic processing machine (more commonly **computers** and their **applications**) to carry out any library activity, such as **cataloguing**, **circulation** etc., or help in the provision of information such as **access** to remote sites or digitally stored **full text** material.

Library management system – LMS
▶ comprehensive integrated **computer**-based system that provides control over all major library

functions including traditional processes such as **cataloguing** etc., statistics provision and more recently developed services such as **access** to an organization's **PC network**, remote **databases** and the **web**.

Library of Congress classification scheme
▶ **classification scheme** with an **alphanumeric notation** developed by the Library of Congress to arrange its collection.

Library of Congress Subject Headings – LCSH
▶ list of **subject headings**, initially designed for use in conjunction with the American Library of Congress **catalogue**, that employs a **controlled vocabulary** with **references** to **broader** and **narrower terms** with a subject **hierarchy**. It may or may not be used in conjunction with the **Library of Congress classification scheme**.

Library resource centre
▶ location that holds a comprehensive collection of all kinds of learning material together with the equipment necessary for their use by teaching staff and students. It does not necessarily include books, but in practice it often does. Usually called a **learning resource centre**.

Library science
▶ collecting, storing and distributing written or printed **records** and material; study of libraries and **information centres** and the **management** of libraries.

Licence agreement
▶ legal agreement between the supplier and user which has conditions on use of material, **software** etc.

LIFO – Last In First Out
▶ **queue** system which processes the last item stored first.

Ligature
▶ two letters written and pronounced as a single **character**. Also called a **digraph** or **diphthong**.

Light emitting diode – LED
▶ semiconducting **diode** that gives off light when a **current** is applied.

Light gun/pen
▶ electric **stylus** used to send a **machine-readable symbol** to a computer.

Light sensitive
▶ material that reacts to light.

Light wand
▶ hand-held **bar code** reader which resembles a pen that is used to read or **input** information via a **bar code**. Also called a **wand**.

Lignin
▶ substance in the cell walls of wood which causes paper made from mechanical wood pulp to turn yellow.

Limited area network
▶ technique for accessing remotely an organization's resources that exist within a larger organization that has a **local area network** (**LAN**) by offering limited interconnectivity to the **host** system.

Limited edition
▶ **edition** of a work with a set number of copies, each copy being numbered and usually printed on special paper. Usually more expensive than an ordinary **edition**.

Limited cataloguing
▶ practice employed to speed up the time and reduce the work involved

by creating limited or shortened **catalogue entries** for those items that do not justify the inclusion of detailed information.

Line drawing
▶ illustration represented by black lines and black areas on a white background.

Line graph
▶ **graph** that draws connecting lines between **data** points.

Line management
▶ organizational structure where line managers can make decisions that affect the organization.

Line printer
▶ **printer** which prints a complete line at a time.

Line speed
▶ rate at which **data** are transmitted over a **communication channel**, usually expressed in **bits per second** (**bps**) or as a **baud rate**.

Line switching
▶ in **telecommunications**, individual **circuits** are interconnected through successive exchanges to provide continuous **transmission.** Also called **circuit switching**.

Linear network
▶ type of **network** in which **signals** from the main **computer** are **input** to each **computer** on the **network** in turn until they are accepted.

Linear program
▶ form of programmed **instruction** which follows a predetermined sequence of increasingly complicated steps. Not the same as **linear programming**.

Linear programming
▶ mathematical technique for breaking problems down into a form suitable for **computer** processing.

Linear searching
▶ machine **search** in which each machine **record** has to be scanned in its entirety and in sequence. Sometimes called **serial searching**.

Lines per inch – LPI
▶ measure of the **resolution** of a **halftone screen**.

Linguistic analysis
▶ construction of mathematical **algorithms** to analyse **natural language**.

Linguistics
▶ scientific study of language.

Link
▶ **1.** generally – **code** which provides **syntax** to a group of terms;
2. information handling – symbols used to relate major **descriptors** or **subject headings** in a **document.** In **postcoordinate indexing**, codes that identify all **descriptors** derived from the same **document,** and have the effect of preventing false correlations between **index terms** and help to clarify the relationship between the **indexing terms; 3.** computing – connection between one **hypertext document** and another. Also called a **hotlink**.

Link analysis
▶ higher quality or frequently linked **documents** are placed at the top of a list of retrieved items.

LIPS – Library and Information PlanS
▶ series of regional surveys in the UK that analysed library and **information services** aimed at

encouraging **cooperation** and closer working relationships.

Liquid crystal display - LCD
▶ clear liquid which turns black when a voltage is passed through it. It provides a **data display** when the liquid crystals are placed between a light source and the observer. Usually used in **notebook computers** and slimline **desktop monitors**.

LISP
▶ **high-level programming language** popular for **artificial intelligence applications** because of the way in which it handles complex **data** structures.

List box
▶ in **Windows**, a **display** of available choices.

List price
▶ price set by the publisher for retail sale of a book. Also called **retail price**.

List processing
▶ any procedure which operates on lists of items. Specialized **high-level programming languages** have been devised to facilitate processing such lists.

Listing
▶ printed **output** from a **computer**.

Literacy
▶ ability to read.

Literary warrant
▶ **1.** information handling – principle of **term** selection for **controlled vocabulary indexing** being empirically derived from the **documents** to be indexed. Sometimes **terms** are selected for their frequency of occurrence in core **documents**. In a **classification scheme**, providing a place for all subject areas that occur in the literature; constructing a **classification scheme** by examining the literature of a subject area so that the resulting scheme corresponds to the material being classified and to the needs of users; **2.** publishing – total sum of material published on a particular subject.

Literature search
▶ search through a number of **documents** to find those that can satisfy an enquiry.

Lithium-ion battery
▶ sophisticated type of rechargeable battery which is light in weight and has a long life.

Lithography
▶ method of printing from a flat surface of stone or metal, where the **image** areas of the plate are coated with water-repellent ink and the non-**image** areas are protected by a film of water. Modern presses use a rubber-covered cylinder to transfer plate **images** to paper. Also called **offset litho**.

Little Endian
▶ ordering the components of a name by size, with the smallest entity first, e.g. individual name, town, region or country. Derived from 'Gulliver's Travels' by Jonathan Swift where there was a dispute about which end of the boiled egg should be broken first.

Loading
▶ entering **data** into a **computer** by means of magnetic **media** (**tape**, **disk**).

Local area network - LAN
▶ **computers, electronic mail, word processors** and other **electronic office** equipment linked by **cable** which are located within a limited geographical area.

Local area wireless network – LAWN
▶ **local area network** which uses high-**frequency** radio waves rather than wires to communicate between **nodes**.

Local collection
▶ books, **maps**, photographs and other material referring to the area where the library is situated. Sometimes called a **local history collection**.

Local exchange
▶ exchange where a number of individual telephone subscribers' telephone lines end.

Local history collection
▶ books, **maps**, photographs and other material referring to the local area where the library is situated; sometimes called a **local collection**.

Local line
▶ **communications channel** which connects a subscriber's telephone line to a **local exchange**.

Local variable
▶ **variable** that only has a meaning within a particular **routine** or function.

Locator
▶ **reference** code that identifies the source of an **article** in an **index**.

Lockout
▶ user denied **access** by a security system; temporary denial of **access** to **commands** when other work is in progress.

Logic circuit
▶ electronic **circuit** that accepts **binary digits** (**bits**) as **input** and produces an **output bit** according to a specific rule.

Logic programming
▶ method of writing **computer programs** which are based on the mathematical study of logical reasoning.

Logical difference
▶ in **Boolean algebra**, given two classes A and B, the logical difference A – B consists of all the items that belong to class A but not to class B.

Logical operator
▶ logical relationship between two conditions such as **AND**, **OR** or **NOT**.

Logical product
▶ in **Boolean algebra**, given the two classes A and B, the logical product A × B consists of those items belonging to both class A and class B.

Logical sum
▶ in **Boolean algebra**, given the two classes A and B, the union or logical sum A + B consists of all items which belong either to A or B or both.

LOGO
▶ high-level **computer programming language** designed to teach mathematics; often used to teach children.

Logo
▶ statement of ownership, address, publication frequency, printer details, subscription rates etc. carried on the last or editorial page of a **newspaper** or on the editorial or contents page of a **journal**. Sometimes called a **mast-head**.

Logoff
▶ sending a **command** to a **computer** to indicate the end of an activity.

Logon
▶ sending a **command** to a **computer** to indicate the start of an activity;

usually requires the use of a user identification **password**.

Look and feel
▶ overall visual appearance and user **interface** of a **computer program**.

Look up table
▶ chart or list which holds information such as a **directory**; table of different values for a **variable**.

Lookalike clone
▶ **computer hardware** or **software** which appears to be the same as other items that are familiar to the user.

Loop
▶ repeating a process in **computer programming** until a predetermined condition is met.

Looseleaf catalogue
▶ book-form **catalogue** which allows the insertion of supplementary or replacement sheets and the removal of outdated sheets.

Looseleaf publication
▶ publication which is issued as separate sheets stored in a ring binder. Updated material can be distributed and filed and out-of-date sheets discarded.

Lotka's law
▶ suggestion made by Alfred J. Lotka that, over a given period of time, a few authors are prolific and account for a relatively large number of publications in a specific field.

Low earth orbiting satellite – LEO satellite
▶ **satellite** which orbits over the polar regions in a low orbit that can communicate with portable handheld **terminals**.

Low-end product
▶ least expensive and least featured product in a manufacturing range.

Low-level language
▶ **programming language** which uses an **instruction** set that can be translated into a **machine code**; it cannot be easily understood by humans.

Low-power standby
▶ energy-saving feature of **laptop computers** and **monitors** connected to a **desktop computer** where parts will be shut down if the **computer** is not used for a few minutes. The use of the **mouse** or **keyboard** switches them back on.

Lower case
▶ small letters as opposed to **capital letters** or **upper case letters**.

LPI – Lines Per Inch
▶ measure of the **resolution** of a **halftone screen**.

LS-120
▶ advanced version of a **floppy disk drive** that is capable of storing 120 **Mb** of **data** on a single **disk**.

LSI – Large-Scale Integration
▶ integration of many **circuits** onto one **silicon chip**, which may contain between 100 and 1000 logical elements.

Luggable
▶ so-called **portable computer** that is awkward or heavy to carry.

Lurk
▶ slang expression for reading a **newsgroup** regularly without contributing any messages; to eavesdrop in a conference, **chat room** or **newsgroup**.

Mm

Machine address
▶ real and unchanging location in **computer memory**. Also called **absolute address**.

Machine-aided cognition
▶ ability of a machine to copy aspects of human intelligence, such as understanding **natural language**, problem solving etc. A **computer** responds by referring to rules that have been programmed into its **memory**. If it responds outside these conditions, it is acting intelligently.

Machine-aided indexing
▶ use of **computers** to automate part of the **indexing** process.

Machine-aided translation
▶ use of **computers** to assist in the **translation** of information from one spoken language to another.

Machine code
▶ form of coded **instructions** suitable for feeding directly to **computer circuits**.

Machine-dependent program
▶ **computer program** that can only be used on one type of **computer**.

Machine independent
▶ **computer program** which has been written without a particular machine in mind, so it can be run on **standard** equipment.

Machine-independent language
▶ **programming language** which can be understood by a wide range of **computers**.

Machine-independent program
▶ **computer program** that can be used on many different types of **computers**.

Machine language
▶ language used by a **computer** to communicate internally; the language that the **computer** uses for its arithmetical and editing functions.

Machine learning
▶ process by which a **computer program** records the results of an action or computation and uses the results to modify future actions or computations.

Machine-oriented language
▶ **programming language** in which each **instruction** has either one or a limited number of **machine code** equivalents. Machine-oriented languages therefore require little reprocessing before being understood by **computers**. They are less easily understood by users.

Machine readable
▶ information that has been coded so that a machine (often, but not always, a **computer**) can be used for processing. Examples are **files** stored on **magnetic tape, punched cards, aperture cards, disks** etc.

Machine-readable cataloguing – MARC
▶ American Library of Congress system developed jointly with the British Library for the creation of **machine-readable bibliographic records**, widely adopted internationally.

Machine-readable data
▶ **data** that can be read directly by the **computer** through an **input device**.

Machine-readable material
▶ material capable of being interpreted by a **computer input device**. Sometimes called an **electronic document**.

Machine-readable record
▶ **record** where the information content is usually in code on **media** such as **punched cards** or punched paper tapes, or on **magnetic tapes**, **disks** or **drums**. This coded information is only retrievable by machine.

Machine translation
▶ automation of the **translation** process from one spoken language to another.

Macintosh
▶ **personal computer (PC)** manufactured by the Apple company.

Macro
▶ series of **instructions** stored as a single item to meet a recurring but individual need.

Macro-virus
▶ type of **virus** able to hide behind the **screen**, for example in the **template** section of a **word processing document**, so that its existence is not immediately apparent.

Magnetic bubble memory
▶ **storage** in which information is encoded on to a thin **film** of magnetic silicate in the form of bubbles. The presence or absence of a bubble in a particular location can be used to denote a **binary digit**. Detection of bubbles is carried out by means of a special sensor which emits an electronic pulse as each bubble passes its read/write **head**.

Magnetic card
▶ **card** with a magnetized surface upon which **data** can be recorded.

Magnetic disk
▶ circular plate with a magnetized surface; it holds a number of recorded tracks, divided into sectors, which provides **storage** for its **random access** capability.

Magnetic disk drive
▶ storage device containing a **disk drive** and the necessary magnetic **read/write heads**.

Magnetic drum
▶ **storage** giving rapid **direct access** and having a large **capacity**.

Magnetic Ink Character Recognition – MICR
▶ automatic recognition of **characters** printed with a special ink. The ink contains magnetic particles which can be detected and traced by appropriate **input devices**.

Magnetic media
▶ materials that respond to magnetism such as **hard disks, floppy disks** and **magnetic tape**.

Magnetic resonance imaging – MRI
▶ **computer**-based method of displaying the internal features of a living body (human or animal) that involves placing the body within a magnetic field.

Magnetic strip
▶ thin band of magnetic material used for coding **data**, which is used on credit cards and in **automatic teller machines**.

Magnetic tape
▶ tape with a magnetic surface on which **machine-readable data** or information such as audio or **video** material can be stored.

Magneto-optical disc
▶ disc made of plastic with a reflective metal coating that is read using a laser beam. Types used in publishing are **CD-ROMs**, **laser discs** and **video discs**. Better known as an **optical disc**.

Magneto-optical technology
▶ combination of **magnetic disc** and **CD-ROM** technologies that produces a high-capacity **storage medium** using a **magneto-optical disc** or **cartridge**. A **laser** beam is used to heat a magnetic coating on the **disc** before information is written on to the coating.

Mail-bomb
▶ sending a huge number of **E-mail** messages to one person or system with the aim of crashing the recipient's system.

Mail bridge
▶ **computer gateway** that forwards **E-mail** messages between **networks**.

Mail gateway
▶ **computer gateway** between two or more **E-mail** systems which can transfer and, if necessary, translate messages between them.

Mail merge
▶ **computer program** that combines names, addresses and other **data** from a **database** with a body of prepared text.

Mail path
▶ **E-mail address** which gives a message route listing the **host** names through which the message must pass.

Mail server
▶ **computer** facility that sends **files** or information in response to **E-mail** requests.

Mailbox
▶ **file**, **directory** or message **queue** on a system by which incoming **E-mail** messages are stored for a particular user or for distribution to a **mailing list** or via a **mail server**.

Mailbox system
▶ any system in which **computer** messages are transferred from one user (or organization) to the **file** of another to await collection.

Mailing list
▶ **online** discussion which is conducted by relaying copies of all messages to all participants using **electronic mail**.

Mailshot
▶ advertisements or letters sent out at the same time to a large number of potential customers.

Main class
▶ in **general classification schemes**, discrete areas of **knowledge** which are coordinate with each other and cover all subject areas.

Main entry
▶ principal **entry** for an item in a **catalogue**, giving the fullest information.

Main logic board
▶ **circuit board** inside the **computer** which holds **ROM**, **RAM**, **microprocessor** and other special **circuits**.

Main memory
▶ place in a **computer** where **instructions** and **data** are stored for fast **access**. Used to be called **core memory**.

Mainframe computer
▶ large **computer** capable of performing many complex **tasks** at the same time while simultaneously providing connection to a hundred or more users and controlling many **peripheral** devices.

Maintainability
▶ ease with which an activity or piece of equipment can be kept in a usable or functioning state. **Software maintenance** can include **file backup**, installation of upgrades etc. Equipment **maintenance** can include performance testing, measuring use **data** etc.

Maintenance
▶ keeping things in working order which includes repairing, testing, adjusting and replacing. Corrective maintenance is carried out after a problem develops while preventive maintenance is carried out before problems develop.

Maintenance contract
▶ legal agreement with a company to provide regular **maintenance** of equipment for a fee.

Maintenance release
▶ revision of a **software program** that corrects small **errors** or introduces a new minor feature.

Male connector
▶ plug that has pins in it that will connect to a **female connector**.

MAN – Metropolitan Area Network
▶ **computer network** that links users in an area usually the size as a city.

Man-machine interface
▶ contact between the human being and the **computer**; procedure or **protocol** that allows a human operator to **access** and operate the system.

Management
▶ coordinating the resources of an organization to accomplish desired goals and **objectives**.

Management accounting
▶ recording and controlling the expenditure of an organization in order to control specific activities. Sometimes called **cost accounting.**

Management audit
▶ study of the relationship between the use of resources (human and physical) and company profitability.

Management by objectives – MBO
▶ **management** approach where quantitative and measurable goals and **standards** have been set so that performance can be evaluated.

Management communication system
▶ system that provides links between users and **computer** technology to transmit information.

Management information system – MIS
▶ system that provides information which supports the **management** functions and **decision-making** processes within an organization.

Management of change
▶ process of implementing a new working situation, with attention being paid to all aspects affected, including staff.

Manpower
▶ staff available in an organization.

Manual
▶ generally – describes something that is done by hand; **2.** information sources – comprehensive publication on a specific subject with concise information. Also called a **handbook**.

Manual indexing
▶ process of analysing manually a **document** or collection of **documents** and presenting the results in recognized groupings (author, subject etc.) that facilitates the **retrieval** of the original **document**.

Manuscript – MS
▶ original version of any **document** (including music scores) usually written by hand; any material in its final form that has been typed but not reproduced. An illuminated manuscript is one that has been written or copied and decorated by hand; often religious in content and prepared in religious houses in the middle ages.

Map
▶ representation of the surface of the earth showing physical features, political boundaries etc.

MARC – MAchine-Readable Cataloguing
▶ American Library of Congress system developed jointly with the British Library for the creation of **machine-readable bibliographic records**, widely adopted internationally.

MARC record
▶ **bibliographic record** of an item produced according to the **MARC** cataloguing system rules.

Margin
▶ white space around a block of text on a page.

Marginalia
▶ written or printed notes or descriptive information given in the **margin** of a book.

Mark sensing
▶ technique for reading pencil marks on specially prepared forms into a **computer**.

Market penetration
▶ market share of a specific product or service.

Market research
▶ systematic gathering, recording and analysing of information relating to the marketing of goods and services.

Markov model
▶ **model** in which probabilities of future events depend only on the current state of the **model** and not how the **model** got to that state.

Markov process
▶ system which produces a sequence of discrete symbols according to previous events in the series.

Markup
▶ instructions on a copy or **layout** for a compositor to follow when typesetting.

Markup language
▶ **1.** computing – method of converting typesetting instructions to **computer** typesetting instruction **code**; **2.** publishing – any language that provides ways to indicate underlining, paragraph breaks, section **headings**, **italics** etc. in text.

Mass communication
▶ means by which **mass media** (information, education and entertainment) is disseminated to as large an audience as possible. Characteristics are that information

moves from the few to the many; it is transmitted swiftly only one way and there is no **feedback** or control by the audience.

Mass media
▶ all forms of **communication** (publishing, radio, television etc.) that disseminates information, education and entertainment to a wide audience.

Mass storage
▶ various devices used for storing large amounts of **data** that is measured in **gigabytes** abd **terabytes**, such as tapes, **optical discs**, etc. Sometimes called auxiliary storage or secondary storage.

Master
▶ original **compact disc** recording of a finished **program**.

Master file
▶ most accurate and up-to-date version of a **computer file** held in a **data-processing** system.

Master page
▶ **template** which defines the overall appearance of every page in a printed **document**.

Master-slave system
▶ **computer** system that controls one or more devices (slaves) and determines when slaves may or may not send messages. Such relationships are common in **teleprocessing networks**.

Mastering facility
▶ capital-intensive production facility where **CD-ROMs** are produced.

Masthead
▶ statement of ownership, address, publication frequency, printer details, subscription rates etc. carried on the

last or editorial page of a **newspaper** or on the editorial or contents page of a **journal.** Sometimes called a **logo**.

Mathematical model
▶ characterization of a process, **object** or **concept** in terms of mathematics, so that **variables** can be manipulated easily. Set of equations which represents the action of a system.

Mathematical operator
▶ **symbol** that governs a mathematical computation: + for add; – for subtract; × or * for multiply; and ... or / for divide.

Matrix
▶ rectangular **array** of quantities arranged in rows and columns.

Matrix printer
▶ **printer** that uses a series of small **dots** to form a **character.** Might be called a **dot matrix printer**.

Mb - Megabyte
▶ a million **bytes**; measure of **storage** capacity.

MBO – Management By Objectives
▶ **management** approach where quantitative and measurable goals and **standards** have been set so that performance can be assessed.

MCA – MicroChannel Architecture
▶ high-performance **channel** for **personal computers** designed by **IBM**.

MCI – Media Control Interface
▶ **platform**-independent **specification** published by **Microsoft** and other organizations in 1990 which controls **CD-ROMs** and other playback units.

MCGA – MultiColour Graphics Array
▶ obsolete **standard** for **display** of information introduced by **IBM**.

Mean
▶ measure of the central tendency obtained by dividing the sum of two or more quantities by the number of these quantities.

Media
▶ specifically, printed or audiovisual forms of **communication**; sometimes used in a general sense for all **communication formats**.

Media centre
▶ library or **resource centre** in a school that provides a range of **media** and related equipment. Also called a **school media centre**.

Median
▶ middle value of a series of values arranged according to size.

Mediated searching
▶ process of **information retrieval** commonly carried out on a **database** by a third party, usually a librarian or other **information professional**, on behalf of those seeking information.

Medium
▶ physical material upon which **data** are recorded, e.g. **magnetic disk**, **magnetic tape** or **punched card**.

Mega
▶ word prefix used to indicate one million.

Megabit
▶ one million **bits**.

Megabyte
▶ one million **bytes**; measure of **storage** capacity.

Megaflop
▶ unit of measurement used to measure how fast a **computer** can carry out mathematical calculations.

Megahertz – MHz
▶ one million **cycles** per second.

Megapixel
▶ **image** containing about one million **pixels** or more.

Memorandum
▶ note which helps a person to remember something or a **record** of events.

Memory
▶ part of a **computer** which holds **programs** and **data**.

Memory bank
▶ set of **memory chips** connected together to form a **memory** unit.

Memory board
▶ **card** or **board** that is added to a **computer** to increase total **memory** which is distinct from plugging more **memory chips** into the **mother board**.

Memory map
▶ table that shows how the **memory storage** in a **computer** is organized.

Memory resident
▶ **computer programs** which are held permanently in the **main memory**.

Menu
▶ list of options or facilities listed on a **computer screen** which allows a user to make a selection.

Menu bar
▶ list of available **menus;** most **applications** have a **file menu**, an edit **menu** and a help **menu**.

Menu-based interface
▶ **user-friendly interface** that provides a selection of options or **commands** from which the user can choose. It is the alternative to a **command interface**.

Menu-driven system
▶ **computer** system or **software** which uses **menu** techniques rather than **commands**.

Merge
▶ bring together two or more **files** or different kinds of information.

Message box
▶ small **window** on the **computer screen** which brings information to the attention of a user.

Meta-information modelling
▶ successful user interaction where information is presented and arranged in ways that are useful to the understanding of previously held mental **models** of the user.

Metacrawler
▶ search tool that translates and sends a **query** to a number of **search engines** and **directories** simultaneously. Results are presented as a single integrated set. More usually called a **metasearch engine**.

Metadata
▶ word that describes **data** about **data**, e.g. a **catalogue**.

Metalanguage
▶ list of terms representing **concepts** that appear in **index vocabularies**, which enables a translation from one **vocabulary** to another. This is accomplished by matching the terms from the **vocabularies** which are to be reconciled with the terms in the metalanguage. Sometimes called an **intermediate lexicon**.

Metasearch engine
▶ search tool that translates and sends a **query** to a number of **search engines** and **directories** simultaneously. Results are presented as a single integrated set. Sometimes called a **metacrawler**.

Metropolitan area network – MAN
▶ **computer network** that links users in an area usually the size as a city.

MHz – megahertz
▶ one million **cycles** per second.

Mice
▶ plural of **mouse**.

MICR – Magnetic Ink Character Recognition
▶ automatic recognition of **characters** printed with a special ink. The ink contains magnetic particles which can be detected and traced by appropriate **input devices**.

Micro-justification
▶ use of **microspacing** to justify text.

Microcard
▶ opaque **card** on which microcopies are reproduced photographically in rows and columns. It resembles a **microfiche**, but has its **images** printed positively.

Microchip
▶ common name for an **integrated circuit** placed on a **silicon chip**.

Microcode
▶ set of **microinstructions** that can be a whole or part of a **microprogram**.

Microcomputer
▶ small **computer** which has a **microprocessor** or **computer chip** as its **central processing unit (CPU)**.

Microelectronics
▶ design and production of **integrated circuits** and **chips**.

Microenhancer
▶ **program** which allows a **micro-computer** to **upload** to and **down-load** from a **mainframe** or **minicomputer** that processes **data** stored on a **disk** in a **micro-computer**.

Microfiche
▶ type of **microform** in which pages of text and **graphics** are photographically reduced and then mounted (usually as a negative image) on a film. Each film usually has the dimensions of 4 × 6 inches, and holds a **matrix** of 7 × 14 pages. The fiche can be read a **frame** at a time using a **microfiche reader**.

Microfiche reader
▶ optical device for illuminating **microfiche** and providing an enlarged readable **image**, usually projected on to a **screen**.

Microfilm
▶ type of **microform** in which photographically reduced pages are mounted in sequence on a roll of film.

Microfilm reader
▶ optical device for illuminating a **microfilm** and presenting an enlarged readable **image** on a **screen**.

Microfloppy disk
▶ old name for a small 3.5 inch **floppy disk**.

Microform
▶ generic term for all forms of micro record, including film in strips (**microfilm**) or sheets (**microfiche**) or opaque cards (**microcard**) on to which pages of photographically reduced documents are impressed. Some form of special magnifying device is required to read any type of microform.

Microform reader-printer
▶ device for reading **microforms** which combines a viewing screen for visual **display** with a mechanism for producing enlarged print on paper copies of the material viewed.

Micrographics
▶ process of reducing **documents** to such an extent that some form of enlargement is required to make them legible.

Microinstruction
▶ single **computer instruction** representing a simple idea such as 'delete' or 'add'.

Microprocessor
▶ single **chip** containing a complete **central processing unit (CPU)**. Sometimes used as a synonym for a **microcomputer**.

Microprogram
▶ **program** written in **microinstructions** that are implemented by **computer hardware**. Such a **program** is not normally accessible to a user.

Micropublishing
▶ publishing information or literature in any **microform,** e.g. **microfilm, microfiche** or **ultrafiche**.

Microsecond
▶ one millionth of a second.

Microspacing
▶ insertion of variable-sized spaces between letters in order to justify text.

Microsoft
▶ large **software** company founded by Bill Gates that has developed such products as **Windows** etc.

Microsoft Disk Operating System – MS-DOS
▶ microcomputer operating system developed by Microsoft.

Microthesaurus
▶ thesaurus covering special fields which is based on a general thesaurus. Sometimes called satellite thesaurus.

Microwave
▶ radio wave with a frequency above 890 megacycles per second.

Middle management
▶ individuals in an organization who are responsible for specific functions and services but do not have final or overall authority.

Middleman
▶ individual who transfers services or products from the producer to the consumer. Sometimes describes the person who provides information to an end user or performs a search on behalf of the end user. Sometimes called an intermediary.

Middleware
▶ computer software that connects two separate applications.

MIDI – Musical Instrument Digital Interface
▶ standards and guidelines for connecting digital musical instruments to a computer.

Migration
▶ in information handling moving material from one form of storage to another, usually more up-to-date. Often used in handling archive material; updating preserved documents or files to be compatible with current versions.

Migration path
▶ marketing term to describe a series of alternative ways whereby a user

of proprietary computing equipment can upgrade an installation to provide increased processing power or additional input or output capacity.

Millennium bug
▶ inability of computers to change date information from years numbered from 2000.

Milli
▶ word prefix used to mean one thousandth.

Millions of Instructions Per Second – MIps
▶ measure of computing power.

Minicomputer
▶ computer that is smaller than a mainframe computer but larger than a microcomputer.

Minifloppy
▶ computer floppy disk measuring 5.25 inches.

Minimal cataloguing
▶ least amount of cataloguing information regarding an item that is regarded as necessary to identify accurately and retrieve that item.

Minitel
▶ French videotex system.

Miniscroll bar
▶ small scroll bar that appears inside a dialog box which lists choices.

Minithesaurus
▶ thesaurus which is a subset of a larger thesaurus usually limited to a specialized subject.

MIps – Millions of Instructions Per Second
▶ measure of computing power.

Mirror site
▶ set of **Web pages** in popular use held on a **server** in the searcher's own county but originating in another country.

MIS – Management Information System
▶ system that provides information which supports the **management** functions and **decision-making** processes in an organization.

Mission-oriented research
▶ research aimed at a particular project or mission, such as landing a man on the moon.

Mixed media
▶ less familiar term for **multimedia**.

Mixed notation
▶ **notation** which uses more than one set of **symbols**: upper- and lower-case letters, numerals, arbitrary symbols etc.

Mnemonic
▶ shortened word or phrase that helps in remembering something.

Mnemonic notation
▶ **notation** whose meaning is easily memorized.

MO jukebox
▶ device that uses **magneto-optical technology** for storing and accessing information, usually a large collection of **discs**.

Mobile telephone
▶ hand-held portable telephone which consists of all necessary **communications hardware** and operates by means of a **cellular communications** systems.

Mock-up
▶ **layout** or rough artwork. Also called a **visual**.

Model
▶ scale representation of a system that allows the **characteristics** to be altered and the effects studied; three-dimensional representation of an **object**.

Model building
▶ construction of a system which simulates a process in the real world.

Modelling
▶ representation of a real activity, place etc.

Modem – MOdulator-DEModulator
▶ device for changing **signals** from the **analogue** or voice **signal** that is accepted by the telephone line to the **digital signal** that can be understood by a **computer**.

Moderated newsgroup
▶ **newsgroup** monitored by an individual or group who have the ability to block messages that are thought to be inappropriate.

Modifier
▶ **term** or phrase which differentiates among the **entries** under a main **term** in an **index entry**.

Modula 2
▶ **high-level programming language** that is written as an extension of **Pascal** in an effort to overcome **Pascal's** shortcomings. Its structure is modular and **routines** can be written and tested before being integrated into other **modules**.

Modular architecture
▶ **computer** system design made up of separate components that can be connected together.

Modular planning
▶ building or office layout which consists of a number of **modules** or units, with no permanent internal walls dividing the working space.

Modular programming
▶ **computer programs** developed as separate **modules** where each one can be developed and tested individually. Commonly used when a team of **programmers** are working on a large **program**.

Modularity
▶ something made up of **modules**.

Modulation
▶ method of changing a **signal** from one **frequency** to another.

Modulator
▶ device that converts an audio or **video signal** into a form which can be transmitted by a **carrier signal**.

MOdulator-DEModulator – modem
▶ device for changing **signals** from the **analogue** voice **signal** that is accepted by the telephone line to the **digital signal** that can be understood by a **computer**.

Module
▶ **1.** generally – self-contained unit that can be used in conjunction with other units or added to an existing system. **2.** computing – part of a **computer program** designed to perform a specific **task**.

Monitor
▶ device like a television **screen** for the **display** of **data** from a **computer**. Also called a **visual display unit** (**VDU**).

Monochrome
▶ **visual display unit** which can **display** only one colour on the **screen**.

Monograph
▶ literally means a single written item, often used to mean a book. In library terms, any printed item that can be described, identified and shelved as a single item.

Monographic series
▶ volumes issued under a **series** title, with each volume having an individual title.

Monolingual thesaurus
▶ **thesaurus** produced in a single language.

Monospaced font
▶ single spaced **font** which allocates the same amount of space to each character. Also called **fixed-pitch font**.

Monospacing
▶ **fonts** where each **character** is allocated the same width.

Montage
▶ combination of drawings, photographs and other material overlaid to form a single illustration for decorative, display or advertising purposes.

Monte Carlo method
▶ generally any method of estimating based on sample observations; more specifically, observing some process where chance plays a part in order to arrive at an estimate.

Monte Carlo simulation
▶ **simulation** method that uses **random numbers** to estimate complex probabilities.

Mooers descriptor
▶ proposal by Calvin Mooers in the mid-1960s that a basic set of approximately 250-350 terms could be selected for a specific subject area to form the foundation of an **indexing** system for that defined subject.

Mooers law
▶ suggestion made by Calvin Mooers that **information systems** will not be

used when it is more painful and troublesome for a **client** to have information than not to have it.

Moore's law
▶ observation by Gordon Moore in 1965 that the number of **transistors** per square inch on **integrated circuits** has doubled every year since the **integrated circuit** was developed.

Moral right
▶ right of authors to be acknowledged as the originator of a work; right not to have their names attributed to work that they did not create; right not to have their work amended in any way that undermines their reputation.

Morphing
▶ formation and alteration of structures using a **computer**.

Morphological analysis
▶ study of words and languages as part of **linguistic analysis**.

Morphology
▶ form and structure of words in a language.

Mosaic
▶ **software** developed by the American National Center for Supercomputing Applications (NCSA) for use on the **World Wide Web**.

Mother board
▶ main printed **circuit board** in a **computer** system, into which other **boards** are connected. Sometimes called **backplane**.

Motion video
▶ **video** that displays a sequence of **images** (**frames**) sufficiently rapidly for the viewer to see a continuous moving picture.

Motivation
▶ interest in undertaking a particular task or activity.

Mouse
▶ handheld device which is used to move an **icon** or **cursor** across a **monitor screen**. It can also be used to move text and illustrations.

Mouse pointer
▶ small moveable symbol (usually an arrow) on the **computer screen** which acts as a **pointing device**.

MP3 – MPEG Layer 3
▶ method of compressing **digital** sound so that **downloading** takes less time and takes up less **disk** space. It has been criticised as tracks can be copied easily.

MRI – Magnetic Resonance Imaging
▶ **computer**-based method of displaying the internal features of a living body (human or animal) that involves placing the body within a magnetic field.

MS – ManuScript
▶ original version of any **document** (including music scores) usually written by hand; any material in its final form that has been typed but not reproduced. An illuminated manuscript is one that has been written or copied and decorated by hand; often religious in content and prepared in religious houses in the middle ages.

MS-DOS – MicroSoft Disk Operating System
▶ microcomputer operating system developed by **Microsoft**.

MUG – Multiuser Game
▶ game which many people can play, possibly by contacting an **electronic bulletin board**.

Multi-tier architecture
▶ computer architecture which separates the interface, the application and the database into layers or tiers.

Multi-user system
▶ time sharing system where many users have access to a computer at the same time. Sometimes called a multiaccess system.

Multiaccess system
▶ time-sharing system where many users have access to a computer at the same time. Usually called a multiuser system.

Multicasting
▶ form of broadcasting in which packets of information are delivered only to specific destinations.

Multilingual thesaurus
▶ thesaurus produced in one or more languages; often printed in parallel columns.

Multimedia
▶ information combining different content types, such as motion video, audio, still images, graphics, animation, text etc.

Multimedia platform
▶ integrated collection of computer and sound- and image-based systems that provide access to multiple formats, including text, graphics, audio, still images, animation and motion video.

Multiple access
▶ ability of a system to receive messages from and transmit them to a number of separate locations.

Multiplexing
▶ transmitting two or more messages simultaneously via the same channel.

Multiplexor
▶ device that uses and controls several communication channels which are sending and receiving messages at the same time.

Multiprogramming/multiprocessing
▶ handling of more than one task by a single computer. Sometimes called multitasking.

Multiskilling
▶ developing several different skills or abilities in an individual.

Multitasking
▶ now taken to be the same as multiprogramming.

Multiuser game – MUG
▶ game which many people can play, possibly by contacting an electronic bulletin board.

Music chip
▶ integrated circuit that can generate musical sounds and tunes.

Musical instrument digital interface – MIDI
▶ standards and guidelines for connecting digital musical instruments to a computer.

Mutually exclusive class
▶ in classification, classes which have no members in common.

Nn

Naive user
▶ user of a **computer program** or **database** who is unaware of **program architecture** but can use one or more features to carry out limited tasks.

Name authority file
▶ list of the names of persons or **corporate bodies** that are approved for use in **cataloguing** or **indexing**.

Name catalogue
▶ **catalogue** arranged so that names of places, people and organizations are interfiled in one alphabetical sequence.

Name indexing
▶ listing and organizing names (personal and company etc.) to be used in the process of identifying and locating **documents**.

Name resolution
▶ mapping an **Internet** name into its corresponding **address**.

Nameserver
▶ **computer** which translates names in **information provider addresses** for other **computers**.

NAND function
▶ equivalent to an **AND** function with a **NOT** function as **output**. Results in a negative **output** if all **inputs** are positive.

Nano
▶ prefix denoting one thousand millionth (ten to the power of minus nine).

Nanosecond
▶ one thousandth of a microsecond, or one thousand millionth of a second; expressed as ten to the power of minus nine.

Nanotechnology
▶ field of science which has the goal of controlling individual atoms and molecules to create **computer chips** and other devices that are thousands of times smaller than are currently available.

Narrowband
▶ refers to a **bandwidth** of up to 300 **Hz**.

Narrower-broader order
▶ **filing order** in which no works on broader subjects file before works on narrower subjects.

Narrower term – NT
▶ in a **thesaurus** the formal **hierarchical relations** between a **genus** and its **species** are indicated by the **narrower term** (**NT**) and **broader term** (**BT**) designators.

National bibliography
▶ list or **catalogue** of all items published in the country. Sometimes it also includes items published about the county or works by authors from the country that have been published elsewhere.

National character
▶ **computer characters** which may vary or be specific in different countries, for example #, $, £ and @.

National Information Infrastructure – NII
▶ American proposal for a high-speed **interactive digital communications** system intended to connect multiple technologies with millions of users.

National information policy
▶ strategy developed for the coordinated development of library and **information services** in a country.

National Research and Education Network – NREN
▶ proposed high-speed **network** being developed in the USA which is being built on the existing **Internet** structure. It will support research and scholarly activities, together with education and research administration.

Natural classification
▶ **classification** based solely on essential properties such as **genus-species relationships**.

Natural language
▶ ordinary spoken or written language.

Natural language indexing
▶ **indexing** method where words are selected from the text of the title, **abstract** or **full text** to provide **index entry points** without any form of **vocabulary control**.

Natural language interface
▶ method of communicating with a **computer application** that relies on the vocabulary and sentence structure found in normal language.

Natural language processing
▶ use of a **computer** to analyse human or **natural language**.

Natural language searching
▶ searching for the occurrence of specific words in the text of titles, **abstracts** or **full text** without any form of **vocabulary control**.

Navigation
▶ process of moving through an electronic **network** and **databases** to find the required information.

Navigator
▶ person who searches an electronic **network** and **databases** to find the required information.

NBM – Non-Book Material
▶ items that are produced in a form other than print.

NCR paper
▶ treated paper which does not require carbon in order to make copies.

Near letter-quality – NLQ
▶ printing by a **dot matrix printer** that provides a higher quality type that is almost as good as a typewriter.

Need to know
▶ security principle which restricts **access** to **classified material** and other information to those who need it in connection with their work.

Needs assessment
▶ determining the needs of a specific group of users.

Negative acknowledgement
▶ **signal** sent by a **receiver** which indicates that **data** have been received incorrectly.

Negative information
► searching for information with the expectation of not finding relevant items in the particular system being searched.

Negative film
► photographic film which produces a clear negative **image** when it is exposed or processed.

Negative selection
► discarding from stock material that is considered to be of no further use. Also called **deselection** or **weeding**.

Negative stock
► photographic film which produces a clear negative **image** when it is exposed or processed.

Nest
► **subroutine** embedded within a **program**; a block of **data** embedded within a larger body of **data**.

Nested logic
► **search statement** where specific parts of the statement are contained inside a broader **search** concept, usually surrounded by **parentheses**.

Nested loop
► **loop** inside another **loop** in a **computer program**.

Nesting
► embedding one **object** in another **object** of the same type.

Net Book Agreement
► agreement in the UK which stated that books could not be sold at less than the price set by the publisher. Public libraries could apply for a licence which allowed them a 10% discount off the price of new books. The Net Book Agreement became redundant in 1995 due to a change in UK legislation.

Netiquette
► behavioural **guidelines** evolved by **Internet** users to make **communication** more friendly and avoid giving offence to users.

Network
► group of physically dispersed **computers** linked to each other by **communication** lines to share **information resources**.

Network access point – NAP
► places in a **network** where individual **backbone providers** can exchange **traffic**.

Network architecture
► **specification** of how a **network** is organized with details of **hardware** and **software** components.

Network computer – NC
► **computer** which is more **Internet**-friendly. **Vendors** could incorporate **Internet** service provision into established **library management systems**.

Network control program
► **software** which monitors and controls **communication** between **host computers** and users in a **network** connection.

Network controller
► **computer** that controls or manages a **network** by receiving and transmitting **data**, sending **files** to the **file** and **print server** and acting as a **memory** store.

Network layer
► in **open systems interconnection (OSI) layer** 3 is responsible for routing **data** across the **network**.

Network literacy
► ability to identify, **access** and use electronic information from a **network**.

Network operating system
▶ **software** that manages shared resources in a **network**.

Network protocol
▶ **handshaking signals** which define how a **work station** sends **data** over a **network** without clashing with other **data transmissions**.

Network server
▶ **computer** system attached to a **communication network** that performs a particular service for other **computers** attached to the same system.

Network topology
▶ physical and logical relationship between the elements or **nodes** of a **network**.

Network user address – NUA
▶ identification given to a **network** subscriber to identify their **address** or place where bills should be sent.

Network user identification – NUI
▶ identification given to a subscriber to a **network** service to identify an authorized user. It may act as a **password** to a system.

Networking
▶ techniques and principles that maintain the **network** system and allow users in different locations to communicate with each other.

Neural network
▶ advanced **computer** processor used for the development of **artificial intelligence** systems, based on the design of the human brain.

Neurolinguistic programming – NLP
▶ set of principles and skills for studying personal excellence in terms of behavioural flexibility, sensory acuity and orientation.

Newbie
▶ slang name for a new user of an **online** service, usually the **Internet**.

Newsgroup
▶ collection of **articles** on a particular subject available via the **Internet**; public **forums** or discussion areas on a **computer network**.

Newsletter
▶ brief publication containing news about a specific organization or activity, usually sent to a limited audience.

Newspaper
▶ **serial** publication issued at stated frequent intervals containing news, opinions, advertisements and other topical material.

Newspaper clipping
▶ item cut or clipped from a **newspaper** or **periodical**. Also called a **cutting** or **press cutting**.

Nexus
▶ point in a system where there are interconnections.

NGO – Non-Governmental Organization
▶ international professional organization whose representatives are not directly appointed by national governments.

Nibble
▶ unit of measurement where one nibble is four **bits** or half a **byte**.

Niche publishing
▶ publishing material in a specialized subject area which is of interest to a limited audience.

NII – National Information Infrastructure
▶ American proposal for a high-speed **interactive digital**

communication system intended to connect multiple technologies with millions of users.

NLP – NeuroLinguistic Programming
▶ set of principles and skills for studying personal excellence in terms of behavioural flexibility, sensory acuity and orientation.

NLQ – Near Letter-Quality
▶ printing by a **dot matrix printer** that provides a higher quality type that is almost as good as a typewriter.

Node
▶ **access** point in a **network**.

Noise
▶ **1.** computing – in **telecommunications** unwanted, usually random, electronic **signals; 2.** information handling – in searching **information systems**, refers to retrieved **documents** which do not deal with the required subject.

Nomenclature
▶ structured system of names for a set of **classes** or things.

Non-book material – NBM
▶ items that are produced in a form other than print.

Non-erasable
▶ **file** or **storage** device that can only be read; **data** can be accessed by the user but cannot be altered.

Non-hierarchical relationship
▶ **term** relationship that is not based on **hierarchy**, e.g. **related term**.

Non-impact printer
▶ **printer** that does not require a type **character** to leave its imprint on the paper by striking an ink ribbon.

Non-print media
▶ material in a library that is not considered to be a book, **journal** or **pamphlet**. It usually requires special treatment, **storage** etc.

Non-volatile memory
▶ **computer memory** which preserves **data** during a power shutdown or loss of power to the **computer**.

Noncompatability
▶ inability of **software** and **hardware** to exchange **data**.

Normal distribution
▶ **frequency** distribution in which the quantities are so distributed that its graphical representation is a continuous symmetrical **bell-shaped curve**. Also called **Gaussian distribution**.

Normalization
▶ in **relational databases**, the process of organizing **data** to reduce duplication.

NOT
▶ **logical operator** or **instruction** in a **computer program** or statement. Often described as a **Boolean algebra** operator.

NOT function
▶ **logical operator** whose **input** is always the inverse of **output**. In **Boolean** terms, not true = false.

Notation
▶ **symbols** which are used to represent the divisions in a **classification scheme**. They may be numerical, alphabetical or a combination of these and are used to indicate subject content and the **filing order** of the scheme.

Note
▶ amplification of the **standard** description of a **document** added by

the cataloguer to identify further or to characterize the item, e.g. to elucidate an obscure title, to show the level of the work or its relationship to other works, to describe the peculiarities in the copy being catalogued etc.

Notebook computer
▶ **laptop computer** developed in the early 1990s which usually has a **screen** and **hard disk drive** and is no larger than a standard notebook.

Notepad
▶ area of **computer memory** used when moving **data** or **graphics** from one **file** or place to another.

Nothing before something
▶ filing method for alphabetical **headings** in which the word is regarded as the filing unit and the space between the words as zero (0). Also called **word by word**.

Notice board
▶ **1.** computing – type of **bulletin board** in an **electronic mail** system on which messages to all users can be left; **2.** management – board that is fixed to a wall to which notices can be pinned.

Novice searcher
▶ person using an **information system** with little or no experience of that system.

NREN – National Research and Education Network
▶ high-speed **network** developed in the USA built on the existing **Internet** structure. It supports research and scholarly activities, together with education and research administration.

NSFnet – National Standard Foundation network
▶ national backbone research **network** in the USA forming part of the **Internet** and interconnecting regional **networks**.

NT – Narrower Term
▶ in a **thesaurus** the formal **hierarchical relationship** between a **genus** and its **species** are indicated by the **narrower term (NT)** and **broader term (BT)** designators.

NTSC – National Television information ServiCe
▶ **standard** for colour television broadcasting in the USA which has 525 horizontal lines per **frame** and 30 **frames per second**.

NUA – Network User Address
▶ identification given to a **network** subscriber to identify their address or place where bills should be sent.

NUI – Network User Identification
▶ identification given to a subscriber to a **network** service to identify an authorized user. It may act as a **password** to a system.

Number building
▶ in **classification**, the process of making a number more specific by adding additional numbers or **notation** taken from other parts of the **classification scheme**.

Number cruncher
▶ powerful **computer** which is programmed to carry out a great many calculations very quickly.

Number crunching
▶ processing large quantities of numerical **data,** usually by large **mainframe computers**.

Numeric data
▶ **data** which consist of numbers.

Numeric database
▶ **database** which provides numeric or statistical information. Sometimes called a **databank**.

Numeric keypad
▶ set of 10 **keys** with numbers plus a decimal point which usually forms a separate group of **keys** on **computer keyboard**.

NVRAM – Non-Volatile Random Access Memory
▶ **integrated circuit memory** whose content can be both read and overwritten as required.

Oo

Object
▶ item of **data** that can be manipulated in a **computer program**; in **artificial intelligence**, a set of **attributes**.

Object Linking and Embedding – OLE
▶ set of **protocols** used to create dynamic automatically up-dating **links** between **documents** and to embed a **document** created in one **application** into a **document** created in another.

Object modelling technique – OMT
▶ technique which expands upon existing **knowledge** of **systems analysis** and design. An **information system** is analysed from a number of different viewpoints to determine three **models**: **object model**, dynamic **model** and functional **model**.

Object orientation
▶ processing method which looks at problems in terms of **objects** that have a recognizable identity.

Object-oriented architecture
▶ **software** structure in which all **files**, **inputs** and **outputs** are thought of as **objects**.

Object-oriented database
▶ **database management** facilities that are offered in an **object-oriented programming** environment. **Data** is stored as **objects** and relationships are defined between **objects**.

Object-oriented graphics
▶ representation of **graphic objects** such as lines, arcs, circles and rectangles by mathematical formulae.

Object-Oriented Programming – OOP
▶ **programming** where not only the type of **data** is defined but also the type of operations or **functions** that can be applied to the **data** structure. The structure thus becomes an **object** that includes **data** and **functions**.

Object program
▶ **program** in **machine language** which has been translated from a **source program** in a **high-level** or **assembly language**.

Objective
▶ specific aim or target that a library or **information service** wishes to achieve.

Oblique type
▶ any form of slanting type; **italic type** usually implies a slope to the right and oblique a slope to the left.

Obsolescence
▶ process of becoming out of date and, by implication, no longer useful. Decreasing use of a **document** or group of **documents** as they become older.

OCR – Optical Character Recognition
▶ identification of printed or written **characters** by a **computer** through

the comparison of the **image** of a text with previously scanned material that has already been recognized and stored by the **computer**. Sometimes called **optical scanning**.

Octal
▶ **notation** which uses the base 8, i.e. numbers 1 to 7.

Octal code
▶ **code** which operates using base 8.

Octave device
▶ term used by Ranganathan for the method of extending the decimal base of arabic numbers by using the figure 9 as an extender, so that it has no numerical value but allows the next eight **digits** to be used equally with the previous ones.

ODA – Office Document Architecture
▶ set of **standards** for exchanging **documents** in electronic form between different **computer** systems.

Off-campus education
▶ educational process where students learn from local centres or from their homes using material supplied to them in printed or electronic form and/or via television, radio etc. Also called **distance learning** or **open learning**.

Off-site access
▶ use of a **computer** from a **terminal** at a geographically distant point. Also called **remote access**.

Off-the-shelf
▶ **hardware** or **software** which can be bought and used in a system. Different from that which is designed and installed to order.

Office Document Architecture – ODA
▶ set of **standards** for exchanging **documents** in electronic form between different **computer** systems.

Offline
▶ **communication** with a **computer** when the user is not directly linked to the **central processor** of that **computer**.

Offline reader
▶ **software** which allows **E-mail** messages to be read and written **offline**.

Offprint
▶ copy of an **article** published in a **periodical** reprinted as a separate item for the author's use. Also called a **separate**.

Offset litho
▶ method of printing from a flat surface of stone or metal, where the **image** areas of the plate are coated with water-repellent ink and the non-**image** areas are protected by a film of water. Modern presses use a rubber-covered cylinder to transfer plate **images** to paper. Also called **lithography.**

Ohm's law
▶ basic law describing the behaviour of electricity.

OLE – Object Linking and Embedding
▶ set of **protocols** used to create dynamic automatically up-dating **links** between **documents** and to embed a **document** created in one **application** into a **document** created in another.

Omission mark
▶ use of three dots (...) in quoted text to indicate that words have been omitted from the original document.

OMT – Object Modelling Technique
▶ technique which expands upon existing **knowledge** of **systems analysis** and design. An **information system** is analysed from a number of different viewpoints to determine three **models: object model**; dynamic **model**; and functional **model**.

On-demand publishing
▶ concept of printing items one at a time from a **computer** store as they are required.

One-man band/one-person library
▶ library or information unit staffed by a single individual.

One-stop shop
▶ **information centre** that aims to provide all information requirements in one place.

One-time pad
▶ coding system that uses a unique **cipher key** each time it is used.

Online
▶ direct **real-time communication** with the **central processor** of a **computer** via a **terminal** or separate **computer**.

Online catalogue
▶ up-to-date and complete list of a library's **holdings** accessible via a **computer terminal**.

Online computing
▶ **computer** system that provides an immediate and up-to-date response to **input** or interrogation from a **remote terminal**.

Online database
▶ **database** that can be accessed via an **online information retrieval system**.

Online documentation
▶ information that is displayed on a **computer monitor screen** as **data** is

processed; information available on a **help screen**.

Online help
▶ help system that can be consulted while using a **computer program** with help text appearing in a separate **window**.

Online host
▶ organization that makes a number of **databases** available for use. Sometimes called an **online supplier, spinner** or **online vendor**.

Online information retrieval
▶ **computer** system that allows the user of an **online terminal** to **access**, search and **display data**.

Online information retrieval system
▶ system in which the searcher has immediate **access** to a **database** via a **terminal** or **visual display unit** (**VDU**) connected through a **telecommunications system**. The **database** can be interrogated directly by the searcher, who develops the **search strategy** interactively and receives immediate **real-time** responses.

Online information service
▶ provides **access** to **databases** stored on remote **computer** systems, available nationally or internationally via a **telecommunications** connection or via an electronic **network**.

Online print
▶ **output** printed as the result of an **online search**.

Online Public Access Catalogue – OPAC
▶ **catalogue** where information is stored on a **database** loaded in a **computer** which can be used directly by a user via a **remote terminal**.

Online registration
▶ facility that allows the purchase and installation of **software** to be registered with the manufacturer.

Online search aid
▶ tool such as a **manual, thesaurus** or **subject heading** list which can be used to facilitate **online searching**.

Online searching
▶ using a **computer**-based **information retrieval system** that has direct online **access** to the **database(s)** available on a **computer** or a **computer network**.

Online supplier
▶ organization that makes a number of **databases** available for use. Sometimes called an **online host, spinner** or **vendor**.

Online system
▶ **computer** system in which all **functions** are performed under the control of the **central processing unit**.

Online vendor
▶ organization that makes a number of **databases** available for use. Sometimes called an **online host, spinner** or **online supplier**.

OOP – Object-Oriented Programming
▶ **programming** where not only the type of **data** is defined but also the type of operations or **functions** that can be applied to the **data** structure. The structure thus becomes an **object** that included **data** and **functions**.

op. cit.
▶ abbreviation for the Latin *opere citato*, which means that a particular work has already been cited.

OPAC – Online Public Access Catalogue
▶ **catalogue** where information is stored on a **database** loaded in a **computer** which can be used via a **remote terminal** directly by a user.

Opaque
▶ material that will not allow light to pass through it.

Open access
▶ library or **information centre** where users can obtain material directly from the shelves.

Open architecture
▶ design of a **computer** system which is published so that other manufacturers can develop compatible accessories and **add-on cards**.

Open entry
▶ **catalogue entry** with an incomplete description because the work is in progress, the library is waiting to complete the set or because the work is a **serial**.

Open learning
▶ educational process where students learn from local centres or their own homes, using material supplied to them in printed or electronic form via television, radio etc. Sometimes called **distance learning** or **off-campus education**.

Open networking
▶ interconnection of cooperating **computer** systems that follows **open systems interconnection (OSI) standards**.

Open system
▶ system which allows a variety of different **computers** and **terminals** to work together freely; system with publicly available **access**.

Open system interworking
▶ establishment of **links** between discrete **computer** systems and **networks** to create a freely interacting **open system**.

Open systems interconnection – OSI
▶ general name for **International Standards Organization** (**ISO**) and **Consultative Committee for International Telephone and Telegraph** (**CCITT**) efforts to facilitate the exchange of information between all types of **computers**. It is a seven-**layer model** for **communications**.

Operand/operator
▶ in a **computer language**, expressions can be expressed as two types of components: operands and operators. Operands are the **objects** to be manipulated and operators are **symbols** that represent specific actions.

Operating manual
▶ book of **instructions** for use in a particular **application**. These are being replaced by help **files** and **context-sensitive help**.

Operating system
▶ permanent **software** within a **computer** which allows it to control the sequencing and processing of **programs** and respond correctly to user requests.

Operations research
▶ scientific methods and techniques for solving operational problems that are used to determine policy and make procedural changes.

Optical character reader
▶ device that scans printed or handwritten **characters** or **graphics** to generate **digital** representations for **computer** processing.

Optical character recognition – OCR
▶ identification of printed or written **characters** by a **computer** through the comparison of the **image** of a text with previously scanned material that has already been recognized and stored in the **computer**. Sometimes called **optical scanning**.

Optical coincidence card
▶ **term entry card** on which **document** numbers are punched as holes in set positions; holes common to more than one **card** are revealed by holding the selected **cards** against a light source.

Optical coincidence system
▶ **retrieval** system in which a hole is punched or notched on **cards** to identify a subject area or **document** number. **Cards** are compared during **retrieval** and notched holes are identified to find relevant information.

Optical computer
▶ **computer** that uses **laser**-generated light with optical crystals instead of microcircuits.

Optical disc
▶ **disc** made of plastic with a reflective metal coating that is read using a **laser** beam. Types used in publishing are **CD-ROM, laser discs** and **video discs**. Sometimes called **magneto-optical disc**.

Optical fibre
▶ thin flexible fibre of pure glass which can carry as much as a thousand times the amount of information possible with traditional copper wire.

Optical scanning
▶ identification of printed or written **characters** by a **computer** through

the comparison of the **image** of a text with previously scanned material that has already been recognized and stored by the **computer.** Usually called **optical character recognition (OCR).**

Optical scanning device
▶ device that scans printed or handwritten **characters** or **graphics** into **digital** form so that they can be processed by **computer.**

Optical storage
▶ may be **read only, write once** or **erasable storage**, which may be either **digital** or **analogue**.

Optical tape
▶ high-**capacity storage medium** that uses **laser** technology and is used to record **digital data.**

Option button
▶ in **Windows**, facility in a **dialog box** which allows one-at-a-time selection of mutually exclusive items.

Optimization
▶ making something work as efficiently as possible.

Optoelectronic computer
▶ system that uses both optical and electronic technologies.

Optoelectronics
▶ electronic components that can generate or detect light.

OR
▶ logical action that compares two quantities to find if either one or both is true. In computer searching, it can be used to connect two conditions.

ORACLE – Optical Reception of Announcements of Coded Line Electronics
▶ **teletext** system of the British Independent Television Authority.

Oral communication
▶ word of mouth, spoken **communication**.

Oral history
▶ recording (usually on tape) of previously unavailable material where individuals speak about first-hand experiences of specific events in their lives.

Organization chart
▶ diagram showing the formal structure of an institution detailing lines of command, staff structures etc.

Organization manual
▶ collection of information relating to a particular institution, covering goals and **objectives**, administration policies, rules and procedures etc.

Organization of information
▶ all processes of listing, arranging, **indexing** and disseminating information with a view to making it accessible to those who seek it.

Organization theory
▶ what is known regarding the behaviour of an individual as a member of an organization as well as patterns of relationships that exist between members of an organization.

Organizational culture
▶ shared beliefs, attitudes, expectations and unquestioned assumptions of the members of an organization. Also called **corporate culture**.

Organizational environment
▶ surroundings, conditions and circumstances that affect an individual's professional life.

Orphan
▶ first line of a new paragraph, **heading** or **subheading** which

appears at the bottom of a page of text.

OSI – Open Systems Interconnection

▶ general name for **International Standards Organization (ISO)** and **Consultative Committee for International Telephone and Telegraph (CCITT)** efforts to facilitate exchange of information between all types of **computers**. It is a seven-**layer model** for **communications**.

Out dent

▶ text **format** in which all lines except the first one in a paragraph are indented. Also called **hanging indent**.

Outage

▶ interval of time when a **computer** system cannot be used because it is being serviced or maintained.

Output

▶ transfer of **data** held in a **computer** system to an external device such as a **printer** or a **visual display unit (VDU)**.

Output device

▶ any piece of equipment capable of receiving information held in the **central processor** of a **computer**.

Output measure

▶ count or combination of counts that enables a library or **information service** to assess the degree to which it is meeting service **objectives.** Sometimes called **performance measure**.

Outreach service

▶ service aimed at a potential **user group** that cannot visit a library or **information service** in person.

Outside margin

▶ **margin** of a printed page that is furthest away from the binding.

Outsourcing

▶ using the services of an external organization to provide a system or service that could be provided internally. Using outside assistance in order to get a specific task or job done. Could mean the use of individuals or organizations such as **bureaux**.

Overhead cost

▶ expenditure which is not directly charged to a particular product or service. Also called **indirect cost**.

Overlaid window

▶ **window screen** which partly or completely covers another.

Overlap

▶ material that is **indexed** by more than one **abstracting** and/or **indexing service**.

Overload

▶ condition that can cause a **computer program** to **crash**, usually brought about by attempting to transfer more **data** than the **memory** can hold or by transferring **data** faster than the **central processing unit** can handle.

Overstrike

▶ in a **dot matrix printer**, printing a **character** twice to make it bolder so that it stands out.

Overwrite

▶ to write **data** to a location on a **tape, disk** or **memory** and in doing so destroying **data** already contained at that location.

Pp

P-E approach
► **management** technique that views service quality as the gap between expectation (E) and performance (P).

PABX – Private Automatic Branch eXchange
► telephone system exchange owned by the user that connects lines internally between extensions without incurring charges, and routes calls to and from the public telephone system.

Packed file
► **file** that has been reduced to the smallest possible size. Sometimes called a **compressed file**.

Packet
► set of **bits** which can be sent over a **network** as a self-contained message. **Data** are assembled in a special condensed **format** for high-speed **transmission**.

Packet assembler/disassembler – PAD
► electronic device which converts **data** into **packets** for **transmission** via a **packet-switched system**.

Packet driver
► **computer software** for **local area networks** that divides **data** into **packets** for **transmission** for **networks** and reassembles **packets** of incoming **data** so that they can be read.

Packet radio
► **communication** between **computers** using amateur radios. They can be connected to the **Internet** and used to send **E-mail**.

Packet-switched system – PSS
► system that transmits **data** in **packets** using **packet-switching** procedures.

Packet switching
► sending **data** in **packets** through a **computer network**. **Data** are broken into **packets** at the **transmission** point and sent at high speed via a **communication network**. The **packets** are re-assembled at the delivery point.

PAD – Packet Assembler/Disassembler
► electronic device which converts **data** into **packets** for **transmission** via a **packet-switched system**.

Paddle
► control device used in **video** games and **microcomputers** to move a **cursor** or **graphic images** on a **screen**.

Page break
► place where one text page ends and another one begins.

Page charge
► charge levied by publishers, usually in scientific or technological subject areas, where authors are

charged for each page of a published **article**.

Page Description Language – PDL
▶ in **desktop publishing**, a **computer language** which allows the description and formatting of combined text and **graphics**.

Page layout/makeup
▶ determination of the dimensions of a printed page in terms of **margin** size, position of page numbers, **headers**, **footers** etc.; setting type for reproduction; overall page layout of type and **graphics** on a page. Sometimes called **composition**.

Page printer
▶ any **printer** that can process a complete page at a time.

Pages per minute – PPM
▶ speed at which **printers** can print pages. Measurement usually used for **laser** and **ink jet printers**.

Pagination
▶ part of a **catalogue** entry or **bibliographic citation** which gives the number of pages in an item.

PAL – Phase Alternate Line
▶ European **standard** for colour **television broadcasting** adopted by the UK and Germany which is also used in Australia and South Africa. It has 625 horizontal picture lines per **frame** and 25 **frames per second**.

Palaeography
▶ study and description of ancient and mediaeval **manuscripts**, **documents** and systems of writing.

Palmtop computer
▶ small **computer** that fits in the palm of the hand or in a pocket. Compared with full-size **computers**, they are limited but are useful for such things as telephone books and diaries.

Pamphlet
▶ small book with paper covers, usually between five and 50 pages. Also called a **booklet** or **brochure**.

Paper-based information system
▶ information system that is based primarily on material produced and stored on paper.

Paperless office
▶ workplace where all material is in electronic **format** and there is no information recorded, distributed or stored on paper. Sometimes thought of as the ideal type of office environment where the **computer**, rather than the typewriter or pen and ink, is the main tool for the production of **documents** and material is generated and stored in electronic rather than paper format. Also called the **electronic office**.

Paperless publishing
▶ electronic storage and distribution of information.

Paradigm
▶ scientific achievement which may pertain to theory, **cognition** or methodology. Example or pattern; words which have the same root, e.g. catalog, **catalogue**, catalogues, cataloging, **cataloguing** and recataloging.

Parallel communication
▶ **data transfer** in which each **bit** is transferred along its own line and **bits** are transferred at the same time.

Parallel edition
▶ publication where different texts of the same **document** are usually printed side by side.

Parallel interface
▶ **interface** that permits **bits** to be transmitted in parallel.

Parallel port
▶ socket in the back of a **personal computer** which is used to connect **peripherals**, usually a **printer**. Often called a **printer port**.

Parallel processing
▶ **computer processing** where more than one task is carried out at the same time, rather than sequentially as in most **computers**.

Parallel transmission
▶ simultaneous **transmission** of information by distinct **channels** or by different carrier **frequencies** over the same channel.

Parameter
▶ arbitrary **constant** that determines the specific form of a mathematical expression. **Variable** which is assigned a specific value so that a **program routine** can be carried out.

Paraprofessional
▶ staff member who does not have professional qualifications but has significant responsibility under the supervision of professional staff. Sometimes called **subprofessional**.

Parentheses
▶ **characters** that enclose text, usually round **brackets** ( ).

Parity
▶ condition where the number of items is always odd or even.

Parity bit
▶ **binary digit** added to a set of **bits** so that the sum of all the **bits** is either always odd or always even.

Parity check
▶ method of testing that uses the number of ones and zeros to establish if **errors** have been made.

Park
▶ locking the **read/write head** of a **hard disk drive** over to a point on the **disk** where there are no **data** stored.

Parliamentary paper
▶ used in the UK to describe a paper published by Parliament.

Parsing
▶ **1.** computing – breaking a **high-level language computer code** into its elemental parts when translating into machine **code**; **2.** information handling – breaking a sentence or **search statement** down into its constituent parts; technique used in the **PRECIS indexing** system.

Part whole relationship
▶ **hierarchical relationship** based on genus/species.

Partial match retrieval
▶ one type of **fuzzy logic searching**.

Participative management
▶ **management** style which encourages employees to be involved in **decision-making** processes regarding job responsibilities and other activities.

Participative problem solving
▶ practice in which employees participate in solving problems that have traditionally only been considered by senior **management**.

Partition
▶ method of splitting large **hard disks** into manageable chunks with each division behaving as if it were a separate **hard disk**.

PASCAL – Program Appliqué a la Selection et la Compilation
▶ **high-level programming language** that has had a great influence on the design of other languages and has

long been popular as a teaching language.

Password
▶ word, **code** or set of **characters** used to identify a user and permit **access** to a **computer** system.

Patch
▶ small **computer program** which fixes a problem within a larger **program**.

Patent
▶ **document** specifying the design or manufacture of an item which gives protection to the manufacturing agent for a set number of years.

Path
▶ **directories** or sub-**directories** used by **DOS** to search for a **command** or a **file** name.

Pathname
▶ sequence of symbols and names that identify a **file**.

Patron
▶ name for a user or client of an information service, **computer** system, library etc.

Pattern matching/recognition
▶ **term** which can be used to cover recognition of any sort of stimulus or **input;** normally used for the **computer** recognition of patterns (implying a reference to something already known) for the purpose of **classification**, grouping or identification.

Pause key
▶ **key** on the **computer keyboard** that can halt temporarily the **display** of **data**.

PAX – Private Automatic eXchange
▶ exchange for a private telephone service within an organization which is not connected to the public telephone **network**.

Pay per view television
▶ **cable television** where the viewer pays for **channels** or **programs** watched; type of television which is broadcast scrambled and can only be viewed using a **decoder**.

PBS – Personal Bibliographic Software
▶ **software** that allows an individual user to re**format references** from a number of different sources into a single bibliographic style.

PBX – Private Branch EXchange
▶ telephone system that connects lines internally between extensions within an institution. Limited **access** to a number of outside telephone lines is also available, generally by dialling 9 followed by the number required.

PC – Personal Computer
▶ small **computer**, usually a **microcomputer,** designed for business or home use.

PC-DOS
▶ **operating system** designed for **IBM personal computers** which is very similar to **MS-DOS**.

PCI card – Peripheral Component Interconnect card
▶ place where **modems** and **sound cards** can be fitted into a **personal computer**. It enables fast exchange of large amounts of **data**.

PCN – Personal Computer Network
▶ **digital** radio **network** that allows users to make and receive calls using a pocket-sized telephone.

PDA – Personal Digital Assistant
▶ **computer** facility that allows a **personal computer** to accept handwriting and drawings, and has **communication** and **artificial**

intelligence capability together with voice recognition. Generic term for any small, electronic personal organizer.

PDMS – Product Document Management System
▶ system that controls product information which might include design details, engineering drawings, product specifications, numerical control, machine tool programs, analysis results, correspondence, invoices etc.

Peek-a-boo system
▶ indexing system developed by W.E. Batten that coordinates single attributes by using holes punched on cards which have to compared to match relevant items. Sometimes called Batten system.

Peer group
▶ group of individuals who are equally knowledgeable in a specific subject area.

Peer review
▶ process by which manuscripts submitted for publication are evaluated by a group of individuals who are experts in the subject area.

Peer-to-peer file transfer/network
▶ in local area networks (LANs), a file-sharing technique in which users have access to the public files on all other workstations.

Pen computer
▶ computer that uses an electronic pen or stylus rather than a keyboard for input.

Performance appraisal/evaluation
▶ assessing the behaviour of employees for the purpose of career development, salary increases and promotion. Also called employee evaluation.

Performance indicator
▶ technique for assessing performance that uses a ratio or some kind of quantification, such as number of items issued per registered user, rather than a simple count of the number of issues.

Performance measure
▶ count or combination of counts that enables a library or information service to assess the degree to which it is meeting service objectives. Sometimes called output measure.

Performance measurement
▶ quantified statement used to evaluate and compare the performance of a library or information service in achieving its objectives.

Period
▶ dot character (.) placed at the end of a sentence in text; separator used in a file name; part of an Internet address. Also called dot or full stop.

Periodical
▶ most common type of serial, published at regular or irregular intervals and carrying primary material.

Peripheral
▶ auxiliary equipment that is attached to a computer, such as a printer, modem, scanner etc., which performs input, output or backing up storage operations.

Peripheral Component Interconnect card – PCI card
▶ place where modems and sound cards can be fitted into a personal computer. It enables fast exchange of large amounts of data.

Peripheral journal
▶ periodical which has only a small number of articles in a particular

subject area; relatively unimportant journal for a particular subject area. Sometimes called a **fringe journal**.

Permanence
▶ resistance of paper to ageing.

Permanent paper
▶ paper which is acid free and manufactured under stringent **specifications** for archival purposes; usually has a pH value of 7 or more.

Permutation indexing
▶ method of generating **index entries** under different **entry** words by using the **computer** to rearrange the subject **terms** assigned to a given item.

Permuted index
▶ **index** generated, usually automatically, from **terms** in the title of an item where each **significant word** is successively positioned as the **entry point** in association with the next **significant word**.

Permuterm index
▶ **indexing** procedure that allows word coordination in pairs of all significant words in the title of a **document**.

Persistent URL – PURL
▶ type of **URL** which acts as an **intermediary** for the real **URL** of a **web** resource.

Personal author
▶ individual responsible for the intellectual content of a work.

Personal bibliographic software – PBS
▶ **software** that allows an individual user to re**format references** from a number of different sources into a single bibliographic style.

Personal computer – PC
▶ small **computer**, usually a **microcomputer**, designed for business or home use.

Personal computer network – PCN
▶ **digital** radio **network** that allows users to make and receive calls using a pocket-sized telephone.

Personal data
▶ information about an individual which may be held on a **computer database** and is subject to restrictions under **data protection legislation**.

Personal Digital Assistant – PDA
▶ **computer** facility which allows a **personal computer** to accept handwriting and drawings, and has **communication** and **artificial intelligence** capability together with **voice recognition**. Generic term for any small, electronic personal organizer.

Personal file
▶ **database** containing information about an individual which is subject to restrictions under **data protection legislation**.

Personal Identification Device – PID
▶ device such as a **card** that can be inserted or connected into a system to provide authorization for a user to use the system.

Personal Information Manager – PIM
▶ **database** of information that is often scattered, such as names and addresses, telephone numbers, notes and memos, appointments and lists of things to do.

Personal networking
▶ acquiring personal and professional contacts often in a social setting to gain professional information or advantage.

PERT – Programme Evaluation and Review Technique
▶ systematic method of planning and implementing a complex

operation which requires accurate scheduling, resource location and programme monitoring, and which is presented in graphic form as a **PERT** diagram.

Pertinence
▶ measure of the closeness of a retrieved piece of information to the answer of an inquiry. The state or quality implying close logical relationship with, and importance to, the matter under consideration. Also called **relevance**.

PEST
▶ analysis of political, economic, social and technological factors that will affect a particular organization or activity in the future.

Phase Alternate Line – PAL
▶ European **standard** for colour **television broadcasting** adopted by the UK and Germany which is also used in Australia and South Africa. It has 625 horizontal picture lines per frame and 25 frames per second.

Phenome
▶ sound unit of language.

Phonetics
▶ identification, description and **classification** of vocal sounds used in speech.

Phosphor dot
▶ element of a **cathode ray tube** which glows to form an **image**.

Photo-CD
▶ system developed by Kodak which transfers ordinary photographs on to a **disk** for permanent **storage** and viewing on a **screen**.

Photocell
▶ device that is light sensitive.

Photocharging
▶ loan transaction system which photographs details of items borrowed and the identification of the borrower.

Photocomposition
▶ typesetting performed by a photosetter.

Phreaking
▶ using a **computer** or other device to trick a telephone system; usually used to make free calls or have calls charged to a different account.

Physical layer
▶ in **open systems interconnection** (**OSI**), **layer 1** which is responsible for actually sending **data** on the **transmission** medium.

Pica
▶ unit of typographic measurement which is made up of 12 points and measures 4 mm.

Pico
▶ word prefix denoting one millionth of a millionth.

Picture management
▶ arranging pictures to be retrieved from a **database** and presented or printed to resemble the original as closely as possible.

Picture telephone
▶ telephone which displays a picture of the person making the call. Also called **video telephone**.

PID – Personal Identification Device
▶ device such as a **card** that can be inserted or connected into a system to provide authorization for a user to use the system.

Pie chart
▶ graphic diagram representing a pie, with portions varying in size to show values or percentages.

PIF – Program for Information File
▶ in the **Windows** system, a special **file** containing settings that tell **Windows** how to run a non-**Windows application**.

Piggyback
▶ fitting one thing on top of another; learning based on previous experience to build a better system.

PII – Publisher Item Identifier
▶ internal numbering system developed by scientific, technical and medical (STM) publishers and used mainly for prepublication control.

PIM – Personal Information Management
▶ **computer software application** designed to help users organize random bits of information. Most **PIMs** include calendar, scheduling and calculation programs.

PIN – Personal Identification Number
▶ number (usually four **digits**) given to users by banks and building societies for use with cash dispensers or **automatic teller machines**.

Piracy
▶ unauthorized commercial recording or copying of material covered by **copyright**.

Pirate software
▶ **software** that has been copied illegally.

Pitch
▶ measurement used in printing which relates to the spacing of **characters**.

Pixel
▶ smallest point in an **image**. **Image resolution** is measured in pixels. A one-**bit** pixel can be only black or white; to represent eight shades of grey from black to white requires three **bits**, while full colour requires many more.

PKI – Public-Key Infrastructure
▶ system of **digital certificates** that is used to verify and authenticate the validity of parties involved in transactions on the **Internet**.

PL/1 – Programming Language/1
▶ **high-level programming language** developed from **FORTRAN** and **COBOL** with a wide range of scientific and business **applications**.

Plagiarism
▶ copying or reproducing someone else's work and claiming it is original work.

Plain text
▶ textual **data** produced in **ASCII format**.

Plasma display
▶ type of **flat-panel display** that sandwiches an ionized gas between two wired panels. It requires more power than **LCD displays** and is not used very often.

Platform
▶ underlying **hardware** or **software** in a **computer** system.

Platter
▶ round magnetic plate that constitutes part of a **hard disk** which is typically made up of a dozen platters.

Plotter
▶ **output device** for reproducing designs on a **computer**.

PMBX – Private Manual Branch eXchange
▶ manually operated **switching** facility or exchange within an organization which provides **access** to the public telephone **network**.

PMEST (personality, matter, energy, space and time)
▶ basic **facets** identified by S.R. Ranganathan, who developed the **Colon Classification** scheme in 1933.

Point
▶ in **Windows,** to slide the **mouse** until the tip of the **pointer** rests on the item chosen.

Point size
▶ measurement of **character** size within specific **fonts**.

Point-and-click
▶ to point at something on the **screen** and **click** the **mouse** button.

Point-of-sale terminal – POS terminal
▶ computer **terminal** used in shops to **input** and **output data** when a sale is transacted.

Pointer
▶ small **symbol** on a **display screen** that moves in response to a **mouse** or a **tracker ball**.

Pointing device
▶ device which allows the user to control the movement of items on a **computer screen**. Pointing devices may be **mice, joysticks, tracker balls, touchpads** and **light pens**.

Poke
▶ high-level **language** term meaning to insert information in a specific memory location.

Polyglot edition
▶ publication giving versions of the same text in several languages, usually printed side by side.

Polyphony
▶ ability to play one or more voice or instrument at the same time.

Polyvinyl chloride – PVC
▶ plastic used in coating or impregnation when **bookbinding** or covering books for waterproofing or **durability**.

Pop-up menu
▶ **menu** that may be made to appear at a user's discretion on top of what was on the **screen** before. After the **menu** has been used, it usually disappears. Similar to a **pull-down menu**.

Pop-up window
▶ **window** which appears (pops up) when a **function key** is pressed or an option is selected.

Pornography
▶ material that is obscene or licentious.

Port
▶ exit or **entry** point from a **central processor**; socket located at the base of the **computer** where additional items can be plugged in.

Portability
▶ ability to move **data** or, more usually, **programs** from one system to another. Complete **portability** requires close adherence to defined **standards**.

Portable computer
▶ **microcomputer** that can be moved around easily between different locations.

Portal

▶ **gateway** to the **web,** which is often subject-specific, that includes a **search engine**, other **links** to relevant sites, a news service, **E-mail** and **chat** groups, as well as a list of **search hits**.

Portrait

▶ printing an **image** on a page in vertical mode used for letters, memos and other text **documents**.

POS terminal – Point Of Sale terminal

▶ **computer terminal** used in shops to **input** and **output data** when a sale is transacted.

Position description

▶ formal written statement which may describe the duties, tasks and responsibilities of a specific post. Also called **job description** or **job specification**.

Post

▶ sending an **E-mail** message usually to a **mailing list** or **newsgroup**.

Postal, Telegraph and Telephone Authority – PTT

▶ official organization(s) that control(s) the **communication** facilities within a country.

Postcoordinate index

▶ **index** system where the **descriptors** or **subject headings** are in the form of separate **headings**, so that a **document** whose subject has more that one element must be given a separate **descriptor** for each element. In **searching**, **documents** entered under each of the **search terms** are compared to find appropriate combinations. This process may be facilitated by the use of optical or mechanical devices.

Posting up

▶ **indexing** items that were originally indexed under **narrower terms** are moved to a **broader term** in a hierarchical structure.

Postmortem dump

▶ **routine** used after a **program** has been executed to analyse how it has functioned.

Postprocessor

▶ **computer** which processes **output** generated by another **computer**.

PostScript

▶ early page description language developed by Adobe Systems, a company that specializes in **typefaces** for **computer-**generated **documents**.

Power down/up

▶ to switch a machine off or on.

Power surge

▶ sudden and transient increase in power voltage which can cause damage to the power supply units of **computers**.

Power user

▶ sophisticated **computer** user who has considerable experience and can use the most advanced features and **applications**.

PPBS – Planning Programming Budgeting System

▶ **management** and financial system which requires the identification of goals, the examination and costing of alternatives to achieve those goals and overall **evaluation**.

PPM – Pages Per Minute

▶ speed at which **printers** can print pages. Measurement usually used for **laser** and **ink jet printers**.

Pragmatic
▶ behaviour that is dictated more by practical consequences than by dogma or theory.

Pragmatics
▶ linguistics study that deals with the use of language.

PRECIS PREserved Context Index System
▶ subject **indexing** system developed by Derek Austin in which the initial set of subject terms is organized according to an established scheme of **role operators**. These are manipulated by the **computer** so that selected words function in turn as the **access points** to the item indexed.

Precision
▶ used, along with **recall**, to evaluate the performance of **literature search**, relating to the ability of the system not to retrieve **records** that are irrelevant.

Precoordinate index
▶ **index** where subjects are represented by **headings** that coordinate a number of single **concepts** as items are indexed.

Preface
▶ formal statement before the text of a book, usually written by the author.

Preferred order
▶ order in which **facets** in a **faceted classification** scheme are arranged.

Preferred term
▶ **term** selected to be used in an **index** as opposed to other **terms** that have not been selected.

Preliminaries
▶ pages of a book that precede the first page of numbered text. Also called **front matter**.

Premastering
▶ organizing information onto **compact disc** to optimize the material being recorded by controlling **disc layout**.

Preprint
▶ **document**, usually a **journal article**, which is printed in advance of the formal publication.

Presearch interview
▶ discussion between an enquirer and information staff (**intermediary**) to determine the exact requirements and formulate a **search strategy**. Also called **question negotiation** or **reference interview**.

Presentation layer
▶ in **open system interconnection** (**OSI**), **layer** 6 which is responsible for sending **data** in proper **format** between the **applications program** and lower **layers**.

Preservation
▶ activities aimed at maintaining material for use, either in its original form or some other **format**. Processes which aim at maintaining archival and library material in their original form or in some other usable form.

Press cutting
▶ item cut or clipped from a **newspaper** or **periodical**. Also called a **clipping**, **cutting** or **newspaper clipping**.

Press release
▶ official statement providing news and other information for **newspapers** and **periodicals** to print.

Press run
▶ number of copies of a publication printed at one time. Also called a **print run**.

PRESTEL
▶ British Telecom's **viewdata** (interactive **videotex**) system which allows subscribers to make bookings, order goods and provides **gateways** to other services.

Preview
▶ in **word processing,** a **document** can be formatted for printing and viewed on the **screen** before actually printing out.

Price's law
▶ law developed by Derek de Solla Price that defines the number of prolific authors in a particular subject field.

Primary material
▶ items that contain actual information: **monographs, journal** articles, **patents, maps,** statistical tables etc.

Primer
▶ elementary **instruction manual.**

Print engine
▶ mechanical part in a **laser printer** which performs the printing function.

Print run
▶ number of copies of a publication printed at one time. Also called a **press run.**

Printed circuit board
▶ plastic **board** on which resistors, capacitors, **silicon chips** and electrical components are mounted.

Printer
▶ **output device** that converts electronic **signals** into print on paper.

Printer/plotter
▶ **high-resolution printer** that can undertake **character** printing and **graphics** reproduction.

Printer port
▶ socket in the back of a **personal computer** which is used to connect **peripherals,** usually a **printer.** Sometimes called a **parallel port.**

Printout
▶ printed paper produced by a **printer** attached to a **computer.** Sometimes called **hard copy.**

Privacy
▶ limiting **access** to personal information held in **computer files;** protection of information about individuals held in **computer** systems so that it can not be disclosed to unauthorized people.

Private Automatic Branch eXchange – PABX
▶ telephone system exchange owned by the user that connects lines internally between extensions without incurring charges, and routes calls to and from the public telephone system.

Private Automatic eXchange – PAX
▶ exchange for a private telephone service within an organization which is not connected to the public telephone **network.**

Private Branch eXchange – PBX
▶ telephone system that connects lines internally between extensions within an institution. Limited **access** to a number of outside telephone lines is also available, generally by dialling 9 followed by the number required.

Private key encryption
▶ security procedure that uses a common **key** (usually a lengthy number) which scrambles a message on **transmission** and deciphers it on receipt.

Private line
▶ **communication channel** with associated equipment provided for the exclusive use of a particular subscriber.

Private sector
▶ commercial, for-profit or not-for-profit organization as opposed to public sector operated by government.

Proactive library service
▶ provision of services which anticipate information needs, rather than responding to demonstrated needs. Sometimes called **assertive library service**.

Probabilistic indexing
▶ **indexing** method used to improve the **recall** ratio of **computer**-based **retrieval** systems by **ranking documents** according to their **relevance** to a subject. This is done by assigning a **relevance** number or **weighting** to each **index term** or statement.

Probabilistic retrieval
▶ technique that assigns a **relevance** number or **weighting** to a request in an effort to improve the **relevance** of **documents** retrieved.

Probability theory
▶ estimate of the likelihood or possibility that a chance event will occur.

Problem-based learning
▶ learning based on individuals solving problems.

Problem-oriented language
▶ **high-level programming language** whose structure depends on the specific nature of the problem with which it is designed to deal.

Proceedings
▶ published **record** of the meetings of an institution or society, often including the text of papers presented.

Processing power
▶ speed at which a **computer** system is able to complete its work, largely determined by the **CPU**.

Processor
▶ normally means the **hardware** component in a system which actually transforms information arithmetically or logically. More commonly called the **central processing unit** (**CPU**).

Product Document Management System – PDMS
▶ system that controls product information which might include design details, engineering drawings, product **specifications, numerical control,** machine tool **programs**, analysis results, correspondence, invoices etc.

Productivity
▶ ability of an individual, organization etc., to produce products, work effectively etc.

Professional development
▶ process of acquiring skills, new competencies etc. with a view to making progress in the profession.

Professional ethics
▶ code of conduct that should guide or govern the activity of a particular professional group.

Professional system
▶ system that supports the individual and the unique needs of a specific professional group.

Profile
▶ details of the **search** elements of a request in response to a user's **information need.**

Proforma invoice
▶ bill which shows the value of goods; usually linked to payment being made before the materials are supplied.

Program
▶ set of **instructions** which enables a **computer** to carry out a specific **task** or, in the case of an **operating system,** to allow other **tasks** to be performed.

Program Appliqué a la Selection et la Compilation – PASCAL
▶ **high-level programming language** that has had a great influence on the design of other languages and has long been popular as a teaching language.

Program documentation
▶ complete technical description of a **computer program** which is built up as **software** is written and is used to support later development or maintenance.

Program for information file – PIF
▶ in the **Windows** system, a special **file** containing settings that tells **Windows** how to run a non-Windows application.

Program generator
▶ **computer program** which helps users to write their own **programs.** It can often take **natural language** and change it into **commands** that the **computer** recognizes.

Program loop
▶ part of a **computer program** that is repeated several times.

Programmable Read-Only Memory – PROM
▶ blank **chip** that can be **programmed** by means of a special machine which leaves the desired pattern on the **chip.**

Programmer
▶ person who writes **computer programs.**

Programming
▶ creation of **codes** which instruct a **computer.**

PROgramming in LOGic – PROLOG
▶ **computer language** developed in France which is used in **artificial intelligence** research.

Programming language
▶ set of **instructions** assembled following set rules to perform specific **tasks.**

Project
▶ undertaking with a defined starting point and defined **objectives** by which completion can be identified.

PROLOG – PROgramming in LOGic
▶ **computer language** developed in France which is used in **artificial intelligence** research.

PROM – Programmable Read-Only Memory
▶ blank **chip** that can be **programmed** by means of a special machine which leaves the desired pattern on the **chip.**

Promotion
▶ publicizing a particular product or service; giving staff an increased job responsibility that moves them up the management structure.

Prompt
▶ **symbol** or message from a system or **computer program** either asking for information or suggesting what might be done next.

Proof
▶ trial printed sheets or copies made before the production run for checking and correction.

Proofreading
▶ checking a **document** for **errors** etc. before final printing.

Proofreading mark
▶ special **symbol** used by proofreaders when making corrections on **proofs**.

Proper name
▶ name by which something is identified; name of the family to which a person belongs. Often called **family name**.

Proportional spacing
▶ use of different **character** widths in printing. Sometimes called **kerning**.

Proportionally spaced font
▶ **font** where the amount of space allocated to each **character** varies with the width of the letter.

Proprietary software
▶ commercial **software** that is covered by **copyright.**

Protected field
▶ **field** in a **database record** or **cell** in a **spreadsheet** which cannot be changed by the user.

Protection
▶ in **copyright**, the legal guarantee of ownership of a printed work under the laws of a specific country.

Protocol
▶ **standard** that allows for the **transmission** of **data** between two **hardware** devices; conventions governing the **format** of messages to be exchanged within a **communications system**.

Protocol stack
▶ set of **network protocol layers** that work together.

Prototype
▶ original **model** built to test a system or service, on which future developments will be based.

Proximity
▶ in **online searching**, words that occur near each other.

Proximity search
▶ **searching** technique in which it is possible to search for a group of **characters** within a defined group of words or **characters** in other groups.

Proxy server
▶ **server** that sits between a **client application** such as a **web browser** and a real **server**. It is used to improve performance and to filter requests.

PSDS – Public Switched Digital Service
▶ US Bell Telephone Company service which provides **full duplex** services operating at 56 **kbps**.

PSS – Packet-Switched System
▶ system that transmits **data** in **packets** using **packet-switching** procedures.

PSS Dialplus
▶ British Telecom's **dial-up service** which provides **access** to the **packet-switched network**.

PSTN – Public Switched Telephone Network
▶ system that includes telephones, local lines, exchanges etc.

PTT – Postal, Telegraph and Telephone Authority
▶ official organization(s) that control(s) the **communication** facilities of a country.

Public domain
▶ **1.** management – areas in a library or **resource centre** where the public have free **access**; **2.** publishing – material that is not protected by **copyright** and is available for anyone to use free of charge.

Public domain program
▶ **program** that can be fully copied, amended or incorporated into other **programs** without charge.

Public domain software
▶ any **software program** that is not protected by **copyright**. It is free and can be used without resriction.

Public-key encryption
▶ **cryptography** system which uses two **keys,** one which is public and generally known and one which is private and secret to the person receiving the message.

Public-key infrastructure – PKI
▶ system of **digital certificates** that is used to verify and authenticate the validity of parties involved in transactions on the **Internet**.

Public lending right
▶ authors living in the UK may register to receive up to £5000 per year from a government fund based on the number of times copies of their books are borrowed from a public library.

Public policy
▶ policy established by government that covers the provision of and **access** to information for the general public.

Public relations
▶ activities aimed at creating and preserving good relations between an organization and the general public.

Public sector
▶ segment of society usually called the general public.

Public Switched Telephone Network - PSTN
▶ system that includes telephones, local lines, exchanges etc.

Publication explosion
▶ unprecedented growth of information and **knowledge**. It is argued that the doubling of printed information every five years threatens human ability to cope with the volume. However, it offers greater **access** to **knowledge** through technological advances in **computers** and **communication** systems. Also called **information explosion**.

Publish or perish syndrome
▶ academic requirement, which may be explicit or implicit, which requires academic staff to write for publication so that the amount published forms part of the person's **evaluation**.

Publisher Item Identifier – PII
▶ internal numbering system developed by scientific, technical and medical (STM) publishers and used mainly for prepublication control.

Puff
▶ description of a book prior to or upon publication to promote sales, often containing quotes from **book**

reviews; information about a book
which appears on the **book jacket.**
Sometimes called a **blurb.**

Pull-down menu
▶ menu giving a choice of **commands** and options that appear when
an item is selected using the **mouse.**

Punch
▶ making holes in a **card** or paper
tape to enter information; piece of
equipment for making such holes.

Punched card
▶ **card** for each item in a collection
which has numbered positions on its
face; a position or combination of
positions is punched to represent the
subject and the **cards** are searched
with mechanical or electrical devices.

Punctuation mark
▶ printing **symbol** that is used to
make text understandable and
grammatical.

Pure notation
▶ **notation** consisting solely of one
set of symbols, e.g. A-Z, a-z or 0–9.

PURL – Persistent URL
▶ type of **URL** which acts as an
intermediary for the real **URL** of a
web resource.

Push technology
▶ information based on user **profiles**
which is automatically delivered to a
user and is available in a range of
formats.

Pushbutton
▶ square shape displayed on a
screen which carries out a specific
action when selected by a **pointer**
or **key.**

Pushdown list
▶ list where the last item added is
placed at the top of a list.

Pushup list
▶ list where the last item added is
placed at the bottom of a list.

PVC – polyvinyl chloride
▶ plastic used for coating or
impregnation when **bookbinding** or
covering books for waterproofing or
durability.

Pyramid coding
▶ **fixed-field** indirect coding system
for **edge-notched cards,** which allows
any number from 0 to 9 to be
encoded into **fields** consisting of five
holes.

Qq

QBE – Query By Example
▶ simple language used to retrieve information from a **computer database management system** by entering a query with a known value which is matched in the **database** to retrieve an answer.

Qualifier
▶ **delimiter** used to distinguish different meanings of words or **terms** that are spelled the same.

Qualitative research
▶ understanding factors and participants in specific situations to reach conclusions that relate to **quality**.

Quality
▶ what something is like; how good or bad something is when compared to a set **standard**.

Quality assessment
▶ promise to live up to customer expectations and a guarantee to provide a service that meets customer requirements.

Quality assurance
▶ **1.** computing – process that ensures that a piece of **software** is of acceptable **quality** and meets the different levels of requirements expected. Usually called **software quality assurance**; **2.** management – examination of all activities of an organization by submitting it to a comprehensive battery of tests with the intention of improving **quality**.

Quality control
▶ process of ensuring that products and services achieve a recognized **standard** of excellence.

Quantitative research
▶ counting, measuring and testing to reach conclusions based on numerical or statistical data.

Quarto
▶ paper size which results when a sheet is folded twice to make up eight pages; traditional British paper size 8 × 10 inches which has been superseded by ISO A4.

Quasi
▶ word prefix that means something that is almost like or seems like something.

Quasi-synonymous relationship
▶ **term relationship** that is nearly but not quite a **synonomous relationship**.

Qube
▶ American **videotex** system developed by Warner Amex Cable Corp.

Query
▶ question put to a **computer database**.

Query by example – QBE
▶ simple language used to retrieve information from a **computer database management system** by

entering a **query** with a known value which is matched in the **database** to retrieve an answer.

Query language
▶ high-level programming language resembling a **natural language** which is designed to make **online searching** easy for inexperienced users; language used in **relational databases**.

Query processing
▶ processing **queries** by either extracting information from a **database** or translating **query commands** from a **query language**.

Query window
▶ **window** that appears on a **computer screen** when an **error** occurs which asks the user what action should be taken.

Questel
▶ French **host** that provides access to French and EU **databases**.

Question answering system
▶ selected **recall** of pre-stored information through extracting selective **keywords** from full or partial texts. System requires a high degree of prior formatting and formulation and is inflexible.

Question mark
▶ **1.** computing – **character** (?) used as a **wild card** in **computer** searching to indicate that any **character** in the position marked will produce a match; **2.** printing – **character** which is placed at the end of a question statement in text.

Question negotiation
▶ discussion between an enquirer and information staff (**intermediary**) to determine the exact requirements and formulate a **search strategy**. Also called **presearch interview** or **reference interview**.

Queue
▶ **jobs** waiting to be processed.

Queuing theory
▶ type of **probability theory** which examines queues and their behaviour in terms of arrival time, service time and queuing discipline.

Quick reference material
▶ reference works that can provide information quickly and easily. Many libraries have a small collection of such works near a staff desk so that questions can be answered quickly. Also called **ready reference material**.

Quickkey
▶ key which can be pressed to bypass **GUI** actions so that tedious **menu**, **icon** or **mouse** use can be avoided. Sometimes called **fast key** or **keyboard** shortcut.

Quicklist
▶ short list of recently used **files** that appears in a **file menu**.

Quicksort
▶ algorithm for rapid **sorting** of large **data files**.

Quit
▶ **command** used to leave or exit a **program** or **computer** system.

Quota sampling
▶ **sampling** method which interviews a specific number of people who have common characteristics: age, gender, income etc.

Quotation
▶ text borrowed from another source which is usually set in **italic** type, indented or surrounded by double (" ") or single (' ') **quotation marks**. Double (" ") or single (' ') marks around text usually indicate that the enclosed text is quoted from another source.

QWERTY

▶ conventional English-language layout of **keys** on the **keyboard** of a **computer terminal** or typewriter, which places the letters q, w, e, r, t and y in this order on the top row.

Rr

R&D – Research and Development
▶ basic research and applied research directed to the design, development and improvement of services and products.

Ragged margin/right
▶ uneven right margin of a printed document, usually when only the left-hand side is justified.

RAM – Random Access Memory
▶ temporary high-power memory which is lost when the computer is switched off.

Random access
▶ 1. access to stored data where the next location from which information is to be obtained is unrelated to the previous location; 2. processing data in an arbitrary fashion without any plan or structure.

Random Access Memory – RAM
▶ temporary high-power memory which is lost when the computer is switched off.

Random number
▶ number generated by computer that cannot be predicted in advance.

Random sampling
▶ method of selecting representatives of a population where each member has a possibility of being selected.

Ranganathan's laws
▶ five laws of library science proposed by S.R. Ranganathan: 1. books are for use; 2. every reader his book; 3. every book its reader; 4. save the time of the reader; 5. the library is a growing organism.

Range searching
▶ search confined to a set of values that are assumed to have been selected in advance.

Ranking
▶ placing documents found as a result of a search in an order that reflects the degree to which they match the search terms used.

Ranking system
▶ method of displaying search results where the ones considered the most relevant are listed first.

Rare material
▶ any material that is old, scarce or difficult to locate in the open or specialized markets. Mainly books, either those printed during the hand printing press period or those of local interest.

Raster
▶ grid on a screen which divides the screen area into sections like a geographic map reference system.

Raster graphics
▶ computer graphics that use a full matrix of pixels, with each pixel

having its own **code**. Also called **bit-mapped graphics**.

Raster image processor
▶ **hardware** and **software** combination that converts a **vector image** into a **bit-mapped image**.

Raster scan
▶ examining a **display** area line by line; used in **computer graphics**.

Rating system
▶ method of determining the suitability of something based on **evaluation** of **characteristics**.

Rationalization
▶ logic used to explain the integration of **information services**.

Raw data
▶ **data** that has not been processed in any way.

RDBMS – Relational Database Management System
▶ system that can handle several **database files** at the same time.

Read-Only Memory – ROM
▶ **storage** device that contains **data** or **programs** which can be read but cannot be changed, written over or erased.

Read-only storage
▶ permanent method of storing **data** in a **computer** so that it can be read many times but cannot be altered.

Read/write head
▶ electromagnetic device which transfers **data** to or from a **magnetic tape** or **disk**.

Readme file
▶ small **text file** that comes with many **software** packages with information that does not appear in the printed **documentation**, usually very recent information.

Ready reference material
▶ reference works that can provide information quickly and easily. Many libraries have a small collection of such works near a staff desk so that questions can be answered quickly. Also called **quick reference material**.

Real time
▶ **computer** operating mode where **data** are received and processed and the results are displayed immediately.

Real-Time Clock – RTC
▶ **chip** which can be set to keep a **computer** informed about the correct date and time.

Real-time processing
▶ processing system that accepts **data** and processes it immediately in **interactive** mode.

Realia
▶ three-dimensional **objects**, such as paintings, **models** etc., that can be used for purposes of illustration.

Reboot
▶ resetting a **computer** system during a computing session.

Recall
▶ used, along with **precision**, to evaluate the performance of a **literature search**, relating to the ability of the system to retrieve relevant **records**.

Receiver
▶ electronic device which detects and decodes transmitted **data**.

Reciprocal
▶ **entry** in an **indexing** system which generates another **entry** when a **cross-reference** is made, for example when entering a synonym or a **preferred term**.

Record
▶ **1.** computing – unit in a **computer file** usually made up of **fields**; **2.** information handling – **bibliographic description** of an item in the published literature or other recorded material. It contains author name(s), title, publisher, date of publication etc.; **3.** management – in business, the result of recording or preserving information on any **media** to preserve information that reflects the position or business of an organization.

Records management
▶ systematic creation, use, handling, control, **storage** and disposal of **records**; application of systematic and scientific control to all the recorded information that an organization needs to do business.

Recovery program
▶ **computer program** that can be used to get back corrupted or deleted **data**.

Recto
▶ right-hand page of a printed book.

Recycling bin
▶ electronic **folder** for discarded **computer files** that can be restored if necessary.

Reduced Instruction Set Chip – RISC
▶ **computer chip** designed to operate with a reduced set of commonly used **instructions** so that faster speeds can be achieved.

Reduction rate
▶ in **micrographics**, ratio between the scale of the original material and the scale of the **microform image**.

Redundancy
▶ reduction of staff or material for a particular activity or service, usually as a cost-cutting exercise.

Reengineering
▶ reorganization that focuses on processes, breakthroughs, breaking with old tradition and rules and creative use of **IT** to facilitate change.

Referee process
▶ process by which **manuscripts** submitted for potential publication in a scholarly or research publication are reviewed by subject experts for comment and approval.

Reference
▶ **instruction** which leads from one **heading** to another; may be made between titles, subjects or names. Also called **cross reference**.

Reference file
▶ **database** containing information relating to **documents** (books, **articles**, **reports** etc.). The information normally contains details of authorship and title, together with place and date of publication. Some **databases** contain **abstracts** and each item is **indexed** to facilitate search and **access**. Also called **bibliographic database**.

Reference interview
▶ discussion between an enquirer and information staff (**intermediary**) to determine the exact requirements and formulate a **search strategy**. Also called **presearch interview** or **question negotiation**.

Reference retrieval
▶ provision of a complete **reference** to an item in response to an information request.

Reference service
▶ provision of information in response to requests.

Referential integrity
▶ feature provided in **relational database management systems** that prevents users or **applications** from entering inconsistent **data**.

Referral service
▶ service which, if unable to provide the information required, refers the enquirer to another potential source or service.

Reformat
▶ deleting **data** on a **disk** that has been used and setting a new **format** which can receive new **data**.

Refresh rate
▶ **image** on the **screen** that is being redrawn constantly many times per second, usually measured in **Hertz**.

Register
▶ temporary **storage** location in the **central processing unit** (**CPU**) which is used to monitor and control **program instructions**.

Related term – RT
▶ **cross reference** to another **subject index term** that is used in a **thesaurus**.

Related work
▶ work that has a relationship with another work, usually a supplement, **index**, **continuation** etc.

Relational database
▶ **database** in which the relationships between the items it contains are formally stated; type of **database** where information is held in a number of separate **files** which are linked by common **keys**, so that **data** can be drawn from several **files** simultaneously.

Relational DataBase Management System – RDBMS
▶ system that can handle several **database files** at the same time.

Relational indexing
▶ technique that concentrates on the expression of precise relationships between **concepts** or ideas using **relational operators**.

Relational operator
▶ **symbol** that represents a relationship between **concepts** or ideas in an **index**.

Relative classification
▶ **classification scheme** that shows relationships between subjects.

Relative index
▶ **alphabetical index**, usually provided with a **classification scheme**, which draws together aspects of a subject that would be scattered by the structure of the **classification scheme**.

Relative location
▶ system of locating **documents** by their positions relative to each other, usually according to **classification notation** or author's name.

Relevance
▶ measure of the closeness of a retrieved piece of information to an enquiry. The state or quality implying close logical relationship with, and importance to, the matter under consideration. Also called **pertinence**.

Relevance feedback
▶ innovative search feature in a **wide area information server** (**WAIS**) that allows the searcher to select relevant material that the search **software** then uses to discover additional material.

Relevance judgement
▶ assessment of the **relevance** of retrieved **documents** in relation to the information demands of the user.

Relevance ranking
▶ **searching** technique that uses **weights** to signify the importance of various **concepts**, either in the item or in the **search profile**, and

produces a list of retrieved **documents** in an order that reflects their **weights**. The most relevant **documents** are at the top of the resulting list.

Reliability
▶ capacity of a functioning unit such as **computer hardware** or **software** to perform required **functions** as expected by users.

Remainder
▶ book which is sold at a reduced price.

Remote access
▶ use of a **computer** from a **terminal** at a geographically distant point. Sometimes called **offsite access**.

Remote control (computing)
▶ any device that can be operated from a distance without connecting wires.

Remote control software
▶ **software** installed in two machines which allows a user at a local **computer** to have control over a remote **computer** using a **modem**.

Remote login
▶ connecting to a **computer** system at a remote location using a **computer network**.

Remote sensing
▶ use of **sensors** and. **telecommunications** to pick up **signals** in one location and send them to a **computer** in another location.

Remote terminal
▶ **terminal** which is in a geographically distinct location from the **processor** it is accessing.

Remote working
▶ office work done from home rather than the workplace, using **computers**

and **telecommunications** to provide an electronic **link** to the office. Sometimes called **telecommuting** or **teleworking**.

Removable cartridge/hard disk
▶ type of **disk drive** system which has **hard disks** enclosed in plastic or metal **cartridges** so that they can be removed in the same way as **floppy disks**.

Repackaging
▶ provision of **information services** or products tailored to the requirements of specific groups of users by rearranging or merging material obtained from different sources.

Repeating key
▶ **key** on a **computer keyboard** that will repeat a **character** over and over again as long as the **key** is depressed.

Repetitive strain injury – RSI
▶ work-related syndrome caused by particular physical movements, often associated with the use of **keyboards**.

Replication
▶ process of creating and managing duplicate versions of a **computer database**.

Report
▶ official **record** of the activities of a specific organization, or details of special activities.

Report generator/writer
▶ part of a **database management system** which extracts information from one or more **files** and presents the information in a specified **format**.

Repository
▶ organization which acquires, stores and distributes material; **storage**

location for material that is kept for archival purposes.

Repro
▶ all stages of prepress camerawork, **scanning** and film makeup.

Reprography
▶ general term for all methods of **document** duplication.

Request For Proposal – RFP
▶ **document** which solicits proposals from prospective bidders for a particular project, system or service.

Request For Quote – RFQ
▶ formalized request for a cost figure or **estimate** for a particular project, system, material or service which allows competing bids to be evaluated.

Request-oriented indexing
▶ **indexing** where the content of a **document** is compared with words used in a **controlled vocabulary** and the **indexer** decides which words to use to **search** for information.

Rerun
▶ repeat a particular sequence or operation.

Rescue dump
▶ recording **data** on a **disk** when a **computer crash** occurs. If this has been programmed to take place automatically **data** loss will not occur.

Research and Development – R&D
▶ **basic research** and **applied research** directed to the design, development and improvement of services and products.

Research front
▶ subject field where there is current research activity.

Reset button
▶ switch or **button** on a **computer** that will begin the start-up procedure similar to a **warm boot** when certain **instructions** are already in **memory**.

Resident font
▶ in **laser printers**, typestyle provided with the printing machine.

Resident routine
▶ **computer program** that remains in **memory** as distinct from one that has to be **input** using a **disk** or **tape**.

Resident software
▶ **software** held permanently in the computer's **memory**.

Resolution
▶ measure of the fineness of an **image**.

Resource centre
▶ collection of material that provides relevant information on specific topics.

Resource management
▶ effective organization and use of all the facilities in a library or **information service**, including material, staff, space etc.

Resource sharing
▶ group of organizations agreeing to use or collect material cooperatively or to share personnel, equipment, facilities, **knowledge** or other resources to reduce costs and increase services.

Response time
▶ time between entering **data** or a **command** into a **computer** and the appearance of a **display** in response.

Retail price
▶ price set by the publisher for retail sale of a book. Also called **list price**.

Retrieval
▶ selection or identification of **documents**; finding a item with known characteristics; and the fetching or delivering of material.

Retrospective conversion
▶ conversion of **records** from an existing **catalogue** into **machine-readable** form; process by which a library acquires copies of existing **machine-readable records** for its own use.

Retrospective searching
▶ **search** request which calls for a **search** to be made for all items published on a specific topic from a specified date.

Returns
▶ unsold stock returned to a publisher by a **bookseller** with the publisher's agreement.

Reverse engineering
▶ recreating a design by analysing the finished product. This could be an illegal action.

Reverse video
▶ **display** of **alphanumeric characters** where the usual foreground and background colours are interchanged.

Review
▶ survey and critical **evaluation** of published material.

Review copy
▶ copy of a book sent to a **newspaper** or **periodical** for critical appraisal and **review**.

Rewritable optical disc
▶ **optical disc** whose contents can be erased and written over with new information.

RFP – Request For Proposal
▶ **document** which solicits proposals from prospective bidders for a particular project, system or service.

RFQ – Request For Quote
▶ formalized request for a cost figure or **estimate** for a particular project, system, material or service which allows competing bids to be evaluated.

Rich text format – RTF
▶ form of a **word processing file** which contains only **ASCII** code but contains all the **commands** that would be contained in a coded **file**.

Right click
▶ **click** on the right-hand **button** on a **mouse**.

Right-hand truncation
▶ reducing a word to its root or stem by cutting off letters at the end, to allow for searching for words with the same stem or root.

Right justification
▶ aligning type to the right hand margin of a printed **document**.

Right sizing
▶ **computer** system **configuration** which is the optimum for a particular institution.

Rights ownership
▶ legal protection provided to an author of a scientific, literary or artistic work.

Rigid classification
▶ **classification** of books based on their position on the shelf rather than according to a **classification scheme**.

Ring-back system
▶ method of contacting a remote **computer** which can be used for security purposes.

Ring network
▶ **network** arranged in a way that permits **terminals** to communicate with one another without having to go via a central **computer**.

RISC – Reduced Instruction Set Chip
▶ **computer chip** designed to operate with a reduced set of commonly used **instructions** so that faster speeds can be achieved.

River
▶ text on a **document** page where the white spaces between words are lined up to seem like a river running down the page.

Robot
▶ machine capable of performing automatically some type of activity which is normally controlled by human beings, usually simple repetitive **tasks**. Shortened form of name is **bot**.

Robotics
▶ study of **robots,** including the development of controlling **software** and building mechanical machines. **Artificial intelligence** techniques are used in their design and production.

Robust program
▶ **computer program** with the ability to resist a **crash**.

Role
▶ **qualifier** which defines the **function** of a **descriptor**, usually in a **postcoordinate indexing system**.

Role indicator/operator
▶ in **information retrieval, code** assigned to a word, e.g. a **descriptor** or **keyword**, which indicates the **role** the word plays in the text where it occurs.

Roll-up menu
▶ **dialog box** which stays open on the **computer screen** while choices are made.

Rollerball
▶ device used to control and send information in a **graphics workstation** or a **personal computer; pointing device** which could be described as an upside-down **mouse**. Sometimes called a **tracker ball**.

ROM – Read-Only Memory
▶ **storage** device that contains **data** or **programs** which can be read but cannot be changed, written over or erased.

Roman character
▶ type **font** containing letters of unemphasized normal type instead of **bold face** or **italic type**.

Romanization
▶ representation of picture-writing alphabets (e.g. Chinese, Japanese) by Roman alphabet letters.

Root directory (computing)
▶ main **directory** of a **hard drive** or **floppy disk** which contains both **program** and **data files** and **sub-directory files**.

Root thesaurus
▶ **faceted thesaurus** produced by the British Standards Institute in 1981 which was intended to be a basic **indexing** tool and guide to technical terminology.

Rotated catalogue
▶ **classified catalogue** in which entries are made under each significant part of the **classification notation**.

Rotated descriptor
▶ alphabetical **index** of all the words used in a list of **descriptors**, where each subject word is rearranged in

the filing position in the context of all the other words within the **string** of **subject headings**.

Rotated index
▶ multiple specific **entry indexing system** in which each element in turn is brought to the **filing position** but the relative order of elements is unchanged.

Rounding
▶ adjusting a number so that a value contains fewer decimal places.

Router
▶ device that connects two **local area networks**. On the **Internet** routers are used to forward **packets** of **data** from one **host** to another.

Routine
▶ set of **instructions** within a **program** that performs a specific **task**.

Royalty
▶ payment made to the author of a book for every copy sold, usually calculated as a percentage of the published price.

RPG
▶ **computer programming language** used to write **programs** that produce complex printed reports.

RSI – Repetitive Strain Injury
▶ work-related syndrome caused by particular physical movements, often associated with the use of **keyboards**.

RT – Related Term
▶ **cross reference** to another **subject index term** that is used in a **thesaurus**.

RTC – Real-Time Clock
▶ **chip** that can be set to keep a **computer** informed of the correct date and time.

RTF – Rich Text Format
▶ form of a **word processing file** which contains only **ASCII** code but contains all the **commands** that would be contained in a coded **file**.

RTFM
▶ abbreviation for 'Read The Friendly Manual'; **instruction** to a **computer** user who is unwilling to look something up.

Rubric
▶ printed headings in a book chapter or section.

Ruly English
▶ English where each word has only one conceptual meaning and each **concept** has only one word to describe it.

Run
▶ execute a **computer routine**, **program** or set of **programs**.

Run-on cost
▶ cost of continuing to print without stopping the press once a certain number of copies have been printed; usually expressed in thousands of copies.

Run time
▶ time it takes for an **application** to be processed.

Running foot
▶ information that is printed at the bottom of every page of a **document**. Also called a **footer**.

Running head
▶ information that is printed at the top of every page of a document; usually carries title and author name. Sometimes called a **header**.

Ss

Salami shaving/technique
▶ **computer** fraud that involves
unauthorized transfer of money from
a number of bank accounts. The
amount taken from each account is
too small to be noticed, but
accumulates into a substantial total.

Sale or return
▶ agreement between **bookseller** and
publisher whereby unsold books can
be returned for credit.

**SALINET – SAtellite Library
Information NETwork**
▶ **satellite communications** system
used to provide library services to
remote parts of Canada.

Sampling
▶ capturing continuous phenomena
by collecting **data** or by taking
periodic snapshots.

SAN – Standard Address Number
▶ unique number for publishers,
libraries and other firms or
organizations.

Sans serif
▶ typeface that has no **serifs** (i.e.
small horizontal and/or vertical lines
added to letters in some **typefaces**).

Satellite
▶ orbiting station that relays **signals**
from ground positions where the
shape of the earth does not allow

direct **transmission**. Transatlantic
telephone calls are transmitted via
geostationary satellites which remain
in a fixed orbit.

Satellite communication
▶ transmitting **signals** between
ground stations using **satellites**.

Satellite computer
▶ small ancillary **computer** used to
relieve a central larger **computer** of
simple time-consuming operations.

Satellite thesaurus
▶ **thesaurus** for a specialized subject
area based on a general **thesaurus.**
Sometimes called a **microthesaurus**.

Scalability
▶ ability of **hardware** or a **hardware**
system to adapt to increased
demands; anything which can be
changed in size.

Scalable font
▶ printing characters or **fonts** that
can be enlarged or reduced in size.

Scan
▶ in **information technology**,
examining material that is available
in **machine-readable format**.

Scanner
▶ device that converts photographs
and text into electronic **format** so
that it can be read by a **computer**.

SCANNET
▶ Swedish **computer network**.

Scanning
▶ examining or producing **data** from the shape of an **object** or drawing.

Scatter
▶ distribution of **articles** in a specific subject area which occur occasionally in a large number of **journals**; related to the concept of **core and scatter**.

Schedule
▶ list of subjects in a **classification scheme** which displays relationships between subjects.

Scheduling
▶ process carried out by a **software program** that coordinates **access** to a shared resource such as a **printer**; operation of a **software program** that is designed to help those involved in organizing and planning meetings, selecting an appropriate date/time, booking necessary resources and issuing **E-mails**.

Scholarly publishing
▶ academic or research-oriented publication of high quality.

Scholarly skywriting
▶ authors mounting their own papers on the **web** in order to make them widely available.

Scholar's workstation
▶ **workstation** that supports all the functions required by a scholar or researcher. Also called an **academic workstation**.

School media centre
▶ library or **resource centre** in a school that provides a range of **media** and related equipment. Also called a **media centre**.

Science indicator
▶ measure which provides information on activities in the physical sciences, sometimes limited to a particular country or region.

Scientometrics
▶ mathematical and statistical analysis of research patterns in the physical and life sciences.

Scope note
▶ indication of the meaning or extension of terms in a **thesaurus** or **subject heading list**, or of a class in a **classification scheme**.

Scrambling
▶ taking **data** and mixing it up using a **code** so that it cannot be understood unless the **code** is known.

Screen
▶ surface of a device such as a **visual display unit** (**VDU**) or **cathode ray tube** (**CRT**).

Screen buffer
▶ location where information displayed on the **screen** of the **visual display unit** (**VDU**) is stored.

Screen dump
▶ making a printed copy of the **computer screen**; it can sometimes be stored as a **file** before printing.

Screen saver
▶ **computer application** which, when a **computer** is switched on but has not been used for a set period, puts a moving **image** on the **screen** to avoid **screen** burn-out.

Scroll
▶ movement of text up and down or across a **visual display unit** (**VDU**) so that the user can view areas of text adjacent to that displayed on the **screen**.

Scroll bar
▶ in **Windows,** facility which allows movement to other parts of a **document** when the entire **document** will not fit on the **Windows screen.**

SCSI – Small Computer Systems Interface
▶ method of connecting devices to a **communications system.** Pronounced 'scuzzy'.

SDI – Selective Dissemination of Information
▶ distribution of a limited amount of information (**references** etc.) that covers an identified area of interest. May be to a single individual or groups of individuals, and is usually on a regular basis.

Search
▶ systematic examination of information in a **database.** The aim is to identify items that satisfy preset criteria which represent an information need.

Search aid
▶ tool that assists in preparing a **search,** such as a **manual** for a particular system or **database, thesaurus,** list of **indexing terms** etc.

Search engine
▶ **online software** tool used to **search databases** and find information on the **Internet.**

Search intermediary
▶ person who conducts a **search** on behalf of another person.

Search language
▶ any language used in the **search** of **databases** in an **information retrieval system** and/or **online searching.**

Search profile
▶ **indexing** terms and other details such as language, date etc. which are used for a specific **search.**

Search record
▶ details of people, documents, **databases** searched and **search terms** used for a specific **search.**

Search save
▶ facility that allows the details of a **search** to be saved in the memory of the **computer,** to be used again when required.

Search statement
▶ **search** terms linked by **logical operators** which represent an enquiry developed to identify information in an **information retrieval system.**

Search strategy
▶ plan of a **search** for information involving specification of needs, choice of **search terms,** degree of **specificity** in searching and how to extend the **search** to **broader, narrower** and **related terms.**

Search term
▶ word, phrase or **notation** used to locate items that may have been indexed under these.

Search time
▶ amount of time required to locate a particular item or **data** in a store.

Searching
▶ process of looking for information in an information store.

Searchware
▶ **computer software** used to search a **database.**

SECAM – Séquential Couleur a Mémoire
▶ **standard** for colour television broadcasting used in France, Russia, Eastern Europe etc.

Second-generation computer
▶ **computer** developed in the early 1960s using **transistors** and **printed circuits**.

Secondary service
▶ printed and machine-based services that give **references** to where information is available in **full text**, **primary** form. Secondary services may contain **abstracts** and **indexes** which aid in identifying the information needed.

Secondary storage
▶ non-volatile devices, such as **computer tapes, disks** etc. used to store data and program instructions. Also called **secondary storage** or **auxiliary storage**.

Security backup
▶ copy of a **disk, tape** or **file** which is kept in a safe place in case the working copy is damaged or lost.

See also reference
▶ **reference** from a **heading** in a **subject index** or a **subject catalogue** from a **term** that is used to another **term** that might also be of use.

See reference
▶ reference from a **heading** in a **subject index** or a **subject catalogue** from a **term** that is not used to a **term** that is used.

Seek time
▶ time it takes for a **read/write head** to reach a **track** on a **disk**.

Segmentation
▶ division of a **packet** of information into smaller **packets** for **transmission** over a **communications** system.

Selective Dissemination of Information – SDI
▶ distribution of a limited amount of information (**references** etc.) that

covers an identified area of interest. May be to a single individual or groups of individuals, and is usually distributed on a regular basis.

Semantic factor
▶ generic **concept** used to indicate important aspects of the meaning of **terms** of a more specific nature.

Semantic network
▶ method of representing **knowledge** in an **expert system** as a **network** of associated **concepts**, using facts as **nodes** linking the lines that represent relationships.

Semantic relationship
▶ relationship between subjects that are stable; reflects the consensus of opinion concerning such relationships.

Semantics
▶ **1.** generally – study of relationships between **linguistic symbols** (words, phrases etc.) and the **objects** to which they refer; the science of meaning; **2.** computing – the meaning of words or **symbols** in **programming languages**.

Semiconductor
▶ any substance which conducts electricity easily when the voltage across it is above a certain value. Semiconducting materials form the basis of **transistors**.

Semiotics
▶ general philosophical theory of signs and **symbols** which deals with their function in both artificial and **natural languages** and comprises **syntactics**, **semantics** and **pragmatics**.

Sensitivity
▶ in an **information retrieval system** this term is sometimes used instead

of **recall**, which is the number of relevant items retrieved in response to an enquiry expressed as a ratio of the total number of relevant items in the system.

Sensor
▶ electronic device that produces an **output** dependent upon the condition or physical state of a process.

Separate
▶ copy of an article published in a **periodical** reprinted as a separate item for the author's use. Also called an **offprint**.

Sequel
▶ complete literary work which continues an earlier work.

Sequential access
▶ 1. generally – reading, writing or searching **data records** one **record** after another; 2. computing – **access** to **data** in a **computer file** in the order in which they are stored until the required **record** is found. Sometimes called **serial access**.

Serendipity
▶ information gained by accident, often as the result of **browsing**.

Serial
▶ publication issued in successive parts that is intended to be continued indefinitely, usually multi-authored and sequentially numbered. Examples of serials are **journals**, **newspapers**, **reports** etc.

Serial access
▶ access to **data** in a **computer file** in the order in which they are stored until the required **record** is found. Sometimes called **sequential access**.

Serial communication/data transmission
▶ **data transfer** in which one **bit** is transferred at a time.

Serial device
▶ **peripheral** device that is connected to a **computer** through a **serial interface**; examples are **keyboard**, **mouse**, **printer**, **modem** etc.

Serial file
▶ **file** in which items are entered one after the other in no particular order.

Serial interface
▶ method of transferring **data** one **bit** at a time between a **peripheral** and the **memory** of a **computer** system.

Serial Item and Contribution Identifier – SICI
▶ standard developed by the American Serials Industry Systems Advisory Committee (**SISAC**) for the coded identification of each issue, **fascicule** or volume of a given **serial** publication and the **articles** it contains. It is published as Z39.56–1991. The Faxon subscription agency has the responsibility for maintaining the **code**.

Serial port
▶ connector at the back of a **personal computer** that is used to connect **peripheral** devices such as **modems** etc.

Serial printer
▶ **computer printer** which prints one **character** at a time along a line rather than a whole line at a time.

Serial processing
▶ processing items in a **data file** in the order in which they are stored.

Serial searching
▶ machine **search** in which each machine **record** has to be scanned in

its entirety and in sequence.
Sometimes called **linear searching**.

Serials control
▶ activity covering **acquisition**, processing, circulation, **indexing** and other aspects of managing **serial** publications.

Series
▶ separate publications issued successively in a uniform style, usually consecutively numbered and having a collective title in addition to an individual title.

Series entry
▶ **entry** in a **catalogue** under the title of a **series**.

Series statement
▶ that part of a **catalogue record** which gives the name and number of the **series** to which the item belongs.

Serif
▶ small horizontal and/or vertical line added to letters in some **typefaces**.

Server
▶ computer **program** and/or **processor** that provides services to users on a **network** to **access files**, control a **printer** etc.

Service bureau/organization
▶ commercial facility which allows **computer** users to lease time on a **central processor** and appropriate **peripherals** to run their **programs**. External body that provides specific services to a library or **information centre**, usually under contract and for a specific fee.

Service program
▶ **program** usually supplied as part of a **software** package or a **computer** system that performs a particular maintenance or **housekeeping**

routine. It may perform such simple tasks as **disk** formatting, copying **files** from one **disk** to another etc. Also called **utility program/software**.

Service provider – SP
▶ organization that stores and offers **access** to information which it does not own via a **communication network**. Not to be confused with an **information provider**.

Service quality
▶ **management model** that concentrates on the reduction of any gap between customer expectations and customer perception of the quality of service provided.

SGML – Standard Generalized Markup Language
▶ standard set of **codes** for presenting **ASCII** text **files** in *italics*, **bold** etc. Became the basis for **HTML**.

Shannon's information theory
▶ information and **entropy** are roughly similar and provide a quantitative measure of the amount of information in a given message.

Shared cataloguing
▶ situation where a number of organizations share in the creation of a **cataloguing** system and/or cataloguing records.

Shared logic
▶ **computer** system in which **logic** is shared between items of **hardware**.

Shareware
▶ computer **program** that has been developed and made available for public use at little or only nominal cost, so that it can be tried by a user to see if it is useful.

Sheaf catalogue
▶ physical form of **catalogue** where **entries** are on paper slips which are filed in binders.

Shelf arrangement
▶ arrangement of items on the shelves in a library. Sometimes called **shelf order**.

Shelf list
▶ list of items in the order in which they appear on the shelves.

Shelf mark/number
▶ number assigned to a shelf and to a book to identify where it is physically placed in the library.

Shelf order
▶ arrangement of items on the shelves in a library. Sometimes called **shelf arrangement**.

Shell
▶ **software** that operates between the user and the **operating system** usually to make the system more **user friendly**.

Shortcut
▶ fast **link** to an **application** or **document** provided by a **desktop icon** or a **key** on the **keyboard**.

Shovelware
▶ **software** that is of little or no value which is offered in an attempt to increase the value of a package.

Shrinkwrap licence
▶ **software** licence that the purchaser is deemed to accept when the **software** package is opened.

Shrinkwrapped program
▶ **computer program** that has successfully completed the **alpha** and **beta test** stages and is ready for commercial release.

sic
▶ Latin abbreviation for "so", "thus", "in this manner"; often used in brackets to indicate that a mistake has been made in the original text which has been noticed but not corrected.

SICI – Serial Item and Contribution Identifier
▶ standard developed by the American Serials Industry Systems Advisory Committee (**SISAC**) for the coded identification of each issue, **fascicule** or volume of a given **serial** publication and the **articles** it contains. It is published as Z39.56–1991. The Faxon subscription agency has the responsibility for maintaining the **code**.

SIGLE – System for Information on Grey Literature in Europe
▶ project sponsored by the Commission of the European Communities to improve the detection, identification, collection and delivery of **grey literature**.

Signal
▶ information transmitted in the form of electrical disturbance.

Signature
▶ **1.** computing – **authentication code** which a user gives prior to accessing a **computer** system; **2.** printing – printed and folded pages in a book usually made up of eight, 16 or 32 pages.

Significant word
▶ word which can be used as an **index** term, especially in a machine-generated **index**.

Silicon chip
▶ wafer of silicon providing a **semiconductor** base for a number of electrical **circuits**.

Silicon Glen
▶ geographical area of Southern Scotland where there are a number of **computer** and **semiconductor** manufacturers.

Silicon Valley
▶ geographical area of California where many innovative information technology companies are located.

Silver halide
▶ compound used to give a light-sensitive coating on photographic paper or film.

Simulation
▶ **1.** generally – representation of some aspects of the real world by numbers or other symbols that can be manipulated easily. **Model** system constructed to allow for different approaches to be tested;
2. computing – use of a **computer program** to represent a physical process or system.

Single staff practitioner
▶ another name for an individual who runs a library or **information service** by themselves. More commonly called **one-man band** or **one-person library**.

SISAC code
▶ **bar code** using 128 symbology to represent the **Serial Item and Contribution Identifier (SICI) code**.

Site name
▶ unique name of a **computer** on a **computer network**. Also called a **host** name.

Slanted abstract
▶ **abstract** that stresses a particular aspect of the **document** which is of interest to a specific group of users.

Smalltalk
▶ currently considered to be the first and best **high-level object-oriented**

programming language. It has never achieved the commercial success of other comparable languages such as **C++** or **Java**.

Slave
▶ device that operates under the control of another device.

SLSI – Super Large-Scale Integration
▶ **chips** containing more than 50 000 **transistors**.

Smart battery
▶ type of battery that provides the **computer** with details of power status so that the **computer** can conserve power.

Smart card
▶ plastic **card** the size of a credit **card** that contains an **integrated circuit** which can record and process a limited amount of information.

Smart terminal
▶ **computer terminal** that has some processing capabilities: more than a **dumb terminal** and less than an **intelligent terminal**.

SMDS – Switched media Megabit Data Service
▶ British Telecom's service offering a 10-megabit line which is used by **SUPERJANET** to form a **Virtual Private Network (VPN)**.

Smiley
▶ graphical language for conveying feelings; based on a pun on **baud**/body language. Sometimes called **baudy language** or **emoticon**.

Snail mail
▶ derisory term for the traditional postal service.

Sniffer

▶ **computer program** or device that monitors **data** travelling over a **network** which can be used legitimately or for stealing information.

Socioeconomics

▶ study of social status and economic position.

Sociolinguistics

▶ study of language in terms of its social context.

Sociometrics

▶ study of sociological relationships and preferences within social groups.

Soft font

▶ type **font** that can be transferred to the **memory** of a **printer** from a **computer** rather than being built into the **memory** of the **printer** or plugged in as a **cartridge**. Also called **downloadable font**.

Soft hyphen

▶ **hyphen** that is automatically inserted when a word falls near the end of a line. Sometimes called a **discretionary hyphen**.

Soft return

▶ automatic creation of a line break which is produced by the **software** settings to maintain the **margins**. Differs from a **hard return**.

Soft vocabulary

▶ imprecise terminology which can have multiple interpretations and will probably require synonyms and qualification in developing a **search statement**.

Software

▶ **instructions**, **programs** or a suite of **programs** which are used to direct the operations of a **computer** or other **hardware**.

Software engineering

▶ disciplined approach to **software** development which takes a problem-oriented approach.

Software house

▶ company which develops **computer software** for other organizations.

Software licence

▶ legal agreement between a publisher of a **computer program** and the person who buys it.

Software quality assurance

▶ process that ensures that a piece of **software** is of acceptable quality and meets the different levels of requirements expected.

SOLINET – SOuth eastern LIbrary NETwork

▶ **network** joining over 200 libraries in the southeastern USA, providing shared **data-processing** facilities and **access** to **bibliographic information** and resources.

Solo librarian

▶ a lone individual who runs a library. More commonly called **one-man band** or **one-person library**.

Something before nothing

▶ arranging words in alphabetical order letter by letter, with the space between words being ignored so that words file together. Sometimes called **letter-by-letter** arrangement.

Sorting

▶ arranging the result of a **search** in a specified sequence for either **offline** or **online** printing. The order may be by author, journal name, geographical area, chronological, classified etc.

Sound card
▶ **expansion card** that allows a **computer** to manipulate and **output** sounds. Also called an **audio card**.

Source, The
▶ American **interactive videotex** system which is accessible via **microcomputers** supplied by the Telecomputing Corporation of America.

Source database
▶ **database** that contains source material such as numerical or **full-text** material.

Source document
▶ original **document** from which **data** are prepared in a form acceptable to a **computer**.

Source language
▶ in **machine translation**, refers to the **language** from which **translation** is made.

Source program
▶ **program** written by a **programmer** which has to be translated into a **machine code** so that it can be processed by a **computer**.

Space character
▶ space which results when the space bar is pressed. Sometimes called a **blank character**.

Spamming
▶ sending unwanted junk **E-mail** messages to a large number of **newsgroups** irrespective of interest of the receivers. The intention may be to advertize a product or service or to be malicious or mischievous.

Spatial information system
▶ name given to a system that includes geographical information, global positioning systems, remote sensing and advanced navigational systems etc.

Special classification
▶ **classification scheme** which has limited subject coverage or has been designed for a specific purpose.

Species
▶ in **classification**, one of the **classes** of things into which a **genus** is divided.

Specification
▶ **document** which gives a precise statement of a process or a service requirement.

Specificity
▶ extent to which an **indexing language** or system allows for the precise statement of the subject of the item being indexed.

Spectrum
▶ in **information technology**, the range of electromagnetic frequencies available in **telecommunications**.

Speech recognition
▶ ability of a **computer** system to understand and act on spoken **input**. Sometimes called **voice recognition**.

Speech synthesis
▶ spoken response from a **computer** system where digitally coded information is synthesized to a resemblance of human speech that can be understood. Sometimes called **voice synthesis**.

SpeechBot
▶ **search** tool that listens to **web-resident** audio **programming**, converts the sound into a textual transcript and then **indexes** those words so that the searcher can type in **queries** and receive **hits** that refer to the appropriate section of audio that is relevant.

Spell checker
▶ **application software** that checks words and identifies possible

misspellings; usually forms part of **word-processing** packages.

Spider
▶ type of search **program** that can be used over a network. Usually called a **knowbot**.

Spinner
▶ organization that makes a number of **databases** available for use. Sometimes called a **host, online supplier** or **vendor**.

Split screen
▶ use of a single **screen** to **display** separate sets of **images** or **data**.

Spoofing
▶ impersonating a user or a machine.

Spreadsheet
▶ arrangement of figures in rows or columns with headings for presentation of financial, statistical or other numerical information; used for financial analysis and **forecasting**.

SQL – Structured Query Language
▶ high-level **programming language** designed for searching for information in **relational databases**, usually within a **client-server architecture**.

SQML – Structured Query Markup Language
▶ **query language** developed by IBM based on **relational database management** principles.

Square bracket
▶ generally used in quoted text to indicate text not in the original document. Used in a **cataloguing record** to indicate information that has been added by the cataloguer which does not occur on the item being catalogued.

SR
▶ international **standard** developed by the **International Standards Organization** (**ISO**); a subset of the **Z39.50 application layer protocol** developed in the USA by the National Information Standards Organization.

SRAM – Static RAM
▶ **random access memory** that does not need to be constantly refreshed, unlike dynamic memory. These **chips** are substantially faster but more expensive than **DRAM chips**. Sometimes called **static memory**.

SSI – Small-Scale Integration
▶ **integrated circuit** with fewer than 10 components.

Stack
▶ method of storing **data** in which the most recent item stored is the first to be retrieved. Often called 'last in, first out'.

Staff appraisal
▶ technique of monitoring the performance of individual members of staff.

Staff motivation
▶ involvement of staff in planning or delivery of services, or encouraging staff to seek further training for **professional development**.

Staff orientation
▶ initial training period for new employees to familiarize them with the organization, other staff members, job responsibilities etc.

Staggered window
▶ arrangement of **screen windows** where each **window** overlaps with a previous one so that the **cursor** can be clicked on any **window** without needing to move a **window** out of the way. Sometimes called **cascade window** or **tiling**.

▶ **STAIRS – STorage And Information Retrieval System**
▶ IBM software for information retrieval.

Stakeholder
▶ person or organization that has an interest in a product or service.

Standalone
▶ ability of a piece of equipment to operate independently of any other equipment.

Standalone indexing
▶ traditional indexes that identify the content of material usually in printed format. For example, the index of a book, abstracting service etc.

Standard
▶ guideline or precise statement for a specific activity or product, level of quality or excellence or a measure of adequacy for a specific purpose.

Standard Address Number – SAN
▶ unique number for publishers, libraries and other firms or organizations.

Standard Generalized Markup Language – SGML
▶ standard set of codes for presenting ASCII text files in italics, bold etc. Became the basis for HTML.

Standardization
▶ producing material that conforms to agreed national or international standards.

Standing order
▶ order to supply specified items, series or periodicals on a continual basis until specifically cancelled. Also called continuation order or till forbid order.

Star network
▶ network design that provides separate cable links to the host computer to form a star shape. In this configuration the separate computers are connected only to the central computer and not with each other.

Start bit
▶ in asynchronous transmission, a single bit transmitted before the bits containing data to indicate that a character is to be transmitted next.

State-of-the-art review
▶ comprehensive and detailed survey of a specific subject area, often containing criticism.

Static RAM – SRAM
▶ random access memory that does not need to be constantly refreshed, unlike dynamic memory. These chips are substantially faster but more expensive than DRAM chips.

Statistical bibliography
▶ use of mathematics and statistical techniques to study communication patterns and publishing in the distribution of information; related to scientometrics. Now called bibliometrics.

Statistical database
▶ database that contains statistical information or data.

Statistical inference
▶ conclusion drawn from the results of a statistical sampling activity.

Statistical sampling
▶ applying procedures to fewer than all the items that compose a population; random techniques are used to select the sample population.

STD – Subscriber Trunk Dialling
▶ direct dialling to a distant location by a telephone subscriber.

STI
► abbreviation for scientific and technical information.

STM
► abbreviation for scientific, technical and medical publishing.

Stochastic
► something which is random, unpredictable and constantly varied.

Stochastic model
► mathematical representation of a system that includes the effect of random actions.

Stochastic process
► system that produces a sequence of discrete **symbols** according to certain probabilities.

Stop bit
► in **asynchronous** transmission, one or two **bits** transmitted immediately after the **data bits** that make up each **character**.

Stop list
► list of **terms** that are excluded from a particular **indexing** or **sorting** system as they are considered to be meaningless or not significant for **indexing** purposes.

Stop word
► word that cannot be used for **indexing**.

Storage
► place in a **computer** where **data** are stored for future use.

Storage capacity
► amount of information which a **storage** device can accommodate. Sometimes also called **memory capacity**.

Store and forward
► automated **communication** method where information is sent

from one **computer** to another, either directly or indirectly, via intermediate **computers**.

Story board
► visual plan of a proposed **video**, **film** or slide presentation.

Strategic audit
► **management** review of current use of information resources within an institution which covers relative value of these, perceptions of expected change and staff capabilities.

Strategic information
► information that relates to a business or company and its ability to market its products, make a profit and to plan for future development.

Strategic plan/planning
► coordination of an organization's activities to achieve specific goals and **objectives** in the face of constant change. Allocation of resources to achieve specific goals and **objectives**.

String
► group of items arranged in sequence according to a set of rules; set of consecutive **characters** in a **memory**.

String search
► using a **string** of **terms** to search a **database**.

Strip index
► **index** in which **entries** are made on strips of **card**, allowing for two or three lines of information to be displayed. Also called a **visible index**.

Structured programming
► process of writing a **computer program** in small, independent parts.

Structured query language – SQL
▶ **high-level programming language** designed for searching for information in **relational databases,** usually within a **client-server architecture.**

Style manual
▶ rules developed by a publisher or printer to ensure consistent practice in spelling, **hyphenation,** capitalization etc.

Stylus
▶ electrical device used to send a **machine-readable symbol** to a **computer.** Usually called a **light pen.**

Subdirectory (computing)
▶ collection of **files** in a **computer** system. Some systems call this a **folder.**

Subdivision
▶ process of dividing a subject into more specific areas.

Subfacet
▶ set of **classes** produced using a single **characteristic** of division within a **facet.**

Subheading
▶ secondary **heading** which qualifies a **main heading.**

Subject analysis
▶ process by which **documents, data** and other information carriers are described and represented according to subject content. Sometimes called **subject description** or **subject indexing.**

Subject authority list
▶ list of **subject headings** which have been accepted for use in a **subject catalogue.**

Subject catalogue
▶ **catalogue** arranged alphabetically either by **subject heading** or in classified order.

Subject description
▶ process by which **documents, data** and other information carriers are described and represented according to subject content. Sometimes called **subject analysis** or **subject indexing.**

Subject entry
▶ **entry** in a **subject catalogue** or **index,** where the **access point** is a **subject heading** or a **classification number.**

Subject heading
▶ word or group of words expressing a subject under which all items on that subject are filed in the **catalogue, bibliography** or **index.**

Subject heading list
▶ alphabetical listing of **subject headings** with a **cross-reference** structure of synonyms, **cross-references** to coordinate subjects and downward **references** to more specific subjects.

Subject index
▶ **index** which identifies the subject content of a publication, library etc.

Subject index term
▶ **index term** that is used to identify a **concept** in a specific subject area.

Subject indexing
▶ process by which **documents, data** and other information carriers are described and represented according to subject content. Sometimes called **subject analysis** or **subject description**

Subject profile
▶ list of **terms** and other **search** requirements (authors' names,

language etc.) that defines a user's interests.

Subordinate subject
▶ more specific subject which comes at a lower level in a **hierarchical relationship**.

Subprofessional
▶ staff member who does not have professional qualifications but has significant responsibility under the supervision of professional staff. Sometimes called **paraprofessional**.

Subroutine
▶ part of a **computer program** which contains a set of **instructions** for a particular task.

Subscriber Trunk Sialling – STD
▶ direct dialling to a distant location by a telephone subscriber.

Subscript
▶ small **character** printed below the line.

Subscription
▶ payment usually made annually for a specific service or publication.

Subscription agent
▶ organization or company which supplies a library with specific **periodicals** on a regular basis and handles all financial and other details for the library or **information centre**.

Subsidiary right
▶ author's rights to literary property after its initial publication; could be for a film, **translation** or **serial** publication.

Suite of programs
▶ number of interrelated **programs** which can be **run** consecutively as a single **job**.

Supercomputer
▶ very fast high-capacity **mainframe computer** capable of very complex rapid calculations.

Superfiche
▶ **microfiche** with a reduction of between 50- and 90-fold such that between 190 and 400 images can be placed on an A6 sheet. It is one of the forms in which **computer output microform (COM)** can be produced.

SUPERJANET
▶ high-performance **wide area network** based on **optical fibre** technology that supports higher education and research in the UK. Supercedes **JANET**.

Superordinate subject
▶ more general subject which comes at a higher level in a **hierarchical relationship**.

Superscript
▶ small **character** printed above the line.

Super Video Graphics Array – SVGA
▶ **graphics display** board which offers more colours and better resolution than standard **VGA** (**video graphics array**).

Support staff
▶ staff members who do not have professional qualifications but have significant responsibility under the supervision of professional staff.

Surfing
▶ exploring the resources available on electronic **networks** such as the **Internet**.

SURFnet
▶ The Netherlands' electronic **communications network**.

Surge protector
▶ device that absorbs bursts of excessive voltage coming through a power line to avoid damage to **software** and **hardware**.

Surrogate
▶ **record** of an item in a **file**, so called because the **record** acts as a substitute for the item.

Survey
▶ details of a specific research activity that has been carried out in a systematic manner.

SVGA – Super Video Graphics Array
▶ **graphics display** board which offers more colours and better resolution than standard **VGA** (**video graphics array**).

Switched media Megabit Data Service – SMDS
▶ British Telecom's service offering a 10-**megabit** line used by **SUPERJANET** to form a **virtual private network** (**VPN**).

Switched network
▶ **communications network** that transports information to a number of different destinations according to the **addresses** provided.

Switching
▶ in **telecommunications**, means of interconnecting users, usually carried out by telephone exchanges.

Switching centre
▶ location where multiple **circuits** terminate and incoming messages can be transferred to the appropriate outgoing **circuit**.

Switching language
▶ **indexing language** developed to act as a bridge between two or more **indexing systems** or **thesauri**.

Intermediate index language that makes cross-**database access** easier by mapping users' queries into the specific **query language** of the individual **database**.

SWOT analysis
▶ identification of strengths, weaknesses, opportunities and threats for a particular organization or activity.

Symbol
▶ picture or sign which represents something.

Symbolic language
▶ **computer program** language that must be translated into **machine language** in order to run; usually a **high-level programming language**.

Symbolic logic
▶ system of logical rules and **symbols** to facilitate exact reasoning about non-numerical factual matter and relationships.

Symmetric encryption
▶ type of **encryption** which uses the same **key** both to encrypt and decrypt messages.

Symposia
▶ collection of papers given at a conference; collection of papers on a specific theme.

Synchronization
▶ processing of hooking a **palmtop computer** to the **desktop PC** in order to share **data**.

Synchronizing signal
▶ **signal** that accompanies the **transmission** of **data**, which can be sent by the transmitting station or from a separate source.

Synchronous
▶ simultaneous action or process; constant time between successive events such as the **transmission** of **bits** or **characters**.

Synchronous transmission
▶ method of transmitting **data** where both devices are controlled by the same clock; messages are sent as a continuous string of **characters** without **gaps**.

Syndetic
▶ interconnections within a system; **cross references** in an **index** or **catalogue**.

Syndetic structure
▶ **cross reference** structure provided between **terms** in an **index**. These **references** may cover synonyms, **related terms** and **broader** or **narrower terms**.

Synonymous relationship
▶ words that mean the same thing.

Synopsis
▶ outline of the content of a **document** or the plot of a play, book, opera etc.

Synoptic
▶ concise publication in a **journal** which presents the key ideas and results of a full-length **article**. It includes an **abstract**, diagrams, **references** etc. and is refereed in the normal manner. The full-length **article** is either published elsewhere or subsequently made available from a **repository**.

Synoptic journal
▶ **journal** which publishes **synoptics** rather than full-length **articles**.

Syntatic analysis
▶ **parsing** a sentence and, on the basis of the derived parts of speech, carrying out further analysis.

Syntactic relationship
▶ relationship that arises from the context of subjects in specific items or from the **syntax**; two **concepts** may appear together within one item but not in another.

Syntactics
▶ theory dealing with formal relationships between signs or expressions and the formal properties of language, separate from meaning and interpretation.

Syntax
▶ **1.** computing – grammatical rules applied to a **computer programming language**; **2.** information handling – way in which relationships between **terms** in an **index vocabulary** are displayed, and the rules for the construction of **terms** that have more than one element.

Syntax error
▶ mistake in the formulation of an **instruction** to a **computer**.

Synthetic classification
▶ **classification** in which accidental properties of things classified are used as the arrangement **characteristic**. Sometimes called **artificial classification**.

Synthetic language
▶ language based on a set of rules established before its use. Sometimes called **artificial language**.

System X
▶ computerized **digital** telephone **switching** system developed by British Telecom which provides connection to the **Integrated Services Digital Network (ISDN)**.

Systematic bibliography
▶ enumeration and **classification** of publications; assembling bibliographic entries into a useful and logical order.

Systematic dictionary
▶ dictionary arranged in broad subject areas rather than in straight **alphabetical order**. Also called a **thematic dictionary**.

Systematic order
▶ order of items where the actual order displays subject or form relationships.

Systems analysis
▶ technique for analysing systems and determining the scope for improved efficiency through the introduction of **computers** and new **information technology**.

Systems analyst
▶ **computer** specialist whose main work is to carry out **systems analysis**.

Systems design
▶ translating a **specification** for a **computer** system to a detailed design.

Systems disk
▶ **computer disk** that holds the **operating system** and other systems **software**. It is needed to **boot** the **computer** when starting.

Systems engineer
▶ **computer** specialist who helps organizations to plan, develop and implement their **computer** systems.

Systems flowchart
▶ **flowchart** diagram which represents the relationship between events in a **data-processing** system and describes the flows of **data** though and within the system.

Systems house
▶ business or company which designs **computer** systems.

Systems integration
▶ **computer** system which coordinates **hardware** and **software** from different suppliers in a particular work environment.

Systems integrator
▶ company or individual who builds **computer** systems by putting together **components** made by different **vendors**.

Systems software
▶ **computer software** that runs the **operating system** and all **utility programs** that operate at a low level.

Tt

Tab
▶ word processing key function that moves the cursor to the next tab stop position. Used to create columns in tables.

Table of contents list
▶ list of items and details of their location in a document given at the beginning of a publication. Also called contents list.

Tactile keyboard
▶ keyboard display laid out on a flat surface which is used by touching the keys with the fingers.

Tactile sensation
▶ information gained through touch that is of use to designers and manufacturers of keyboards, joysticks etc.

Tag
▶ character or digit attached to a record or field; additional information added to items of data to characterize its type or field. Sometimes called a flag.

Talking book
▶ book recorded on tape, designed for blind or partially sighted people. Also called audio book.

Talking newspaper
▶ tape cassette containing news, magazine articles, sport etc., designed for blind or partially sighted people. Also called audio newspaper.

Tape cassette
▶ video tape or audio tape in a container which can be inserted into a camera, projector or reading device.

Tape drive
▶ device for winding and rewinding magnetic tape.

Tape recorder
▶ machine that records signals and data on to magnetic tape.

Tape streamer
▶ magnetic tape drive used as a back-up to a magnetic disk.

Target disk
▶ disk on to which a user copies information.

Target language
▶ in machine translation, the language into which a document is to be translated.

Tariff
▶ charges made for the use of facilities provided by a common carrier.

Task
▶ whatever an individual or a computer is set to do; refers to a single job or a component of a job, rather than to the entire workload.

Task switching
▶ ability of an operating system or operating environment to enable a

user to switch from one **program** to another without losing the place in the first **program**.

Taxonomy
▶ science of **classification**; the study of names and the naming of **generic** assemblies.

Tbit – TeraBit
▶ in engineering one million million; in computing number closest to a million million **bits**: 1 099 511 600 000.

Tbps – terabits per second
▶ one million million bits per second.

TCP/IP – Transmission Control Protocol
▶ **Internet host**-to-**host protocol** that allows **computers** which are dissimilar to connect to the **network**.

Teamware
▶ **computer software** that allows colleagues, especially in different locations, to collobarate on projects using the **Internet** and the **World Wide Web**.

Tear sheet
▶ page or pages torn or extracted from a printed publication.

Technical report
▶ publication that describes the current status of research, specific activity or investigations in a scientific or technological area.

Technical services
▶ all procedures relating to obtaining, organizing and processing library material to make it ready for use.

Technological change
▶ developments in systems and services that must be considered when planning future developments.

Technological gatekeeper
▶ individual in an organization who keeps up with technology and brings relevant details to the attention of colleagues.

Technological innovation
▶ new development that can improve a process or service.

Technology transfer
▶ taking systems and services from one country to another and ideally applying them in an appropriate manner useful to that country.

Technostress
▶ stress that individuals experience when faced with technology that they find difficult to use or understand.

TEDIS – Trade Electronic Data Interchange System
▶ action plan drawn up by the European Community to popularize **electronic data interchange** (**EDI**).

Telco
▶ abbreviation for **telecommunications** company.

Teldata
▶ Danish **videotex** system.

Telecom Australia
▶ Australian **telecommunications** agency.

Telecom Gold
▶ British Telecom's **electronic mail** service.

Telecommunications
▶ generally any form of **signal transmission**, specifically the **transmission** and reception of **data** in the form of electromagnetic **signals**, using **broadcast** radio or **transmission** lines.

Telecommunications network
► physically dispersed **computers** connected by **telecommunication channels.** Sometimes called **communication network.**

Telecommuter
► individual who works from home using a **computer** and **telecommunications** to provide an electronic link with the office.

Telecommuting
► use of **computer, fax** and other office tools at home so that an individual can work at home rather than in the office. Sometimes called **teleworking.**

Teleconferencing
► facility for holding a meeting that is controlled by a **computer,** which allows people in different locations both to see and talk to each other directly. Sometimes called **computer conferencing.**

Telecopier
► device for **facsimile transmission.**

Telecottage
► name for a home when work is done from home rather than an office using **computers, fax, networks** etc.

Teledata
► Norwegian **videotex** system.

Telefacsimile
► full name of a message sent by **fax.**

Telefax
► photocopying machines linked together for image transmission; West German and French **facsimile transmission** service.

Telefax 201
► Dutch **facsimile transmission** service.

Teleglobe Canada
► Canadian government organization for overseas **telecommunications.**

Telegraph
► method of transmitting electrical **signals,** using simple on-off conventions to provide the **code.**

TelE-mail
► American **electronic mail** system.

Telemarketing
► selling products via the telephone.

Telematics
► synthesis or **convergence** of several disciplines such as **telecommunications, information processing** and **office technology.** Sometimes used as a synonym for **information technology.**

Telemetry
► transmission of **data** to and from a remote piece of equipment which is used for measuring, such as a weather **satellite.**

Telenet
► American **packet-switched telecommunications network.**

Teleordering
► ordering material using a communication system, e.g. **Internet.** Usually called **E-commerce.**

Telepack
► American **telecommunications** service combining voice and **data channels.**

Telepen
► electronic **bar-code** reader.

Telephotography
► name in the USA for the **transmission** of news pictures using **facsimile transmission.**

Telepresence
▶ use of a special headset to send and receive information about a situation or problem. The headset contains a camera, microphone, speaker and a small **display screen**.

Teleprinter
▶ printer used to send and receive **telex** messages via the telephone line.

Teleprocessing
▶ **data processing** and **transmission** using **computers** and **telecommunications channels**.

Telesat
▶ Canadian **communications satellite**.

Teleset
▶ Finnish **videotex** system.

Teleshopping
▶ the use of **interactive videotex** to select goods for purchase and to place orders.

Telesoftware
▶ **computer software** transmitted via **videotex**.

Télésystème
▶ French **host** system.

Télétel
▶ French **videotex** system.

Teletex
▶ **CCITT** name for a system which transmits **data** between **terminals**.

Teletext
▶ **generic** name for a one-way **broadcast** information service which displays information using text and simple **graphics** on a television **screen**.

Teleworking
▶ office work done from home rather than the workplace using **home**

computers and **telecommunications** to provide an electronic link to the office. Sometimes called **remote working** or **telecommuting**.

Telex
▶ world-wide **telegraphic** service established by Western Union which permits interconnection between **teleprinters**.

Telidon
▶ Canadian **videotex** system.

Telnet
▶ standard **TCP/IP protocol** for remote **terminal** connection service.

Template
▶ plastic or paper diagram that can be placed over the **keyboard** to show the different functions of **keys**; sheet of plastic with **command** boxes and **menus** that can be used with a **digitizing tablet**; in **spreadsheets** and **database applications**, a blank form which shows what **fields** exist; a style sheet that can be used in **word processing**.

Tera
▶ prefix that stands for the number one million million.

Terabit – Tb
▶ in engineering one million million bits, in computing number closest to a million million: 1 099 511 600 000.

Terabits per second – Tbps
▶ one million million **bits** per second.

Term
▶ word or group of words that is used to identify subject content of material.

Term co-occurrence
▶ words used to identify subject content that occur together in **documents**.

Term entry system
▶ postcoordinate indexing system in which each card represents a concept; numbers that represent documents which deal with that concept are posted on the card. Sometimes called item on term system.

Term frequency
▶ words used to identify subject content that occur frequently in material that has been found as the result of a search. The material with the most terms will probably be judged to have higher relevance.

Term relationship
▶ identification of precise relationship of one term to another, i.e. broader, narrower or related.

Term weighting
▶ giving a value to terms used in a search statement, whereby the highest value or weight is given to those terms considered the most useful or relevant to the search request.

Terminal
▶ device for sending and/or receiving data over a communication channel, which usually has a keyboard and a visual display unit (VDU).

Terminal adapter
▶ device that connects a computer to an external digital communications line such as an ISDN line.

Terminal digit system
▶ entering document numbers on Uniterm cards according to their final digits so as to ensure a random scatter of numbers across the face of the card and thus facilitate the scanning which is necessary with this kind of postcoordinate system.

Terminal emulator
▶ making a computer respond like a particular type of computer which allows access to a mainframe computer or bulletin board service with a personal computer.

Terminal server
▶ device that connects terminals or other equipment to a local area network.

Terminate and Stay Resident – TSR
▶ DOS computer programs which stay in the memory such as a calculator, clock, thesaurus etc.

Tertiary education
▶ commonly accepted as formal academic education obtained after secondary level education, usually through a university or other college of higher education. Usually called higher education.

Tertiary material
▶ publication which reviews and evaluates material on a specific subject; bibliography or catalogue that provides a guide to material on a specific subject.

TeX
▶ macro processor that promotes complete control over typographical formatting.

Tex
▶ program devised by D.E. Knuth which allows text including mathematics to be input at a computer terminal.

Text box
▶ in Windows, rectangles where information can be entered by the user.

Text database/file
▶ database which contains the text of original documents.

Text database management system
▶ software that combines word-processing functions with a database management system (DBMS).

Text editing
▶ editing text on a computer.

Text editor
▶ program provided as part of an operating system or with a programming language which is used to enter and amend source programs or text files.

Text file
▶ data file consisting of characters that can be read by a standard word processor.

Text flow/wrap
▶ word-processing feature that allows for a diagram or a picture to be surrounded by text.

Text management system
▶ file containing both text and data which combines the search ability of a database with word-processing capability.

Text processing
▶ computer editing and production of textual material; often used as a synonym for word processing and for text management (including systems for storing and retrieving text).

Text-processing system
▶ computerized system designed to edit and manipulate text, which is then output in a specified medium and format.

Text retrieval
▶ retrieval of actual document text rather than a bibliographic reference.

Text-retrieval system
▶ computerized system that allows the retrieval of documents.

Text TV
▶ Swedish teletext system.

TFT – Thin Film Transistor screen technology
▶ technology used for high-quality images on laptop computer monitors and flat-panel displays.

Thematic dictionary
▶ dictionary arranged in broad subject areas rather than in straight alphabetical order. Also called systematic dictionary.

Thermal printer
▶ printer that produces images by pushing electronically heated pins against special heat-sensitive paper.

Thermography
▶ any printing process which uses heat.

Thesaurofacet
▶ faceted classification which has a structured thesaurus as an index.

Thesaurus
▶ vocabulary of controlled indexing terms organized so that relationships between concepts are explicit. A thesaurus provides vocabulary control by giving the index terms to be used, grammatical form, spelling, use of singular and plural etc., synonymous relationships, use of proper names and definition of terms. A thesaurus may be arranged in alphabetical order or it may have a systematic or classification arrangement.

Thesaurus display
▶ presentation of a thesaurus which shows the term relationships and the tree structure.

Thesaurus maintainance
▶ process of keeping a **thesaurus** up-do-date by adding new **terms**, establishing **term relationships**, etc.

Thesis
▶ treatise prepared as part of an academic study leading to a higher degree. Also called a **dissertation**.

Thin film transitor screen technology – TFT
▶ technology used for high-quality **images** on **laptop computer monitors** and **flat-panel displays**.

Third-generation computer
▶ **computer** developed in the late 1960s using **integrated circuits**.

Third World
▶ countries in Africa, Asia, Far East and Latin America which are considered to be underdeveloped.

Throughput
▶ amount of work processed during a specified time period.

Throwaway
▶ free **newspaper** containing mainly advertisements that is designed to be thrown away.

Throwout
▶ page which folds out from a book or a journal. Sometimes called a **foldout** or **gatefold**.

Thumbnail
▶ miniature **graphic** representation of an **image** which can be used to view **graphics** or **files** before they are opened or printed.

Tic Tac
▶ French **viewdata** system.

TIDA
▶ Spanish **data communications network**.

Tiling
▶ arrangements of **windows** in a graphical **interface** system so that they do not overlap. Sometimes called **cascade window**.

Till forbid order
▶ order to supply specified items, **series** or **periodicals** on a continual basis until specifically cancelled. Also called **continuation order** or **standing order**.

Time and motion study
▶ systematic analysis of the time spent and the actions taken in the performance of a specific **task**.

Time management
▶ effective use of time to gain maximum advantage of time spent on a specific **task**.

Time out
▶ time when a **computer** automatically logs off if no **input** received.

Time sharing
▶ sharing of **computer** time between a number of users by high-speed **switching** of processing time.

Timeliness
▶ feature of information delivery which means it is provided as it is needed by a user.

Title catalogue
▶ **catalogue** arranged alphabetically consisting of titles of works.

Title entry
▶ **entry** under the title of work in a **catalogue** or **index**.

Title page
▶ right-hand (**recto**) page of a printed book which carries full title, author and publisher details.

Toggle
▶ on-off switch that allows a user the choice of two alternatives.

Token Ring
▶ method of controlling traffic on a **local area network** (**LAN**).

Tomography
▶ medical **imaging** technique in which a sequence of x-ray **images** are used to build up a three-dimensional representation.

Toner
▶ special type of ink used in copying machines and **laser printers**.

Tool
▶ different kinds of **software** which help the **programmer** to construct correct and efficient **programs**.
A collection of such **software** is sometimes called a **toolkit**.

Toolbox
▶ collection of **icons** displayed on a **computer screen** that represent frequently used **commands**.

Toolkit
▶ collection of different types of **software** which are used by a **programmer** to construct correct and efficient **programs**.

Top term
▶ in a **thesaurus**, the broadest term used in a **hierarchical relationship**; top of a **genus** listing.

Top-down management
▶ **management** style in which decisions and directives are made by high-level staff and passed on to lower-level staff with little or no input from the lower level.

Top-down programming
▶ **computer programming** technique which defines the overall outlines of a **program** first and fills in the details later.

Topographical catalogue
▶ **catalogue** of books or geographical names relating to places.

Topographical index
▶ **index** of books relating to places.

Topology
▶ physical layout of a **network**; the way in which the **transmission** media are interconnected to form a complete system.

Total Quality Management – TQM
▶ comprehensive method of **management** which covers people, recruitment, **staff development** and training, systems and processes. It is often used to move an organization to develop new ways of doing things.

Touch pad
▶ flat device that senses when it is touched; used to control a **cursor** or switch a device on or off.

Touch-screen terminal
▶ **terminal** with a **screen** that is sensitive to touch; the positions touched are recorded by the **computer** as coded **signals** for **data input**.

Touch sensor
▶ **computer** controlled **robot** that has a sense of touch which allows it to manipulate small objects or move about a room.

Tower
▶ **hardware** that contains a number of stacked **CD-ROM drives**.

Tracing
▶ record of all entry **headings** generated by a **document** in a particular **catalogue**, usually kept attached to the **main entry**.

Track
▶ **path** along which a sequence of **signals** can be impressed on a recording **medium**.

Tracker ball
▶ device used to control and send information in a graphics **workstation** or a **personal computer**; pointing device which could be described as an upside down **mouse**. Sometimes called a **rollerball**.

Trade discount
▶ **discount** allowed by a publisher to a **wholesaler** or retail bookshop.

Trade name
▶ legally protected name given by a manufacturer to a particular product.

Trade press
▶ publication aimed at a specific trade or business area.

Trademark
▶ legally protected design used by a manufacturer to identify a particular product; unique printing mark which identifies an individual company.

Tradicoms
▶ British **electronic data interchange (EDI) standard** for the **transmission** of commercial messages in the **book trade** for the **transmission** of orders and invoices.

Traffic
▶ messages which pass through a **communication system**.

Training
▶ developing skills, awareness and expertise of professional and non-professional staff to enable them to undertake specific **tasks**.

Transactional analysis
▶ scientific study of individual or group behaviour when communicating with other individuals or groups.

Transactions
▶ published records of a meeting, usually containing **abstracts** or text of papers presented. Also called **conference proceedings**.

Transborder data flow
▶ electronic transfer of **data** or information across national boundaries; owing to regulations it is often more restricted than **communication** within national geographical areas. Also called **cross-border dataflow**.

Transceiver
▶ **terminal** which can transmit and receive information.

Transducer
▶ generally a device for converting energy from one form to another. In **information technology**, an **input** or **output** device designed to convert **signals** from one medium to another.

Transfer file
▶ **file** that carries **data** from one processing stage to another.

Transfer rate
▶ speed at which **data** can be transferred from one **peripheral** device to another.

Transistor
▶ electronic device made of **semiconducting material** which can be used to amplify or switch **signals**.

Translation
▶ **document** that has been transferred from the original language to another language.

Translation right
▶ permission to translate a publication from one language to another.

Transliteration
▶ transcribing the **characters** of one language into the **characters** of another.

Transmission
▶ generally the electrical or electromagnetic transfer of energy. In **information technology**, usually refers to the transfer of **data signals** from one point to another.

Transmission speed
▶ rate at which **data** is sent and received which is usually expressed as a **baud rate**.

Transient voltage
▶ fluctuation in standard power voltage which could be caused by a **brownout** or **power surge** that could damage **computer hardware** or **software**.

Translator (computing)
▶ **computer program** that can convert from one **programming language** to another.

Transpac
▶ French **packet-switching telecommunications network**.

Transparent
▶ **computer** activity that is not seen by the operator.

Transponder
▶ device that both receives and transmits **data**.

Transport layer
▶ in **open systems interconnection** (**OSI**), **layer 4** which is responsible for end-to-end communications.

Transputer
▶ complete **computer** on a single **integrated circuit** especially designed to run with others in a **parallel processing** environment.

Tree network
▶ **computer network** arranged along separate lines which are connected to the main **cable** similar to the branches of a tree.

Tree-and-branch filing system
▶ **computer filing** system where all **files** are stored in **directories** similar to **folders** in **filing** cabinets.

Tree structure
▶ **hierarchical** system used in **indexing** and **classification** to organize material from a general (root) to a specific (**branch** and leaf) concept.

Triple X – XXX
▶ **protocol standards** such as **X.3/X.28/X.29** used in an **X.25** network.

Trojan horse
▶ destructive **computer program** that masquerades as a benign application. Unlike **viruses**, it does not replicate itself but claims to get rid of **viruses** while it introduces them into the **computer** system.

Troubleshoot
▶ look for and locate the possible source of a **hardware** or **software** problem so that it can be corrected.

Truncation
▶ shortening or cutting off part of a **search term** so that it can be matched against other **terms** with the same stem or root; it may **left-hand** or **right-hand truncation**, i.e. letters cut from the beginning or end of the word.

Trunk
▶ **telecommunications channel** that carries **signals** between **switching** centres, usually over long distances.

Trunk exchange
▶ British exchange which controls the **switching** of **trunk** calls.

Truth table
▶ table used by **programmers** to write **computer programs** which

finds out whether a statement is true or false.

TSR – Terminate and Stay Resident
▶ **computer program** which stays in the **memory** such as a calculator, clock, **thesaurus** etc.

TT – Top Term
▶ in a **thesaurus**, the broadest **term** in a **hierarchical relationship**; top of a **genus** listing.

Tube
▶ originally a short term for the **cathode ray tube**, but now often used as a synonym for **screen**.

TULIP
▶ early experiment designed by Elsevier Scientific Publishers and 15 American institutions of higher education involving **bitmapped** page **images** from 45 **journals** in materials science.

Turing test
▶ test named after Alan Turing who broke the Enigma **code** that is used in **artificial intelligence**. Human operators communicate from a **remote terminal** to determine if a **computer** or a human being is responding.

Turnaround time
▶ time required to reverse the direction of a **transmission**; time between submitting a **job** to a **computer** and getting the results back.

Turnkey system
▶ complete computerized system installed by a single supplier who takes total responsibility for the production, installation and operation of all the **hardware** and **software.**

Turtle
▶ **pointer** that moves across the **computer screen** leaving a trail which can be used to draw **pictures**.

Tutorial
▶ **computer program** intended to guide a learner in the use of a **program**.

Tymnet
▶ American **packet-switched telecommunications network** operated by Tymshare Inc.

Typeface
▶ specifically-named type style.

Typography
▶ art of designing type for printing; arrangement or general appearance of typographical material.

Tweaking
▶ making small changes to fine-tune **software** or **hardware**.

Twisted pair cable
▶ **cable** that has two independently insulated wires that are twisted together. One carries the **signal** while the other is grounded and absorbs **signal** interference. Superseded by **coaxial cables** and **fibre-optic cables**.

Two-tier architecture
▶ **client/server computer** architecture in which the user **interface** runs on the **client** while the **database** is stored on the **server**.

Type size
▶ height of **capital letters** in a type **font**, usually measured in point units.

Uu

U – Use/Use instruction
▶ in a **thesaurus**, indicates that a synonym is the **preferred term** and should be used instead of the one selected.

U-matic
▶ **video cassette** produced by Sony.

UAP – Universal Availability of Publication
▶ International Federation of Library Associations and Institutions (IFLA) programme aimed at making publications as widely available as possible to users wherever needed as an essential element in economic, social, educational and personal development.

UBC – Universal Bibliographic Control
▶ programme that calls for making basic **bibliographic descriptions** of all publications issued in a specific country universally and promptly available in an internationally acceptable form.

UDC – Universal Decimal Classification
▶ system developed from the **Decimal Classification** which attempts to treat all fields of knowledge as a unified pattern of interrelated subjects; maintained by the International Federation for Information and Documentation (FID) based in The Hague.

UF – Used for/Used for instruction
▶ in a **thesaurus**, indicates that the term used is the **preferred term** and is used instead of other **terms** that are listed.

UHF – ultra-high frequency
▶ radio **frequency** that operates between 300 and 3000 **megahertz,** which allows large amounts of **data** to be transmitted.

ULSI – Ultra-Large-Scale Integration
▶ **microprocessors** with approximately 100 000 **components**.

Ultrafiche
▶ **microfiche** with such small **images** that 3000 pages can be mounted on one 4 × 6 inch fiche.

Ultrasonic
▶ sound that is over 20 **kilocycles** per second and too high to be heard by the human ear.

Ultrasonics
▶ technology involving the use of **ultrasonic** waves.

Umbrella information provider
▶ in **viewdata**, an **information provider** who provides services to other **information providers**.

Unbundling
▶ in the buying and selling of **computers,** separation of charges for **hardware** and **software**.

Underground press
▶ publishing press which prints, in secret, material usually aimed at overthrowing a government or other authority, or promoting subversive or unacceptable political views. Sometimes called **alternative publication**.

Underrun
▶ shortage in the number of copies printed.

Uncertainty
▶ measure of how imprecise information is handled by **expert systems** and **decision support systems**.

Uncontrolled vocabulary
▶ **index**ing system where **terms** used to **index** material have not been controlled by synonyms or **term relationships**.

UNESCO coupon
▶ scheme for providing coupons that can be used as foreign currency payment for educational, scientific and cultural material.

Unexpurgated edition
▶ **full text** of a work which may contain objectionable material.

Unicode
▶ term used by Joe Becker of Xerox in 1987 to define a unique universal **character**-encoding **standard** which represents multilingual **character sets** using a 16-**bit** code for a total of 65 536 **characters**.

Uniform title
▶ distinctive title of a work that has appeared under a number of different titles which is used in a **catalogue** as an **access point**.

Uniform Resource Characteristic – URC
▶ method of encoding **Internet** resources including types of **uniform resource identifier (URI)** and based on **Standard General Markup Language (SGML)**.

Uniform Resource Identifier – URI
▶ general way of addressing resources available on a **network**, including **URLs** and **URNs** via the **World Wide Web**.

Uniform Resource Locator – URL
▶ location or **address** for a resource available on a **network** via the **World Wide Web**.

Uniform Resource Name/Number – URN
▶ proposed way of describing resources available on the **Internet** that is based on content rather than location. This would overcome the problem of constantly changing **URLs**.

UNIMARC – UNIversal MAchine-Readable Cataloguing
▶ **standard format** which specifies **tags**, **fields** etc. to be used in **bibliographic records** supplied in **machine-readable** form.

Union catalogue
▶ **catalogue** showing the items held by a number of libraries, who may be members of a **network** or **cooperative**.

Unit entry
▶ standard **catalogue** entry that provides full details of the item which can be used in different sections of the **catalogue** by adding different **headings**, such as author's name, **classification notation**, **subject headings** etc.

Uniterm

▶ identification of subject content by the use of single words as **index** terms.

Uniterm card

▶ **index** system where a **document** number is written on separate **cards** which each carry a single **subject heading**.

Uniterm indexing

▶ system of **indexing** developed by Mortimer Taube which uses a single term to describe **documents**. These **uniterms** are then used to retrieve **documents**.

Universal Availability of Publications – UAP

▶ International Federation of Library Associations and Institutions (IFLA) programme aimed at making publications as widely available as possible to users wherever needed as an essential element in economic, social, educational and personal development.

Universal Bibliographic Control – UBC

▶ programme which calls for making basic **bibliographic descriptions** of all publications issued in a specific country universally and promptly available in an internationally acceptable form.

Universal character set

▶ facility on a **printer** which permits any **standard typeface** to be chosen when printing a **document**.

Universal Decimal Classification – UDC

▶ system developed from the **Decimal Classification** which treats all fields of knowledge as a unified pattern of interrelated subjects; it is maintained by the International Federation for Information and Documentation (FID) based in The Hague.

Universal Product Code – UPC

▶ **bar code** used in the USA which is compatible with the **European Article Number**.

Universal serial bus – USB

▶ **standard** for connecting **peripherals** to **personal computers** quickly and easily.

UNIX

▶ **operating system** which is a general-purpose multiuser interactive system written in **C**.

Unjustified text

▶ printing style which has equal word spaces, resulting in lines of text being of different lengths so that the right-hand **margin** is uneven.

Updating

▶ **1.** generally – adding current information to a publication or a **file 2.** computing – adding recent additions to a **database** as a normal process of **file** maintenance. In evaluating a service it may be necessary to know how often it is updated.

Upgrade

▶ new version **software** or **hardware** designed to replace an older version, usually incorporating improvements.

Uploading

▶ process of transferring **data** or information held in a local **computer** system to a remote **computer** with a larger **storage** capacity.

Upper case

▶ capital letters as opposed to **lower case** or small letters.

Upsizing

▶ **1.** computing – moving from a smaller **computer** configuration to a larger and usually more expensive one; **2.** management – moving from a lower-level, usually less expensive, system to a larger and usually more expensive one.

Upward reference
▶ direction from a less specific to a more specific **subject heading** in a **catalogue** or **index**; in a **thesaurus** the reference from a **narrower term** to a **broader term**.

Upwards compatibility
▶ ability of a system to run **files** created by an older **software** version by a later version.

Usability
▶ success or otherwise of a **computer** system to fulfil its functions to meet user requirements.

USB – Universal Serial Bus
▶ **standard** for connecting **peripherals** to **personal computers** quickly and easily.

Use – U/Use instruction
▶ in a **thesaurus**, indicates that a synonym is the **preferred term** and should be used instead of the one selected.

Used for instruction/Used for/UF
▶ in a **thesaurus**, indicates that the term is the **preferred term** and is used instead of other **terms** that are listed.

Used term
▶ **term** selected to be used in an **index** as opposed to other **terms** that have not been selected.

USENET
▶ European name for the worldwide **network** of **computers**; service that transmits news.

User aid
▶ tool that assists a user in the **search** process: could be a **manual**, **thesaurus**, list of **subject headings** etc.

User behaviour
▶ how users of a system or service respond when using. Often studied to identify system or service improvements.

User education
▶ formal instruction for users and potential users of library and **information services**; information programme that shows users the sources and services available in a library or **information centre** so that they can use them effectively. In the USA called **bibliographic instruction**.

User expectation
▶ what a user expects of a system or service.

User feedback
▶ users' comments on and reaction to a system or service; often collected to identify system or service improvements.

User-friendly
▶ any service, system or other facility that is easy to learn and to use.

User group
▶ group of individuals who have a common interest and can be provided with information as a group rather than individually.

User interest profile
▶ definition of the information needs of an individual expressed as a series of **index** headings.

User interface
▶ **interactive system** that allows the user to communicate with a **computer** system while having little or no knowledge of system complexity.

User need
▶ what a user requires from a system or service.

User profile
▶ details of user's requirements from a system or service.

User satisfaction
▶ degree to which a system or service meets the needs of the user; details often collected to identify system or service improvements.

User study
▶ study of users within a particular **discipline** or those using a particular system or service.

User training
▶ training users to use a particular system or service.

User's knowledge
▶ information held, understood and available for use in the brain of the person with the information need, which is added to when the information **search** generates additional information.

Userkit
▶ device for improving and simplifying **access** to **online information retrieval systems** which enables **search statements** to be prepared before going **online**; provides **access** to international systems using stored **host addresses, passwords** and **logon** sequences.

Utility
▶ **software package** of general usefulness which can be incorporated into other **programs** or used in conjunction with them. In the USA publicly available **information services** are sometimes described as **information utilities**.

Utility program/software
▶ **program** usually supplied as part of a **software** package or a **computer** system that performs a particular maintenance or **housekeeping routine**. It may perform such simple tasks as **disk** formatting, copying **files** from one **disk** to another etc. Also called a **service program**.

Vv

V series recommendation
▶ series of recommendations covering various aspects of **data communication** over **networks**, including **transmission speed,** operational mode etc., which are endorsed by the **Consultative Committee for International Telephone and Telegraph (CCITT).**

Vaccine
▶ **software program** residing in the **memory** which watches for **virus** activity by noting **file access** and **programs** that are loaded.

Vade mecum
▶ guide, **handbook** or **manual** which can be carried for reference purposes.

Validation
▶ checking that values are within an accepted range and that there are no mistakes.

Validity
▶ extent to which repeated **applications** of a process obtain the same result.

Value
▶ in computing numbers, dates, names, etc. on a **cell** in a **spreadsheet.**

Value-added common carrier
▶ **common carrier** that does not establish **telecommunications links** but leases them from other **carriers.**

Value-added network – VAN
▶ service that uses **common carrier networks** for **transmission** and provides additional services using separate additional equipment, such as **store and forward message switching, terminal** and **host interfaces.**

Value-added service
▶ service that provides information and expands or quantifies it, or evaluates its **relevance.**

Variable
▶ aspect that is susceptible to change.

VBNS – Very high Bandwidth Network System
▶ **network** being developed in the USA. Not intended for general use, it will be used for **network** research and very high-tech science.

VCR
▶ video cassette recorder developed by Philips, now replaced by **V2000 format.**

VDT – Visual Display Terminal
▶ originally this meant an **online display** but it is often used as a synonym for a **visual display unit** (VDU).

VDU – Visual Display Unit
▶ device equipped with a **cathode ray tube** for the visual **display** of information. Usually connected to a **keyboard** for **inputting** and editing information.

Vector
► **1.** computing – **pointer** that refers to a component part of an **image** that is represented in terms or dimensions or coordinates, such as **pixels** on an **image**; **2.** research – mathematical term for a one-dimensional **array** or list.

Vector graphics
► **computer graphics** that use line drawing **displays** which are used in **computer-aided design**.

Velotype
► **keyboard** design which requires minimum hand movement, which increases keying speed.

Vendor
► organization which makes a number of **databases** available for use. Sometimes called a **host**, **online supplier** or **spinner**.

Venn diagram
► diagram representing the terms of a precise statement which are shown by overlapping circles.

Verification
► checking of **data** which has been copied from one source to another to identify mistakes.

Veronica – Very Easy Rodent-Oriented Internet-wide Index to Computer Access
► early **search** tool developed for Internet searching.

Verso
► back of a right-hand page (**recto**); a left-hand page of a printed book.

Vertical file
► cabinet with a number of drawers used to store **cuttings, pamphlets,** correspondence etc., usually stored in folders.

Vertical scrolling
► movement of text on a **screen** one line at a time up or down the **screen**.

Very high Bandwidth Network System – VBNS
► **network** being developed in the USA. Not intended for general use, it will be used for **network** research and very high tech science.

Very high frequency – VHF
► **frequency** range between 30 and 300 **megaHertz** used for local radio and **cellular telephone** networks.

Very large-scale integration – VLSI
► **electronic circuits** constructed on a single **chip** with a complexity from over 10 000 **transistors** up to 100 000 **transistors**.

Very low frequency – VLF
► **frequency** range below 30 000 **hertz**.

VGA – Video Graphics Array
► **standard** for the display of information on the screen of the **personal computer** (**PC**) developed by **IBM**, now superseded by **SVGA**.

VHF – Very High Frequency
► **frequency** range between 30 and 300 **megaHertz** used for local radio and **cellular telephone** networks.

VHS – Video Home System
► **video cassette** system developed by JVC.

Video
► general term implying a **visual display**. Often used to mean a **video cassette**.

Video bandwidth
► maximum rate at which **dots** of illumination such as **phosphor dots** can be displayed on a **screen**.

Video camera
▶ camera that records **images** on **magnetic tape** which can be played back on a **video recorder.**

Video cassette
▶ device for visual recording (especially of television programmes) on to **magnetic tape** contained in a plastic housing.

Video cassette recorder
▶ machine connected to a television set which can be used to record both sound and pictures on **magnetic tape.** Also called a **video recorder.**

Video conferencing
▶ method of providing audio and visual communication between remote sites in order to conduct a conference. Sometimes called **teleconferencing.**

Video disk
▶ **disk** on which visual **images** are electronically recorded. Sound may or not be included.

Video game
▶ game controlled by a **computer** in which the **computer** may oppose the human player. It typically uses fast animated **graphics** and synthesized sound. Sometimes called **computer game.**

Video Graphics Array – VGA
▶ **standard** for the display of information on the screen of the **personal computer** (PC) developed by **IBM,** now superseded by **SVGA.**

Video home system – VHS
▶ **video cassette** system developed by JVC.

Video player
▶ machine connected to a television set which can be used to play but not record **videos.**

Video Random Access Memory – VRAM
▶ fast **computer memory chips** that are used to store **images** to be displayed on a **computer screen.**

Video recorder
▶ machine connected to a television set which can be used to record both sound and pictures on **magnetic tape.** Also called a **video cassette recorder.**

Videophone/video telephone
▶ telephone that displays a picture of the person making the call. Sometimes called **picture telephone.**

Videotel
▶ Italian **videotex** system.

Videotex
▶ generic name for systems that can display text on a television **screen.** Information may be either **broadcast,** such as **CEEFAX** and **ORACLE** in the UK, or transmitted over telephone lines.

Videotext
▶ West German and Swiss **teletext** system. Sometimes used for or confused with **videotex.**

Viditel
▶ Dutch **viewdata** system.

Vidon
▶ Canadian **viewdata** system.

Viewdata
▶ information system that transmits text over the telephone to a television **screen,** allowing users to interact with the system for such activities as **teleshopping.** Hong Kong **videotex** system.

Viewtel
▶ American **viewdata** system.

Viewtel 202
▶ British **viewdata** system.

VIRIS – Visual Information Retrieval InterfaceS
▶ visual **access** tool that allows the user to use the **mouse** to **click** on to **dots** in two-dimensional space which represents **document** content to retrieve either a **document** summary or **full text**.

Virtual community
▶ **online** facility with a commercial orientation which is built around a specific focus and which integrates content and **communication** to provide **access** to a broad range of published information and advertisements.

Virtual distributed catalogue
▶ **catalogue** where there is no one central **catalogue** but a number of **catalogues** that can be searched as though they are a single **catalogue** using **Z39.50 client software**.

Virtual electronic library
▶ group of **web sites** (usually academically oriented) each dealing with a specific subject that is updated and maintained by volunteers. They are organized hierarchically with **hyperlinks** used to located the cited **document**. Ongoing initiative of the American Committee on Institutional Cooperation (CIC) whereby the 13 participating libraries and their users will have seamless **access** to the total information resources of libraries, plus **access** to all other resources available worldwide.

Virtual environment
▶ **application** of **virtual reality** to support teaching and learning by providing a realistic environment to give practical experience of a situation while remaining in the classroom.

Virtual library
▶ library which has its resources extended through **access** to **bibliographic data, full text, images** and other information that exists in **electronic format**. It can integrate internal and external resources from **information providers, database services**, other libraries etc.

Virtual memory
▶ linking of the main **memory** of a **computer** with external **storage** in such a way that they can function as one **memory** with a larger **capacity**. Sometimes called **virtual storage**.

Virtual morality
▶ name given to responsible **guidelines** for appropriate use of information in **cyberspace**. Sometimes called **cyberethics**.

Virtual organization
▶ organization which **outsources** some business activities; conceptual organization which is abstract and exists in the minds of those involved; organization built using virtual links using **information technology**.

Virtual path
▶ location of a **directory** or **file** on a **host** as observed by a remote user accessed via the **World Wide Web**.

Virtual private network – VPN
▶ private **network** maintained by a public telephone company on behalf of an organization which is capable of sophisticated systems of **encryption** to ensure that only authorized users have **network access**.

Virtual reality
▶ **computer** generation of realistic three-dimensional artificial worlds in which humans, usually equipped with head-mounted three-dimensional **displays**, interactive

gloves and possibly whole-body suits, can be immersed in surroundings which they are free to explore and interact with in **real time**, using natural skills such as looking at something from different angles, moving, pointing, grasping, listening and talking.

Virtual reality helmet
▶ method used to enter and navigate through a **virtual reality** environment. The helmet allows three of the senses (sight, touch and hearing) to interact with the **computer** which can track the user's actions.

Virtual reality library
▶ computerization of the physical structures which libraries use to order the information resources that they contain: floors, rooms, shelves etc.

Virtual storage
▶ linking of the main **memory** of a **computer** with external **storage** in such a way that they can function as one **memory** with a larger capacity. Sometimes called **virtual memory**.

Virtual union catalogue
▶ **catalogue** where there is no one central **catalogue** but a number of **catalogues** that can be searched as though they are a single **catalogue** using **Z39.50 client software**.

Virus
▶ hidden **routine** inserted into the **programming** or **software** of a **computer** system which can corrupt **data** and result in serious damage. Spreads from **computer** to **computer** when **disks** are exchanged and opened or **files** downloaded and opened.

Virus checker/detector
▶ special **program** which checks **disks** for **viruses** and identifies and removes the specific **virus** found.

Visible index
▶ **index** in which entries are made on strips of card, allowing for two or three lines of information to be displayed. Also called a **strip index**.

Visual
▶ layout or rough artwork. Also called **mock-up**.

Visual aids
▶ films, slides and other visual material used in teaching.

Visual Display Terminal – VDT
▶ originally this meant an **online display** but it is often used as a synonym for a **visual display unit** (VDU).

Visual Display Unit – VDU
▶ device equipped with a **cathode ray tube** for the visual **display** of information. Usually connected with a **keyboard** for **inputting** and editing information.

Visual Information Retrieval InterfaceS – VIRIS
▶ visual **access** tool which allows the user to use the **mouse** to **click** on to **dots** in two-dimensional space which represents **document** content to retrieve either a **document** summary or **full text**.

viz
▶ abbreviation for *videlicet*, meaning namely.

VLF – Very Low Frequency
▶ frequency range below 30 000 **Hz**.

VLSI – Very Large-Scale Integration
▶ electronic **circuits** constructed on a single **chip** with a complexity equivalent to over 10 000 **transistors** and up to 100 000 **transistors**.

Vocabulary control
▶ indexing system where **index** headings are screened, **cross**

references assigned and new **terms** have to be authorized before they can be used.

Voice activation
▶ device that can be trained to respond to the human voice.

Voice answerback
▶ system in which a **computer** gives responses to a user's commands in the form of prerecorded voice messages.

Voice band
▶ **bandwidth** of normal speech: 300–3000 **Hz**.

Voice data entry
▶ entering information into a **computer** system using the human voice via a microphone.

Voice-grade channel
▶ **channel** suitable for **transmission** of speech which has a range of sound **frequencies** from 300 to 3000 **Hz**.

Voice input/transmission
▶ another name for **speech recognition**.

Voice mail/messaging
▶ electronic system for transmitting and storing voice messages which can be accessed later by the person to whom they are addressed.

Voice processing
▶ harnessing **computer** technology to the telephone so that calls can be handled more efficiently; **generic term** which covers **voice mail**, audiotext, **mailboxes**, enhanced call processing etc.

Voice recognition
▶ ability of a **computer** system to understand and act on spoken **input**. Sometimes called **speech recognition**.

Voice synthesis
▶ spoken response to a **computer** system where digitally coded information is synthesized to a resemblance of human speech that can be understood. Sometimes called **speech synthesis**.

Voice synthesizer
▶ method of producing audible **output** of **computer**-based text that can be understood.

Volatile memory
▶ **memory** which loses its information when power is cut off or interrupted.

Vortal
▶ **web site** which focuses on content and allows users to interact through **chat lines** and/or **E-mail**.

VPN – Virtual Private Network
▶ private **network** maintained by a public telephone company on behalf of an organization which is capable of sophisticated systems of **encryption** to ensure that only authorized users have **network access**.

VRAM – Video Random Access Memory
▶ fast **computer memory chips** that are used to store **images** to be displayed on a **computer screen**.

Ww

Wafer
▶ thin slice of **silicon** which forms the basis of a **chip**.

WAIS – Wide Area Information Server
▶ system for accessing **databases** on the **Internet**.

WAN – Wide Area Network
▶ **network** that connects buildings or offices over a large geographical area.

Wand
▶ hand-held **bar code** reader which resembles a pen that is used to read or **input** information via a **bar code**. Also called a **light wand**.

Warm boot/start
▶ **restarting** a computer which is already running.

Watermark
▶ generally a design impressed into paper during manufacture. Papermaker's device or design that can be seen when the paper is held up to the light. Commonly found in handmade and writing paper.

Watermark magnetics
▶ system for encoding information on to a **magnetic strip**.

WBT – Web-Based Training
▶ training courses delivered via the **World Wide Web** which allow individuals to take the courses at

their own speed and in their own time.

Web
▶ short name for the **World Wide Web (WWW)** which is a **network** of a vast and growing number of **information servers** initially developed by CERN, European Laboratory for Particle Physics, in Geneva. It covers information on many different subject areas in many forms.

Web address
▶ characters that identify a file that is available on the **World Wide Web**.

Web browser
▶ **software** program which is used for **navigation** on the **Internet** and the **World Wide Web**.

Web camera
▶ small camera that plugs into the **computer** to record **video** and still pictures for **web sites** or to allow two people to see each other when engaged in **video conferencing**.

Web master
▶ name for the person or department responsible for setting up, putting information in and maintaining **World Wide Web pages**. Sometimes called **Infomaster**.

Web-Based Training – WBT
▶ training courses delivered via the **World Wide Web** which allow

individuals to take the courses at their own speed and in their own time.

Web page
▶ page available on the **World Wide Web** which provides text, pictures, audio and **video** to people accessing the **web**.

Web ring
▶ group of **web sites** that share a common interest and are used as an alternative to **search engines**.

Web server
▶ **computer program** that provides **files** and **data** to **web** users.

Web site
▶ page or pages on the **World Wide Web** which contain information.

Web space
▶ amount of **memory** allocated by an **information service provider** to a user who wants to build a **web site**.

Webliography
▶ subject guides available on the **World Wide Web** which are compiled from printed publications, **OPACs, online** lists and searchable **databases**; list of **web site** names.

Weeding
▶ discarding from stock materials that are considered to be of no further use. Also called **deselection** or **negative selection**.

Weight
▶ appearance of a character in a **typeface** (e.g. bold, light etc.)

Weighted searching
▶ **retrieval system** in which **terms** are assigned a value to indicate their relative importance in representing the subject matter of the **document**.

The use of weighted **indexing** allows the **output** of a search to be displayed according to the degree of match between **document indexing** and **search** requirement.

Weighting
▶ device to increase **precision**; each **descriptor** is given a score which indicates the degree of importance of the **concept** it represents in the **document** being indexed; in mechanized systems this can be used to rank **documents** retrieved according to the weighting assigned to the **descriptors** that produced them.

Welcome page
▶ main **web page** for a person or organization. Sometimes called a **home page**.

Wet carrel
▶ **carrel** or work area that is wired to provide electrical and **network** capabilities.

Wetware
▶ **human resources** (i.e. people) involved in all aspects of **computer** development and use.

Wholesaler
▶ person or firm that purchases books in large quantities from a publisher and resells them to **booksellers**.

Wide area network – WAN
▶ **network** that connects buildings or offices over a large geographical area.

Wide Area Information Server – WAIS
▶ system for accessing **databases** on the **Internet**.

Wideband
▶ **bandwidth** of the order of 48 000 Hz.

Widow
▶ short last line of a paragraph that appears at the top of a printed page.

Wild card
▶ character that is used in a search which allows any previously specified character to be accepted.

WIMP
▶ acronym for Windows, Icons, Mouse and Pull-down menus or alternatively Windows, Icons, pull-down Menus and Pointing.

Winchester disk
▶ type of hard disk sealed in a chamber which provides a clean, dust-free environment.

Window
▶ feature on a microcomputer system which allows more than one application to be viewed on the screen at the same time.

Windows
▶ graphical user interface for IBM-compatible personal computers (PCs) developed by Microsoft.

Windows application
▶ application that will only run in a Windows environment.

Wired glove
▶ device used to interact with virtual reality that contains sensors which respond to finger movements which are transmitted into the virtual reality system. Some gloves can measure wrist and elbow movements. Also called a cyberglove.

Wireless (computing)
▶ networks that are connected by radio communication rather than wires, cables or optical fibres.

Wireless terminal
▶ portable handheld terminal that can communicate with a computer by radio.

Wiswesser line notation
▶ representation of the structure of chemical compounds by a string of characters that can be handled with ordinary textual material.

Wizard
▶ automated feature which guides a user step-by-step through a complicated process.

Woodcut
▶ hand engraving on a wood block, used in early printed books.

Word
▶ group of characters representing a unit of data and occupying one storage location.

Word by word
▶ filing method for alphabetical headings, in which the word is regarded as the filing unit and the space between them as zero (0). Sometimes called nothing before something.

Word frequency
▶ number of times a particular word occurs in the text of a document.

Word processing
▶ producing and editing text using a personal computer, usually with a keyboard, visual display unit (VDU) and an associated printer.

Word-processing package
▶ software programs for entering and editing text.

Word wrap
▶ moving a partially keyed word to the next line if it is too long to fit on the current line.

Words per minute – wpm
▶ measure of speed of **transmission** in telegraph systems.

Work flow/ work flow analysis
▶ movement of **documents** through an organization.

Worker's knowledge
▶ information held, understood and available for use in the brain of the person with the information need.

Workload
▶ amount of work a person or a **computer** is expected to do.

Workstation
▶ place where a user has **access** to such facilities as telephone, **telex**, **facsimile**, **personal computer**, **word processor**, **data transmission terminal**, **viewdata** and perhaps even a **videophone**, from one integrated unit. Sometimes called an **electronic office**.

Workware
▶ technology which is idea- or work-centred rather than process-centred.

World Wide Web – WWW
▶ **network** of a vast and growing number of **information servers** initially developed by CERN, European Laboratory for Particle Physics, in Geneva. It covers information on many different subject areas in many forms. Often abbreviated to the **web**.

WORM – Write Once Read Many
▶ **optical discs** on which information cannot be altered or erased once it has been recorded.

wpm – words per minute
▶ measure of speed of **transmission** in **telegraph** systems.

Write once
▶ technology that allows a user to write **data** on an **optical disc** once only.

Write protect
▶ magnetic **disk** or **diskette** which has a device that prevents the **data** on the **disk** from being changed. Information cannot be added to the **disk** unless this device is removed or repositioned.

WWW – World Wide Web
▶ **network** of a vast and growing number of **information servers** initially developed by CERN, European Laboratory for Particle Physics, in Geneva. It covers information on many different subject areas in many forms. Often abbreviated to the **web**.

WYSIAYG
▶ acronym for 'what you see is all you get'.

WYSIWYG
▶ acronym for 'what you see is what you get'. **Screen display** which is exactly the same as what is printed out on paper.

WYSIWYP
▶ acronym for 'what you see is what you print'.

Xx

X Windows
▶ standard **network protocol** for graphics-oriented **applications.**

X/Open
▶ **consortium** of European **computer** manufacturers who are promoting the adoption of **open systems interconnection (OSI) standards.**

X.3
▶ CCITT recommendation defining the function of a **PAD** and its mode of operation.

X.25
▶ CCITT recommendation defining the **interface** between a **computer** or a **terminal** and a **packet-switched network.**

X.28
▶ CCITT recommendation defining the **interface** between a **terminal** and a **PAD.**

X.29
▶ CCITT recommendation defining the control **packet format** between the **PAD** and remote **computers.**

x-height
▶ height of the **lower case** letter x in a **font** which determines the size of the **font.**

Xerography
▶ technique whereby an electronic **image** of a **document** is formed on a **drum.** The **drum** picks up a black

powder by electrostatic attraction. The powder is then deposited on to blank paper and fused into it by heating to form the final reproduction of a **document.**

XGA – EXtended Graphics Adapter
▶ IBM **graphics standard** that includes **VGA (video graphics array)** and supports **resolutions** up to 1024 **pixels** by 768 lines.

XML – EXtensible Mark-up Language
▶ simplified version of **Standard General Markup Language** designed specifically for **web documents.**

Xmodem
▶ **file transfer protocol** designed for use over public telephone **networks** which supports **bulletin boards,** etc.

XUI – X User Interface
▶ tool to be used when running **applications programs** under **X Windows.**

Yy

Y2K
► abbreviation for the year 2000.

Year 2000 problem
► concern that many **applications** could only handle twentieth century dates and would have problems in the year 2000. Also called the **millennium bug**.

Yellow press
► sensational **periodicals** and **newspapers**.

Ymodem
► improved version of the **Xmodem file transfer protocol** which can send information in larger blocks.

Zz

Z39
▶ committee of the National Information Standards Organization of the American National Standards Institute which develops **standards** relating to library and **information science** and other publishing activities.

Z39.50
▶ **protocol** for use over a **network** that allows a user to frame a question that can be understood and processed by all **computers** attached to that **network**. This **protocol** can be used in searching **library catalogues**. Often referred to as **ANSI Z39.50**.

Zero hits
▶ **search** activity which generates no relevant or useful items.

Zeroband budgeting
▶ **management** system that requires an organization to identify priorities and justify activities from point zero, i.e. without prior assumptions, in order to examine priority ranking and identify **hidden costs**.

Zine
▶ **alternative publications** which started in the 1960s. Usually they had an ephemeral lifespan with idiosyncratic and often anti-establishment content. Usually regarded as **artefacts** of popular and/or underground culture.

Zipf distribution
▶ named after George Kingsley Zipf, who studied word counts in specific texts where, if ranked in order of **frequency**, the **frequency** would be proportional to their rank.

Zipf-Bradford distribution
▶ studies which have compared **Bradford's distribution** and **Zipf distribution** to show that they are two different ways of examining the same phenomenon.

Zipf's law
▶ law named after George Kingsley Zipf, which states that a person will view the solution of an immediate problem against the estimate of a probable future problem.

Zmodem
▶ sophisticated **file transfer protocol** developed from the **Xmodem**.

Zoom
▶ facility in art and **graphics software** which magnifies an area on the **screen**.

Bibliography

In compiling this dictionary, a number of other terminology guides and glossary sections of textbooks were checked to identify candidate terms that should be included. The major ones are listed below, but this should not be regarded as a complete or definitive list.

Aitcheson, J. (1994) *Communication and information thesaurus*. English edn. Paris: Unesco

Bradley, P. and Hanson, T. (1994) *Going online and CD-ROM*. 9th edn. London: Aslib

Buchanan, B. (1976) *A glossary of indexing terms*. London: Clive Bingley

Cawkell, A.E. (1993) *Encyclopaedic dictionary of information technology and systems*. London: Bowker-Saur

Collin, S.M.H. (1995) *Dictionary of multimedia*. London: Peter Collin

Collin, S.M.H. (1996) *Dictionary of information technology*. 2nd edn. Teddington: Peter Collin Publishing Ltd

Deeson, E. (1997) *Collins dictionary of information technology*. Glasgow: HarperCollins

Diodata, V. (1994) *Dictionary of bibliometrics*. New York: Haworth Press

Downing, D., Covington, M.A. and Covington, M.M. (1998) *Dictionary of computer and Internet terms*. 6th edn. New York: Barron's

Graham, J. (1991) *The Penguin dictionary of telecommunications*. Revised and updated by Sue J. Lowe. London: Penguin

Gunton, T. (1993) *The Penguin dictionary of information technology*. 2nd edn. London: Penguin

Hansen, B. (1997) *Dictionary of multimedia: terms and acronyms*. 1998 edn. Chicago: Fitzroy Dearborn

(1998) *Hutchinson dictionary of computing, multimedia and the Internet*. 2nd edn. Oxford: Helicon

Illingworth, V. and Pyle, I. (1996) *Dictionary of computing*. 4th ed. London: Oxford University Press.

Illustrated dictionary of information technology (1955) London: Bloomsbury Books

Margolis, P.E. (1999) *Random House Webster's computer & Internet dictionary*. 3rd edn. New York: Random House

Meadows, A. J. *et al.* (1987) *Dictionary of computing information technology*. 3rd edn. London: Kogan Page

Milstead, J.L. (1994) *ASIS thesaurus of information science and librarianship*. New Jersey: Learned Information

Nader, J. (1998) *Prentice Hall's illustrated dictionary of computing* (1997) 3rd edn. London: Prentice Hall

New International Webster's pocket computer dictionary of the English language. (1997) new revised edn. USA: Trident Press

Peacock, J. and Barnard, M. (1990) *The Blueprint dictionary of printing and publishing*. London: Blueprint

Penford, D. (1997) *EP, multimedia and communications glossary*. Leatherhead: Pira International

Pfaffenberger, B. (1998) *Webster's new world dictionary of computing*. 6th edn. Hemel Hemstead: Simon and Schuster

Prytherch, R. (1995) *Harrod's librarians' glossary: 9000 terms used in library management, library science, publishing, the book trades and archive management*. 8th edn. Aldershot: Gower

Pugh, E. (1987) *Pugh's dictionary of acronyms and abbreviations*. 5th edn. London/Chicago: Library Association/American Library Association

Rowley, J. (1992) *Organizing knowledge: an introduction to information retrieval*. 2nd edn. Aldershot: Ashgate

Sawoniak, H. and Witt, M. (1992) *New international dictionary of acronyms in library and information science and related fields*. 2nd revised and enlarged edn. Munich: K.G. Saur

Schultz, C.K. (1968) *Thesaurus of information science terminology*. revised edn. Palo Alto, California: Comunication Services Corporation/Pacific Books

Sinclair, I. (1997) *Collins dictionary of personal computing*. 2nd edn. Glasgow: HarperCollins

Stevenson, J. (1997) *Dictionary of library and information management.* London: Peter Collin

Stokes, A.V. (1984) *Concise encyclopaedia of information technology.* 2nd edn. Aldershot: Gower

Tayyeb, R. and Chandna, K. (1992) *Dictionary of acronyms and abbreviations: library, information and computer terms.* Ottowa: Canadian Library Association

Verma, S. (1998) *Computer, Internet and multimedia dictionary.* London: Sangam

Watson, J. and Hill, A. (1993) *A dictionary of communication and media studies.* London: Edward Arnold

West, B. (1991) *Basic computing principles.* 2nd edn. NCC: Blackwell

Whitcombe, A. and Beckwith, P. (1992) *An illustrated information technology dictionary.* Cheltenham: Stanley Thornes

Young, H. (1993) (ed.) *Glossary of library and information science.* Chicago: American Library Association